clean
sweep

DEDICATION

For Michael, my father. Thanks for helping me
in so many practical ways over the decades.

Published in 2004 by Bay Books, an imprint of Murdoch Magazines Pty Ltd.

Chief Executive: Juliet Rogers
Publisher: Kay Scarlett

Creative Director: Marylouise Brammer
Designer: Vivien Valk
Photographer: Sue Stubbs
Editorial Director: Diana Hill
Project Manager: Sarah Baker
Copy Editor: Georgina Bitcon

Printed by Tien Wah Press. PRINTED IN SINGAPORE.
First printed in 2004.
© Text, design and illustrations Murdoch Books® 2004.

Acknowledgments
The author and publisher would like to thank the following for supplying products for photography.

Canningvale, Phone 1800 801 178, for the towel (p. 184); **Castone**, 31 Ocean Street, Woollahra NSW 2025, Phone (02) 9363 5794, for the cushions (p. 211); **Funkis Swedish Forms**, 23c Curlewis Street, Bondi NSW 2026, Phone (02) 9130 6445 for the natural brushes (cover, pp. 1, 4, 38–9, 68, 298, 334); **Humble Beginnings**, 209 Avoca Road, Randwick NSW 2031, Phone (02) 9326 4383, for the slippers (p. 267) and the nightie (p. 268); **Off Centre**, 110 Curlewis Street, Bondi NSW 2026, Phone (02) 9365 7111, for the mixing bowls (pp. 82–3); and **Papaya Studio**, 15B Transvaal Avenue, Double Bay NSW 2028, Phone (02) 9362 1620, for the silk throw (p. 211).

clean sweep

THE ULTIMATE GUIDE TO DECLUTTERING, DETOXING AND DESTRESSING YOUR HOME

ALISON HAYNES

bay books

contents

managing your house

Housekeeping is about so much more than cleaning a house. Until the 15th century cleaning was a peripheral activity to the central tasks of preparing food, gathering and chopping wood and other fuel, keeping the house warm and carrying water. Laundry is not much of a problem when you don't have a change of clothes. When the animals that are your livelihood need feeding, who's going to worry themselves about dust on the mantelpiece?

What is the clever house?

Now that we live in a time of excesses, we have new considerations. Our precious belongings — be they laptops, loofahs or lingerie — need caring for. These days we think more about the environmental impact of our actions — whether it's flushing cleaning product residues down the drain, or the amount of clean water and fossil fuels we use in heating water to wash our clothes. We are increasingly aware that just because a chemical removes stains effortlessly or a paint wears on year after year, it does not guarantee that it's non-toxic and safe near children, or even safe to use regularly.

Added to that, we want our houses to be havens. Somewhere we can escape to, away from the hurly burly of weekly grocery shopping, office politics or playground banter. Our houses are more than roofs over our heads — they are also our homes.

Clever housekeeping incorporates a number of interrelated ideas: that a house should be healthy; that living in it and maintaining it should not take an undue toll on the environment; that it should be comfortable and safe to live in, not unnecessarily expensive to maintain, and efficient to run on a day-to-day basis.

The cleverest of clever houses incorporates all of these aspects. In fact, it is hard to do otherwise. For instance, when you choose to clean your bathroom with safe and gentle bicarbonate of soda instead of a proprietary cleaner, you are not only making a 'green' choice that could save money and has less impact on the environment, you are also creating a healthier and safer home environment for you and your family. When you plant a deciduous tree that will shade your house in summer and allow light and warmth in winter, you are making a 'green' choice that could ultimately represent a saving on your power bill (a saving for both you and the environment), increase the comfort of your home and contribute to a healthier atmosphere. Clever indeed!

So let's take a closer look at all the aspects of a clever house.

Healthy house

A healthy house benefits from sufficient fresh air entering, with enough ventilation to ensure indoor air pollutants are regularly removed. Good ventilation also ensures a house is not too humid, which in turn helps keep it free from excessive mould and bacterial growth.

A healthy house is supportive and considerate of allergy sufferers. Simple measures can help: letting beds air; opening windows for ventilation; cleaning basins and keeping a check on mould growth around plugs and taps. Knowing how to effectively clean and, where necessary, disinfect around the house keeps bacterial populations below disease levels. It also encompasses knowledge of the cleaning products we use that may irritate or even poison in the wrong doses and in the wrong hands. The more we know about the chemicals that we encounter every day, the more we can make informed choices about their use.

A healthy house accommodates the various needs of all members of the family — even the family pet — and still remains healthy.

Increasingly, too, the notion of a healthy house covers choices in furniture, carpets, curtains and decorating options — we don't put lead in paint any more but are there other substances in some paints we might wish to avoid if we knew more?

Green house

An environmentally friendly house is an energy-efficient and comfortable one — warm in winter, cool in summer, light enough in key rooms and pleasant to be in because it is well ventilated and smells fresh. The green house takes an easier toll on the environment — and also on the pocket. Ideally, it is sited and landscaped to take maximum advantage of the sun's light and warmth in all the seasons of the year. It relies less on non-renewable energy sources (such as coal) by making the best use of low-impact, renewable energy sources, such as sun and wind. The green house is a low-polluting one, not only in terms of the energy sources it uses, but also in the products that are used within its walls. Because it is also a healthy house, the green householder chooses low-toxic, natural cleaning products in preference to harsh and polluting chemicals. It conserves water and reuses it when possible.

Recycling is a vital component of the green philosophy. From water and organic waste to recyclable building materials and packaging, the green house minimizes its production of garbage and landfill. The options available to householders for

reducing the impact of their homes on the environment are growing daily and range from something as simple as choosing reusable cloth bags over plastic at the supermarket, to solar water heaters, signing on to green power sources, and even selling solar-produced electricity back to the local grid.

Efficient and safe house

When you run an efficient house, the money you save can go on other expenses such as holidays or music lessons, or in a bigger house it can ensure you are able to make ends meet. There are numerous ways to save money here and there — from turning off the fridge when you go on holiday, choosing energy-efficient appliances, and fixing a leaking tap, to growing a few vegetables (even a pot of herbs on a windowsill) or shopping in bulk.

But being efficient does not just mean being energy efficient. The efficient house ideally has a place for everything and (on a good day) everything in its place. Clutter is reduced to a minimum. In an efficient house, there is a list of emergency numbers near the phone, you can always find your umbrella, and that bill that needs to be paid today is right to hand — not buried somewhere in the middle of a mountain of papers on the dining room table!

A safe house is not only a healthy one — it also provides a physically safe environment where inhabitants of all ages can feel secure. Safety measures are often a matter of commonsense and very little financial outlay. The safe house has fire alarms, circuit breakers, child-proof safety devices for toddlers, security rails in the bathroom for the elderly or infirm, outdoor lighting, a readily accessible first aid kit, and a lockable storage space for medicines and other dangerous substances.

How clever is your house?

The following chapters of this book will give you all the information you need to choose your individual path to creating your own clever house. If you feel the urge to change the way you run your home, you're more likely to be successful if you adapt it, and your lifestyle, gradually. You could start with less toxic cleaning materials and decorating products, and consider the more expensive items such as furniture or flooring, energy-efficient whitegoods or solar water panels, as they need replacing. If you feel overwhelmed by clutter, tackle one room — or even one cupboard or one shelf — at a time. And remember, even the smallest changes can make a big difference. You'll be running a clever house before you know it.

the clever house

Let's explore the various aspects of the clever house in more detail. Once you are familiar with the basic concepts, you can apply them to every room in the house, and even to the garden.

WE ARE BORN AT HOME, *live at home, and we must die at home, so that the comfort and economy of home are of more deep, heartfelt and personal interest to us, than the public affairs of all the nations of the world.*

Motto of *The Magazine of Domestic Economy* (1835)

the clever house

Healthy house

Making your house healthy involves thinking about something as basic as the air you breathe — is it as clean as you think? It's about taking measures to make that air as clean as possible — from reducing pollutants to ensuring that your home is adequately ventilated and damp-free. And it's about making sure that your home environment is comfortably clean and fresh — especially for allergy sufferers.

The air we breathe

Sources of pollution outside the house are immediately apparent. Emissions from cars and factories, for example, are often visible and may even smell. We like to think, in contrast, that our homes are havens of pure, clean air. But our homes have changed. Double glazing is more common, draughty windows and doors less common. We seal up the house for energy efficiency by draught-proofing and insulation. Central heating has largely replaced open fires which create a draught of their own, continually drawing new fresh air into the home.

Coupled with the fact that people in industrialized countries spend somewhere between 75 and 90 per cent of their time indoors, this means we increasingly rely on the quality of indoor air. In many houses it is not being mixed regularly with air from outdoors, 'fresh' or otherwise. In addition, new materials for furnishing and decoration are not always the inert substances we believe they are. Many substances send gaseous molecules into the air in a process that has been called 'out-gasing'. Although some of these are associated only with the installation of, say, a carpet, others — such as the glues in particle board furniture or urea-formaldehyde foam — continue to emit gases for years.

Paralleling this change in the chemical environment of our homes is a rise in a range of diseases and conditions such as allergies, multiple chemical sensitivity and chronic fatigue syndrome.

Whether or not you are affected by particular chemicals you are exposed to in your home or work life, such as pesticides or formaldehyde, depends on a number of factors, including your immune system (which may be compromised by lack of sleep, infection or stress) and the degree of exposure. People can become used to their body's response to chemicals, but only for so long.

The numerous potential sources of indoor air pollution include cigarette smoke, combustion by-products, biological pollutants, volatile organic compounds and a number of other chemical pollutants, such as heavy metals and asbestos.

SICK BUILDINGS

In the 1970s, the term 'sick building' was coined to describe the situation where a group of people occupying a building reported a range of symptoms associated with being in the building. Typical complaints include lethargy and fatigue, headache, dizziness and nausea, irritation of mucous membranes, sensitivity to odours, eye and nasal irritation, rhinitis (runny nose) and nasal congestion as well as feelings of general malaise. Theories as to the causes include air contamination, poor design, inadequate maintenance and faulty ventilation. Low levels of pollutants may act together; humidity may be a factor. In 1984, the World Health Organisation reported that as many as 30 per cent of new and remodelled buildings worldwide 'may have generated excessive complaints related to indoor air quality'.

Tobacco smoke is unhealthy for all

Cigarette smoke is a complex mixture of more than 4000 chemicals, some in gas form and others as solid particles. Smoke at home can cause rhinitis, pharyngitis (inflammation of the throat), a congested nose, persistent cough, headaches, wheezing and irritation of the conjunctiva (the membrane that covers the white of the eye and lines the eyelids). In addition, it can worsen respiratory conditions. Children — even more so, babies — are particularly vulnerable to problems from tobacco smoke. It can trigger the onset of asthma and make an existing asthma condition more severe and more difficult to control. Long-term exposure to tobacco smoke is linked with breathing and lung disease as well as exacerbated respiratory and cardiovascular disease and changes in the body's immune system.

FRESH AIR Place a few slices of lemon in a shallow dish of water to rid a room of the smell of cigarette smoke.

Increased ventilation helps but it does not eliminate the health risks associated with tobacco smoke. Family members may be less exposed if you insist that smokers go outside to smoke. Some high-efficiency air cleaners can remove some of the particles in tobacco smoke but most cannot remove the gaseous pollutants.

Combustion by-products

When we burn fuel to produce heat or light, the combustion of that fuel also produces by-products, such as carbon monoxide, nitrogen dioxide, sulphur dioxide, soot, formaldehyde and hydrocarbons, such as butane, propane and benzene.

BURNING ISSUES

You might think only of a smoky fire, but all heating devices produce combustion by-products to some degree — even a state-of-the-art gas cooker. Most modern heating devices have built-in safety mechanisms, but ancient or faulty devices, or those used inappropriately, can poison the air.

- **Wood stoves and open fires** Both wood and coal smoke contain numerous pollutants, including carbon monoxide. Most of these by-products should go up the chimney, but in the case of inefficient and poorly designed flues, some may enter the room. Wood smoke also contains carcinogens, while coal smoke contains sulphur dioxide – once responsible for city smogs. Open fireplaces are romantic but wasteful of energy and polluting. Sealed units, such as sealed combustion stoves, are more efficient, safer and also environmentally cleaner, especially if you burn matured, dry wood.
- **Gas appliances** These appliances for cooking, hot water and central heating produce carbon monoxide, carbon dioxide, nitric oxide and nitrogen dioxide, small amounts of formaldehyde and sulphur dioxide. Old models with pilot lights or faulty burners produce more toxins than newer, well maintained ones.
- **Kerosene (paraffin) heaters** These heaters release numerous noxious gases and much moisture, and are not recommended for long-term use. It is essential to keep a window open or ensure other ventilation while they burn.
- **Miscellaneous burners** Even oil lamps, incense burners, candles and aromatherapy lamps produce combustion by-products.

Some of these by-products, such as carbon monoxide, are particularly poisonous to the elderly, the growing foetus and people with cardiovascular or lung disease, and are fatal in high concentrations. Carbon monoxide poisoning sometimes mimics flu.

WHAT COLOUR IS YOUR FLAME? The flame on a gas burner — for instance, the stove or water heater — should burn blue. If it's orange, it may be faulty and need servicing.

Other gaseous pollutants can cause a variety of symptoms including dizziness, headaches, nausea, fatigue, a fast heartbeat, wheezing, persistent cough, and eye and upper respiratory tract irritation. Burning fuels may also trigger an asthma attack in some people.

Biological pollutants

When scientists talk about biological air pollution they mean viruses and bacteria passed around by animal and human occupants of homes; insect and animal visitors — usually of the unwelcome variety — that shed allergens; and fungi and bacteria, which grow in water reservoirs and on surfaces.

Although a number of factors determine the level of biological agents that are released into the air, humidity is one of the most significant. High humidity encourages the proliferation of the house dust mite as well as many forms of fungus. It is a particular problem after flooding, or in a continually damp carpet, and in poorly ventilated bathrooms and kitchens. In addition, several household appliances produce moisture, and therefore ideal conditions, for bacteria and fungus. The culprit appliances are humidifiers, dehumidifiers, air-conditioners and drip pans under the cooling coils of fridges.

Microbes may also linger in some heating, ventilating and air-conditioning systems — sometimes for very obvious reasons, such as air intake pipes situated near spots contaminated by bird and animal droppings; at other times because of humidification systems, or cooling coils.

HOT STUFF: IS YOUR HEATER SAFE?

Faulty or incorrectly installed or maintained heaters can produce elevated levels of pollutants. Check that your heater is running efficiently and safely.

- Make sure that vented appliances are properly installed with external vents.
- Investigate any odours produced when a heater is in use.
- Have all heating devices such as water heaters, clothes dryers and furnaces regularly serviced by a professional.
- Clean fireplaces and stoves for wood and coal seasonally.
- Old heaters may lack safety devices such as cut-off mechanisms, which shut the heater off if poisonous carbon monoxide reaches a dangerous level. Consider investing in a new one.
- Never try to heat the room by leaving your gas oven door propped open, or by burning charcoal in a portable grill.
- Reduce the total number of combustion appliances in your home.

Biological pollution can cause infections, hypersensitivity diseases and toxicosis (where biologically produced toxins cause a direct toxic effect).

A well known disease associated with indoor air contamination is legionnaire's disease. This is a type of pneumonia caused by the agent *Legionella pneumophila* that is associated with cooling systems and whirlpool baths. Other diseases associated with poor indoor air quality include tuberculosis and humidifier fever, a flu-like illness thought to be caused by biological toxins and related to exposure to amoebae, bacteria and fungi found in humidifier reservoirs, air-conditioners and aquaria.

Allergic reactions, ranging from rhinitis, nasal congestion, inflammation of the conjunctiva, hives and asthma, may be triggered by a number of biological agents. Notable culprits include moulds, dust mites, cockroaches, rodents, birds, cats and dogs. In addition, natural furnishing fillings such as feathers, and the plant fibre kapok may also act as allergens.

TO REDUCE BIOLOGICAL HAZARDS

Good living practices can significantly decrease your exposure to dangerous levels of biological pollutants.

- Check that all your living spaces are adequately ventilated — open windows regularly, and let air blow through the house.
- Make sure all air-conditioning, humidifying and dehumidifying equipment is maintained according to the manufacturers' instructions and that no water is allowed to stand in them.
- Repair leaks and seepage promptly. Thoroughly clean and dry water-damaged carpets and building materials within 24 hours of damage or consider removing and replacing them.
- Use exhaust fans in the bathroom and kitchen, and vent your clothes dryer to the outside.
- Be aware of the family's exposure to pets.
- Vacuum carpets and upholstered furniture regularly.
- Cover mattresses with anti-dust mite covers.
- Wash bedding and soft toys frequently at a high temperature to control dust mites.

Volatile organic compounds

Other sources of indoor air pollution are substances commonly referred to as VOCs — or volatile organic compounds. They include formaldehyde, many pesticides, solvents such as benzene and perchloroethylene and a number of cleaning agents. VOCs contain carbon, hence the term 'organic', and as they evaporate easily at room temperature, they are described as 'volatile'. Most are derived from petrochemicals.

How harmful are VOCs?

Experts disagree over the level of problems they cause. Some hold the view that for the vast majority, VOCs do not cause any trouble, while for the sensitive few they can be irritating and trigger allergy-like symptoms. Another school of thought regards the accumulated vapours from VOCs as toxic and nearly all VOCs as irritating.

Most VOCs are synthetic but some — such as the citrus aroma of an orange — are natural. The range of problems they can cause includes conjunctival irritation, nose and throat discomfort, headache, allergic skin reaction, nausea, fatigue and dizziness.

Concentration of VOCs tends to be higher inside than outdoors. In some cases, in a study by the Environment Protection Agency of the United States, indoor levels were found to be ten times higher than outdoors. The worst health offenders are considered to be formaldehyde, organochlorines and phenolic compounds (see below). The worst exposure is from house decorating, housework and pest control.

Name that VOC

The three worst VOCs are found in a wide range of household products.

- **Formaldehyde** Used as a preservative and a binder in industry. Crops up in hundreds of household products, including furniture and fabric.
- **Organochlorine** Broad group of often powerful chemicals. Includes many pesticides, solvents, cleaning fluids, PVC (polyvinyl chloride) and PCBs (polychlorinated biphenyls). (See the entry under 'The chemicals of pest control', page 347.)
- **Phenols** Include phenol (carbolic acid), which is a common disinfectant. Other phenols are synthetic resins, used in hard plastics, paints, fabric coatings and varnish.

SPOTLIGHT ON FORMALDEHDYE

Formaldehyde, used as a binder and preservative, has been classified in some countries as a probable human carcinogen. Opinion varies as to how serious a risk it is. Some say the amounts in household products are mostly too minute to worry about for most people, although those with allergies may find them irritating. Another theory is that although individual product levels are small, the cumulative effect may be large, especially in an enclosed space.

The most serious levels are found in board-based products widely used in flooring, shelving (especially flat-packed furniture), foam-backed carpets and underlay, and paint preservatives.

In everyday doses formaldehyde can be irritating to the conjunctiva and upper respiratory tract. These symptoms are temporary, depending on the length of exposure, and can produce a range of symptoms, from tingling sensations in the eyes, nose and throat to chest tightening and wheezing. A portion of the population, including asthmatics, is considered to be hypersensitive to formaldehyde.

Formaldehyde was a component of urea formaldehyde foam insulation (UFFI), an insulation product used in construction until the early 1980s. Formaldehyde resins are still commonly used in finishes, plywood, panelling, fibreboard and particle board. It also crops up in furniture and in fabric finishes, curtains and mattress ticking.

VOCs around us

The average home contains more than 40 VOCs and there are thousands of products we use, some on a daily basis, that emit VOCs at room temperature. Most come from a remarkably long list of unremarkable household items.

- Household products, such as fabric softeners, rug cleaners, paints, lacquers and their thinners, paint strippers and pesticides
- Personal items, such as scents and hairspray
- Dry-cleaning fluids
- Building materials and home furnishings
- Office equipment, such as some copiers and printers
- Office products, such as correction fluids and carbonless copy paper
- Graphics and craft materials such as glues, adhesives, permanent markers and photographic solutions

HOW HIGH IS YOUR VOC EXPOSURE?

The greater your number of 'yes' answers, the higher your risk of exposure to VOCs.

Do you:

■ live in a mobile home or a new home containing lots of pressed wood products?

■ handle chemicals for craft, graphic arts and photography in your job or hobby?

■ use chemical cleaners extensively in the home?

Have you recently:

■ acquired new pressed wood furniture?

■ renovated the house?

■ used pesticides, paints or solvents?

How to reduce your exposure to VOCs

■ Ensure your house is well ventilated, and increase ventilation when using products that emit VOCs.

■ Do not store opened containers of unused paints and similar materials inside the home.

■ Avoid sources of VOCs wherever possible.

■ Avoid permanent press fabric and mattress ticking if you are sensitive to formaldehyde.

Board and VOCs

The popular building material, board, is made from wood components bonded with glue or resin that is made with the VOC formaldehyde. The term 'board' includes laminated board, chipboard (also called particle board), hardboard and MDF (medium density fibreboard). As it is cheap and versatile, board is used in flooring, roofing, shelving and furniture — most mass-produced modern furniture contains some board. Veneer furniture, which might look like solid timber, is actually a thin layer of 'solid' wood overlaying a board structure (or carcass, as it is known).

Board out-gases by far the highest levels of formaldehyde in the first few weeks and months of its life, after which these levels gradually decrease. MDF contains the highest level of formaldehyde, while laminated board furniture leaks the least.

To reduce your exposure to formaldehyde from board furniture, try to air new furniture for a week or two in a dry place under cover; paint exposed board with several layers of paint or varnish; and, where possible, choose solid wood, glass or metal instead (for shelving, for instance).

Other chemical pollutants

Air can also carry other pollutants, such as the heavy metals lead and mercury, as well as asbestos and the gases radon and ozone.

LEAD

Lead poisoning can have a long-term impact on children's development. Toxicity in children can manifest itself as an acute illness with symptoms of irritability, abdominal pain, marked ataxia (lack of coordination and clumsiness), and seizures or loss of consciousness. Symptoms in adults include headache, nausea, weight loss, constipation, fatigue and personality change.

Children can get lead poisoning if they ingest flakes or dust particles of old lead-containing paint. Although the lead content of petrol has been reduced in many countries, even in those where it is now banned in petrol, in places of heavy traffic lead remains in nearby soil and can become airborne and enter dwellings either through windows and doors or on feet. Lead is also a constituent of numerous art and craft materials and, worryingly, PVC toys. Polyvinyl chloride, or PVC, is a widely used plastic that sometimes contains the poisonous metals lead and cadmium as stabilizers. (It also contains plasticizers, which may also be dangerous if ingested.)

See 'The living room', page 245, for advice on dealing with lead paint in your home.

MERCURY

The presence of lead in old paint has been widely publicized; not so the presence of mercury in new paint. Some interior latex paints contain phenylmercuric acetate, or PMA, as a preservative. PMA is now banned in the United States.

ASBESTOS

Long-term exposure to asbestos can cause cancer. It was once widely used in structural fireproofing, and may still be found in heating systems, acoustic insulation, ceiling tiles and shingles in older houses. It was also formerly used in fireplace gloves, ironing board covers and some hair dryers. When material containing asbestos is damaged or starts to disintegrate, microscopic fibres are dispersed into the air — for up to 30 years. If they find their way into human lungs they can cause asbestosis (usually only seen in people whose work has brought them into regular exposure to asbestos), lung cancer, and other lung and gastric illnesses.

ASBESTOS ALERT

If you suspect there is asbestos in your house, do not on any account attempt to remove it yourself, as further disturbance may disperse more fibres into the air. Removal may not even be the best course of action. In some cases it is safer to cover and contain it. Contact your local authority for advice and information on local regulations concerning asbestos.

RADON

Radon is a naturally occurring, colourless, odourless radioactive gas which is a leading cause of lung cancer in the world. It occurs naturally in some types of rock, ground water and soil, and may enter a house by seeping up through cracks, drains and concrete if the house is built on radon-containing ground. Concentrations of radon can become high in houses that are well sealed and well insulated but insufficiently ventilated.

OZONE

Turn off the equipment in your home office when it is not in use, as it gives off ozone, a poisonous gas already present naturally in small concentrations in the air. It is an irritant to the eyes, nose, throat and respiratory tract.

How chemicals harm your health

Chemicals that perform wonders with your cleaning and washing are, understandably perhaps, not to be taken lightly. Many are powerful substances with the potential for harm within the home. They can range from mildly irritating to cancer causing.

On the other hand, substances of little risk are unlikely to cause anyone health problems, or certainly only very minor ones, although chemically sensitive people may have to hunt around before finding formulas which do not give them trouble.

When used in the context they are designed for, and in the safest possible way, many substances cause very few problems for most people. For instance, some laundry detergents cause skin and eye irritation with prolonged direct contact, but present no problem when used to wash clothes. On the other hand, if you are sensitive to a chemical in a particular brand of laundry detergent, you may find sheets washed in it are intolerable.

How toxic a substance is to the user depends not only on its chemical make-up, but also on how often it is likely to be used, in what quantities and under what circumstances. Using a highly toxic solvent to 'save' a favourite and expensive dress on a one-off basis, perhaps the only time in a whole year, is very different from using that solvent every day for hobby purposes.

Here are some of the issues to bear in mind when choosing household chemicals.

- Allergens **Chemicals may trigger allergic reactions (involving the immune system) in one person and responses due to a sensitivity in another. Labelling allows consumers to avoid allergens that cause them trouble, when those substances are identified. Two difficulties arise, however: it is possible to be allergic to almost any chemical; and labelling of household cleaners and chemicals is often absent or incomplete. This is particularly true of colours and perfumes.**

- Corrosive substances **Many strong cleaning agents are also corrosive or caustic — that is, they can burn the skin, eyes and even internal organs if ingested or inhaled by accident. Corrosive substances can be found in bleaches.**

- Flammable chemicals **Some chemicals are highly flammable while others are volatile — that is, they turn to gas at room temperature.**

- Irritants **Many substances are irritating to the skin, mucous membranes (these are the moist surfaces lining, for instance, your nose and your gut), the respiratory tract and, especially, the eyes. Almost all commercial household cleaners contain potential irritants.**

See 'What's in a name?', page 332, for a closer look at the chemicals in your home.

FROM DUST TO DUST *A six-room house in the city may accumulate as much as 40 pounds of dust in a year.*

David Pearson, *The New Natural House Book* (1998)

A NOSE FOR TROUBLE

Trust your nose. If part of your house smells bad, it may signal health or building maintenance problems.

- **Damp smells** suggest the need for more ventilation to reduce moulds, or a possible leak somewhere.
- **Fishy or 'locker room' smells** are indicative of bacterial growth.
- **Stale air smells** and a 'stuffy' atmosphere in bedrooms and other rooms mean it's time to open the windows.
- **New paint and new carpet smells** are often indicative of VOC emission. Ensure good ventilation until the smell disappears.
- **Fragrances** in cosmetics, toiletries and perfumes are a common allergy trigger; non-scented varieties may cause fewer problems.
- **Dry-cleaned clothes** should be aired outside if possible, until the smell has gone.

Safety checklist for household cleaners

Keep this checklist in mind every time you buy or use a chemical cleaner in your home. Remember that the most polluted rooms in your home are the bathroom, laundry and kitchen, rooms where most chemical cleaning products are used.

- Read the labels on cleaning products for advice about the ingredients, how to use and store the product, and how much to use.

- Never mix products as they can cause chemical reactions with toxic by-products. For instance, when sodium hypochlorite (found in many household bleaches) and hydrochloric acid (found in urine and some toilet cleaners) are mixed, the gases chloramine and methyl chloride are produced. Serious exposure can cause a disturbance in the body's acid balance as well as permanent blindness. When household bleaches are mixed with substances that contain ammonia, acrid fumes of chloramine are produced.

- Be careful when mixing hot water with chlorine-containing compounds such as chlorine bleach or disinfectants that may contain aldehydes. Doing so increases your exposure by releasing chlorine gas and formaldehyde gas, which you may inhale.

- Leave products in their original containers so you can identify the contents. This reduces the likelihood of someone using a product inappropriately and also provides vital information in the case of accidental poisoning.

- Never put household cleaning products in food or drink containers.

- Keep all household cleaning products away from children. Children are at risk from accidental poisoning by household chemicals. About one-fifth of all poisoning cases in children are due to household and garden chemicals, including solvents. If you have children, lock your household chemicals in a cupboard well out of their reach.

- Only use as much as you need for the job.

- If you are pregnant, avoid chemical exposure as much as possible.

- Good ventilation reduces the potential for inhaling toxic fumes. If you can smell a chemical, you can breathe it too. Use products in a well ventilated place: use them outdoors whenever possible, and when indoors, open windows. Take plenty of breaks for fresh air.

- Do not eat or drink when using hazardous products.

- Clean up, and seal all containers after the job.

Clever DIY

Renovating and decorating involves using chemicals that need handling with care. In addition, removing old fittings can disturb and expose unhealthy materials.

- Be careful of mould patches when stripping old wallpaper.

- Some people are prone to contact dermatitis from carboxymethylcellulose found in some wallpaper pastes, so wear protective gloves.

- When painting, ensure good ventilation until the smell disappears. Or choose low-odour, environmentally friendly paints.

- Check preservatives.

- Choose water-based polyurethane varnishes and paint strippers.

- Restrict the use of wood preservatives to outbreak areas such as woodworm and decay.

▤ Seal in formaldehyde on exposed board with a coat of paint.

▤ If using board for home improvements, make sure your work area is
well ventilated. Work outside if possible and wear a dust respirator face
mask when sawing. Consider airing the board outside under cover for a
week before working with it, and paint or varnish it to seal as much
formaldehyde as possible.

▤ When fitting new cupboards, consider fitting them right up to the ceiling
to maximize space and reduce dust collection points.

Defeating damp

A damp house is not a healthy one: it's all too easy for moulds and other fungus,
bacteria and mites to proliferate. Fixing dampness first requires identifying the
source of the problem.

▤ Rising damp is water rising from the ground. It is usually prevented by a
damp course which may need fixing or replacing after a number of years.

▤ Penetrating damp occurs when water comes through a wall after heavy
rain, possibly because of a leaking downpipe or gutter, or an entry point
above the damp course.

▤ Condensation forms when water condenses from humid air and settles
on cold surfaces such as windows or cold spots in poorly heated and
badly ventilated rooms.

TO REDUCE DAMPNESS

■ Check damp courses. In old houses they may be non-existent or disintegrated to
the point where they are useless.
■ Check downpipes, gutters and window surrounds. Rust or blockages might be
causing water to flood or leak into vulnerable areas.
■ Wipe condensation away from windows.
■ Ventilate bathrooms and kitchens.
■ Improve insulation. This helps to eliminate cold spots which, in turn, reduces
condensation and associated mould growth.

Allergy and the healthy house

Allergies can cause a range of symptoms from the irritating — such as a runny nose or a mild rash — to the life threatening, such as a severe asthma attack or anaphylactic shock. Living with an allergy such as hay fever or asthma is an unfortunate reality for many children and adults. What's more, the incidence of these problems is rising sharply — in some places the incidence of asthma has doubled over two decades — and doctors cannot say why.

While some allergies, such as hay fever, tend to be more severe outside the house, home sweet home can also harbour allergy triggers, or allergens. The main triggers around the house are dust mites, moulds, pollen spores and particles of skin and saliva from pets. These are all capable of triggering a range of allergy symptoms, especially ones involving the respiratory tract. All these triggers can also be found in household dust — hence an emphasis on tackling dust in the home.

War on dust

If family members suffer dust-related allergies, there are a number of dust traps to avoid.

- Padded headboards, especially buttoned ones.
- Clutter and ornaments, unless they are behind glass.
- Books on open shelves.
- Heavy curtains. (Blinds, including roller blinds, are a better option, and vertical Venetian blinds collect less dust than horizontal ones.)
- Forced heating systems. (Vent coverings can help trap dust and prevent it from circulating in the house.)
- Carpets. (Tightly woven short-pile carpets are less dusty than long, loose weaves, but hard flooring, such as timber or tile, is even better.)
- Cracks between floorboards. (Seal cracks to prevent dust blowing up from the space beneath.)
- Evening cleaning in the bedroom. (Clean earlier in the day, as cleaning can stir up dust in the air that takes a while to settle.)

The invisible enemies

Dust mites

House dust mites love warmth, humidity and, as their name suggests, dust. They are tiny — 0.1 mm (0.004 in) long — but they cause havoc to people who are allergic to their droppings. The term 'house dust mite' applies to about ten species of the Pyroglyphidae family of the arachnids. They thrive at a temperature of about 25°C (77°F) and relative humidity of 75–80 per cent, eating the skin flakes that humans shed constantly. Just like humans, house dust mites love soft furnishings — mattresses, pillows, soft carpets and upholstered furniture. They proliferate in conditions of humidity and poor ventilation, so good ventilation and moisture-reducing practices, such as fans in the bathroom and kitchen, help keep populations down.

See 'The bedroom', pages 273–6, for practical tips on dealing with dust mites.

MIGHTY NUMBERS OF MITES A double bed mattress can support a population of up to two million house dust mites. Under the right conditions a new mattress's mite population can reach this figure in just three months.

Mould

There are more mould spores in the air than any other biological particle: record counts are as high as 160 000 spores in each cubic metre (35 cubic ft) of air, compared to record counts of 2800 pollen particles per cubic metre (35 cubic ft). Reducing dampness is the first line of defence against moulds. Even simple measures such as wiping away condensation and opening up windows can help. In addition, look out for mould growth sites, such as old food and pot plants.

Pollen

People allergic to pollen need to be extra careful about what they let into the house, be it through an open window or on the soles of their shoes. People with severe pet allergies may decide not to own a pet at all, while others may find that as long as they are scrupulous about vacuuming, or they do not let a pet sleep on the bed, their symptoms are manageable. See 'Living with pets', page 37, for more ideas about living in harmony with animal friends.

Out-gases

A growing body of opinion classes unwanted reactions to the fumes from paints, fuel and furnishings as allergies. There is also the suggestion that excessive exposure to these fumes (which includes out-gasing) could make individuals more sensitive and more likely to develop classical allergic reactions. It is a controversial field, but as a general rule, water-based paints, stains and adhesives give off fewer odours and out-gases than solvent-based finishes. Smooth wall finishes offer fewer niches for allergens.

The importance of being ventilated

Good ventilation is a cornerstone of the healthy house and should start from the ground up.

The chemical residues from building materials are less of a problem with good sub-floor ventilation, which is also critical for the control of dry rot and termites.

Ventilation removes stale and polluted air, and replaces it with less polluted air from outside. It also removes excess humidity (water vapour in the air), replaces oxygen and removes carbon dioxide. Dry air is bad news for house dust mites who need relatively humid air to allow them to absorb water. Dry air also decreases the level of out-gassing of chemicals from household items.

Some ventilation occurs as air blows through spaces in a building's structure: through walls, gaps in windows, under doors and so on. As warm air rises, it escapes through the top of a building, pulling in more fresh air lower down. This is known as natural ventilation.

Windows of opportunity

To increase natural ventilation around your house, try the following tips.

- ▨ Living areas **In hot weather, encourage cross-ventilation in the cooler evening by opening the windows on opposite sides of the house.**

- ▨ Bedrooms **Sleeping with the windows open, or opening them when you get up, reduces humidity and helps reduce the dust mite population. If cold air brings on asthma symptoms, air bedrooms during the day. If you suffer from pollen allergy, air bedrooms during the afternoon when the pollen count is at its lowest.**

- ▨ Bathroom **Open the bathroom window after bathing and showering to allow moisture to escape, but keep the door closed so steam doesn't enter the rest of the house.**

- ▨ Kitchen **Open the windows when cooking, but close the doors to the rest of the house.**

- ▨ All rooms **On a sunny day, open the blinds and pull back the curtains, as heat kills dust mites.**

Air control systems

Ventilation and other air control systems can assist where natural ventilation is not sufficient. There are a number of different types.

▧ Passive ventilation **In specially designed passive stack ventilation, warm moist air rises up through ducts leading from the kitchen and bathroom ceilings to outlets in the roof. Fresh air enters through grilles in the living room and bedrooms, replacing the stale air. It uses no fans, relying solely on the characteristic of warm air to rise.**

▧ MVHR (mechanical ventilation with heat recovery) **This system can be fitted while building new houses, or installed later in single storey buildings. The house needs to be well insulated and reasonably airtight. It consists of a central unit with an exhaust fan, inlet fan and a heat exchanger. It supplies fresh air via ducting and air inlets to living rooms and bedrooms, and extracts stale air from the kitchen and bathroom. Air from the outside is filtered before being circulated inside.**

▧ Air filters **These can remove particles or gases and are used in forced air-heating and air-conditioning systems, air-filtering units and vacuum cleaners. Activated charcoal, a specially treated porous charcoal, is one type. A gaseous filter that removes most volatile organic compounds except formaldehyde is another. Activated alumina is sometimes added to remove the latter.**

AIR CLEANERS

Several products — including ion generators, ozone generators, mechanical air filters, electronic air cleaners and hybrid air cleaners (which combine techniques) — are marketed as air cleaners.

Ion generators act by charging particles in a room so they are attracted to surfaces such as walls and tabletops. Rubbing these surfaces can cause the particles to be re-suspended in the air. They may remove small particles such as those in tobacco smoke but cannot remove gases or odours, nor are they effective in removing larger particles such as pollen.

Ion generators indirectly generate ozone, which is itself a lung irritant.

■ Extended surface This is a particulate filter made from fibreglass or polyester fibres held together by synthetic resin. It can filter many particulates and pollen.

■ HEPA (high efficiency particulate air) This is a powerful extended surface particulate filter that removes 97 per cent of particles as small as 0.3 microns (0.00001 in). Used in conjunction with a charcoal filter, it will also remove smoke.

■ Electrostatic This plastic filter captures particulates by static electricity. It is fairly efficient for removing pollen and mould spores but not for particles smaller than 6 microns (0.0002 in).

■ Electrostatic precipitator This system imparts a negative charge to particles in the air such as dust, mould spores and pollen grains, which are then attracted to the positively charged collecting plate.

■ Partial house system A partial ventilation system supplies fresh air to upstairs rooms and extracts stale air from the bathroom. It can be supplemented by a kitchen range or stove hood downstairs and by single room heat recovery ventilation units or air inlets in living rooms.

■ Single room units A supply fan, exhaust fan and heat exchanger in a room can help control humidity and air quality, and may be useful, for instance, in the bedroom of someone who suffers from a dust allergy.

Improve your ventilation

There are several measures you can take to improve the ventilation in your home.

■ Fit extractors, also called exhaust fans, in the bathroom and kitchen. Exhaust fans need to be discharged to the outside air and not to an enclosed garage where they can cause problems of condensation, mould and rot. They are useful in wet rooms such as bathrooms as well as in garages and workshops where they can remove fumes.

■ Install an overrun timer on the extractor fan in very steamy bathrooms.

■ Fit air grilles, also known as trickle ventilators, into the window frames of living rooms and bedrooms.

■ Maintain air-conditioning systems, especially filters.

Living with pets

Medical studies demonstrate that pets help to keep us healthy as they have a comforting and calming effect. They can, however, create more dirt, and if a member of your household suffers from allergies, you may need to take extra care looking after a pet and its belongings.

Ensuring good ventilation and cleaning regularly can minimize the effect of pet allergens; keeping pets out of bedrooms and off beds will also help to reduce exposure to allergens.

Common pet allergies

While you can, in theory, be allergic to any animal, there are some pets that are more likely to cause problems.

- **Cats** These animals are known for their meticulous grooming, which usually consists of much licking from head to tail. When the saliva dries, it flakes and floats off, landing on surfaces around the home. It is this dried saliva that contains the allergen protein which can trigger allergy symptoms such as asthma and a runny nose in sufferers. The particles are so light and small they spread easily, and even a tiny amount can be enough to cause problems. Cat saliva flakes are also highly persistent and unless a place is washed thoroughly after a cat leaves, they can remain for years.

- **Dogs** Allergens are present in saliva and skin particles. These may be carried by fur, but the hairs themselves do not trigger allergic reactions.

- **Mice** The urine of small creatures such as mice and hamsters is a common allergic trigger.

Pet etiquette

Minimize the transfer of bacteria and other disease-causing organisms from pets to humans.

- Wash your hands after handling a pet, especially before eating.
- Keep cats and other mobile pets off food preparation surfaces.
- Give pets their own plates and bowls – do not share family ones – and wash them every day.
- Do not encourage begging at the table.

Keeping pets clean and odour-free

Homes with pets often smell of the pets themselves. Regular attention will minimize odours and keep the pets themselves comfortable and free of fleas and lice.

- Cages, perches, baskets and toys need regular cleaning in hot soapy water. A salty rinse and drying in the sun disinfects without leaving harmful residues.
- All bedding should be washed frequently and dried in the sun, if possible.
- Pets themselves also need regular grooming and bathing.
- Allow pets outside for some of the day, if possible.
- Regularly remove droppings from litter trays – more than daily if necessary.
- Place the tray in an area of good ventilation.
- Don't leave litter trays near where food is prepared or eaten.
- Wash litter boxes frequently in hot sudsy water.
- Frequently vacuum any areas in the house used by pets.
- Increase the frequency of shampooing of carpets and upholstery.
- Use bicarbonate of soda between shampoos on carpets and upholstery: sprinkle generously, leave for 15 minutes then vacuum.

SEED-FLICKING BIRDS To prevent seed showers from spraying surrounding floors or tabletops, wrap a length of fabric around the bird cage.

On the nose

- The smell of pet urine on concrete is difficult to remove. To deodorize it, scrub the surface with a solution of half white vinegar and half water, or spray with undiluted methylated spirits.
- To deodorize a smelly litter tray, wash it in hot soapy water, rinse in salt water then white vinegar and hot water, and dry in the sun.

BATHING A PET
- Use a non-slip mat in a tub to ease fears of slipping.
- Cover the drain with an inverted tea strainer to prevent hairs sliding down the drain and blocking the pipes.

Banish fleas

There are many species of flea, but the main ones to worry about in the home are the ones that prefer humans, cats and dogs (Siphonaptera). If you have a cat or a dog, tackling its flea infestation − or even better, making sure one doesn't happen in the first place − is the priority.

- Vacuuming is the number one defence against fleas. As well as removing the fleas themselves, it also removes eggs and larvae. But vacuuming fleas does not kill them, so you'll need to replace the vacuum bag after each session (and seal the full bag in a plastic bag and leave it in the sun to kill the fleas, before disposing of it). If you have a non-disposable bag, place a little pyrethrin insecticide inside the bag before you begin.

- Wash your pet every week. Ideally, use shampoos that contain essential oils such as pennyroyal, eucalyptus and tea-tree or add 1 drop of lemon grass or citronella oil to your pet's regular shampoo. If you're considering mainstream shampoos, malathion is the least toxic. Others may contain methoprene and pyrethroid products such as permethrin.

- Wash your pet's bedding frequently in hot soapy water. In a high infestation period such as midsummer it's a good idea to do this at least weekly.

- To repel fleas and deodorize, wipe over pet belongings with water to which a few drops of tea-tree oil have been added. Use it also as a final rinse for a kennel floor and litter trays. (Do not use it undiluted as it is poisonous when concentrated.)

- Comb your pet with a flea comb.

- Consider steam cleaning rugs and upholstery seasonally.

- For a bad infestation, use a pyrethrin treatment in cracks, crevices, carpets and your pet's bedding or sleeping places. This paralyses the fleas, allowing them to be vacuumed up.

- Flea powders containing dust of rotenone and pyrethrins are not highly toxic but do not last long and need to be reapplied frequently.

- As a last resort, use a permethrin/methropene flea bomb. The former chemical kills adult fleas while the latter stops new hatchlings reaching maturity.

- Your vet may recommend monthly skin treatments and quarterly injections which also break the flea life cycle. It may be necessary to use other control methods too, however, as these only take effect once a flea has bitten its host.

SUNNING PET FURNITURE When possible, put pets' cages, boxes and bedding (without the pet!) in the sun for a few hours to air, deodorize and disinfect.

Green house

A green house is also a healthy house — the two go hand in hand. When you decide to make your house 'greener', you are making a decision that affects not only your own household but the wider environment as well. 'Going green' means making your home as energy efficient as possible; treating all resources as precious rather than something to be thoughtlessly squandered; and in lots of small but important ways, reducing your impact on a fragile planet.

Saving energy makes sense

Many of the principles of an ecologically sound house also make economical sense. A house that has been designed to be energy efficient should be a naturally comfortable one too. Building a house from scratch allows you to situate, orient and shelter the building to make the best of renewable sources of energy. Ideally, living spaces should face north in the southern hemisphere (and south in the northern hemisphere) to take greatest advantage of the sun for light and warmth in both summer and winter. If you are renovating or extending an existing house, consult an environmental architect to discuss options for low-energy designs.

Even if you are not planning to build, consider a few energy-efficient principles.

- **Use the sun and wind where possible for energy, relying less on supplementary, non-renewable energy. This can be as simple as pegging out the washing rather than using your dryer — sun and wind are free.**

- **Think of the local environment: plant native trees and flowers, compost organic wastes, garden organically and use natural pest control. Use low-flush or waterless toilets, and collect, store and use rainwater.**

SOLAR ENERGY

Sun-powered electricity, harnessed by solar panels on the roof, can run all your house's appliances and heat water for the bathroom and kitchen. In a solar hot water heater, the sun directly heats up water in small pipes, which is stored in a tank for later use, usually in conjunction with a gas or electrical heater to boost the temperature of the water. Photovoltaic cells on the roof convert the sun's energy to electricity, which can be diverted to the fridge, sound system and washing machine. In some systems surplus electricity is sent to the main electricity grid.

- Use green materials and products. The green ideal is to use non-toxic, non-polluting products from sustainable and renewable sources, produced with low energy and low environmental and social costs, which are biodegradable or easily reused and recycled.

- Paint the exterior of a house with light-coloured paint to help reflect unwanted radiant heat.

- Shade all windows when it's warm or hot. Windows are a main entry point for heat and light — highly desirable in winter, but potentially overheating in summer. Consider ways of shading windows in the summertime — for example, with awnings and deciduous trees.

- Create a healthy indoor climate by allowing the house to breathe. Use natural materials and processes to regulate the temperature, humidity and air flow.

- If you live in a hot climate, open up and ventilate the house at night when the air is cooler.

- Allow sunlight and daylight to penetrate your home, and rely less on artificial lighting.

Every little bit counts

You'll be surprised at how quickly even small savings turn into big ones — for both you and the environment.

- Install a solar or energy-efficient hot water heater. Since water heating accounts for up to 50 per cent of a home's energy use, installing one of these heaters saves in energy bills as well as pollution.

- Choose energy-efficient appliances when buying new ones. Many countries have star ratings to make the choice easier. Top-rated fridges, freezers, washing machines, dryers, dishwashers and air-conditioners are much less polluting and also cheaper to run.

- Install a water-efficient showerhead. These usually pay for themselves in the first year of use. The shower is the largest user of household hot water and accounts for around 20 per cent of the greenhouse pollution in the average home. These showerheads use less water, reducing both pollution and heating costs.

- Insulate your home. Save on heating and cooling bills as well as the pollution these processes produce.

- Consider ways of adding thermal mass to your home if you live in a climate with cool winters. Thermal mass describes heavy building materials such as brick, stone or thick ceramic tiles that are slow to heat and slow to cool. In the winter they warm up in the day and continue to radiate heat in the evening, while in summer they protect against excessive heat, especially when shaded. New brick, tile or concrete flooring is an obvious way of adapting an existing home to include greater thermal mass.

- Use appliances only when you really need them. For instance, use a broom in the garden, not a motorized leaf blower.

- Use appliances efficiently and maintain them well so they work optimally.

- Defrost your freezer every three months to prolong its life and ensure maximum efficiency.

- Don't leave the fridge door open unnecessarily. For every minute it is open, it takes three minutes to cool down again.

- Turn off your fridge and leave the door ajar when you go on holiday.

- Switch off lights when they are not in use.

- Replace your most frequently used light bulbs with compact fluorescents: each bulb uses around a quarter of the electricity needed for a standard bulb and will prevent the emission of half a tonne or ton of greenhouse pollution over the life of the bulb. If you fitted all your lamps and lights with energy-efficient bulbs, you could reduce your lighting costs by 80 per cent.

- Turn off microwaves, TVs and sound systems at the power point — they use power even when they are not operating.

- Wash clothes in cold water if you're satisfied with the result. Consider pre-soaking heavily soiled garments first.

- Wear adequate clothing when the weather cools and don't attempt to heat the entire house to the same temperature. Keep one or two rooms cosy by shutting the doors to the rest of the house.

TYPES OF INSULATION

Bulk insulation
Bulk insulation reduces the flow of heat that occurs by conduction. It comes in several different forms.

- Batts and blankets made of materials such as rockwool, fibreglass, acrylic fibre, wool and eel grass.
- Loose-fill material made from cellulose fibre.
- Rigid lightweight boards such as polystyrene and polyurethane, and materials such as straw and wood fibres that can act as a lining when mixed with binders.

Reflective insulation
To be effective, reflective insulation must have an air space next to it. It reduces heat transfer by reflecting heat on its warm side and not emitting much heat on its cool side. Reflective insulation usually comes in one of the following two forms.

- Reflective foil laminate (RFL) is made from aluminium foil laminated onto both sides of a stiffer backing.
- Reflective coating on the underside of corrugated metal or on the back of plasterboard.

Composite reflective and bulk insulation
This type of insulation has reflective foil laminated onto one side of a bulk material.

Insulate for comfort

Effective insulation helps houses in both warm and cool conditions, as it slows down the transfer of heat in and out of a building, thus making the building more energy efficient in terms of heating or cooling costs. You can cut these costs by an estimated 20 per cent by installing appropriate insulation in your home. Insulation is rated according to its suitability for different climates, so make sure you use the type most suitable for yours.

Where should you insulate?

Ceilings, walls and windows are all candidates for insulation.

The ceiling and roof area is the most important spot to insulate, as it is there that a house loses most heat in winter and gains unwanted heat in summer. Reflective insulation is the best choice for preventing the warmth of the summer sun entering, while bulk insulation stops heat already in the house from escaping. Effective roof insulation, therefore, uses a combination of the two.

Walls can be insulated with rigid polystyrene boards, by injecting expanded polystyrene into the wall cavity, fitting bulk insulation between wall studs and by fixing reflective foil laminate to the wall studs. You or your builder need to take care that insulation does not form a bridge in cavity walls for moisture to travel across. Vapour barriers are also necessary on the warm side of the insulation to prevent moisture condensing on both it and the wall surface. In a cold climate this should be at the inside lining, and in hot climates where rooms are air-conditioned, at the outside lining.

Windows are a prime candidate for insulating as glass is an excellent conductor of heat. Reduce heat lost at windows by using any of these methods.

- **Fit heavy curtains and pelmets made from material with a close weave. The air between the curtains and window acts as insulation.**

- **Install fitted insulated panels such as shutters at the window, either inside or out.**

- **Double glazing is a good option for colder climates. Two sheets of glass are separated by a gap of 12–20 mm ($1/2$–$3/4$ in).**

THE VALUE OF INSULATION

The effectiveness of insulation is expressed as its R value. The higher the R value, the greater the insulating effect. As the best insulation for your house depends on its climatic location, you should contact local energy information centres for advice.

If you are making alterations, the existing structure will also affect your needs. Roofing generally requires insulation with a greater R value than external walls. Flooring insulation may also be an option, depending on your home and its location.

Weather proofing

Weather proofing the house helps keep out cold draughts and rain. Consider taking the following measures.

- **Apply weather strips to external doors.**
- **Seal gaps under skirting boards, around the edge of window frames and under windowsills.**
- **Check the ceiling for gaps where pipes leave roof spaces.**
- **Fill the cavity of outside walls with insulation in order to stop unwanted air leakage.**

Getting water wise

According to the World Health Organisation (WHO), the absolute minimum amount of water a person needs every day is 5.6 L (1.5 gal). In 1970 the WHO surveyed 91 countries and found an average water use of 22.7 L (6 gal) per head per day for people who used a public hydrant. In most countries consumption was below 45.4 L (12 gal) per head per day, but in the United States it was 272.5 L (72 gal) per head per day.

TOILET TRICKS Up to one-third of water used in the home is flushed down the toilet. Save water by fitting a dual flush to your toilet cistern. Consider, too, ways to reuse bath/handbasin water.

See 'The bathroom', pages 188–91, for more water-wise tips.

Water supplies the world over are strained to produce enough clean water to meet population demands without drying up reserves. Conserving water not only takes the strain off your local supplier but also reduces pollution, as water processing requires energy, which in turn creates pollution. Saving water can also save you money as, increasingly, local suppliers are charging for the amount of water a household uses.

THIRSTY GARDENS There are many ways to conserve water in the garden: plant natives that are adapted to the environment and therefore less thirsty; collect rainwater; and find ways to reuse household water.

See 'The outdoors', pages 312–17, for water-saving garden tips.

Hot issues

Heating water burns up money as well as produces pollution. Try these simple ideas for reducing your hot water usage.

- Take quicker showers. Cutting your shower time from 10 minutes to 5 could save as much as 27 000 L (5939 gal) of water a year.

- Fix dripping taps. Forty-five drops a minute is ten baths of water a year.

- Don't rinse dishes under a running hot tap. Use a sink or bowl full of water instead.

- Avoid turning the hot tap on for small quantities of water. This leaves the pipes full of hot water, which cools and is wasted.

- Turn off the hot water system if you'll be away from home for more than two or three days.

- Insulate your storage tank. Between 15 and 20 per cent of the cost of running an electric hot water service is due to heat losses from the storage tank. Reduce losses by wrapping the tank in foil-backed insulating blanket held in place with ducting tape. (Do not add extra insulation to gas systems as they may overheat.)

- Install solar hot water heaters if possible when making big changes on your house.

- Install an on-demand system if you have a choice, as they are the most efficient — you are not paying to heat stored water.

- Locate new hot water systems near where you use hot water to cut the amount of hot water and energy lost through cooling in pipes.

DO YOUR BIT TO STOP GREENHOUSE POLLUTION

It might seem like an insurmountable problem, but you can make a difference.

- **Drive less** Shop locally where possible; use public transport or walk or cycle.
- **Use an efficient car** Fuel-efficient cars can produce up to 30 per cent less greenhouse gas than inefficient ones. Keeping a car engine well tuned keeps emissions down too.
- **Use green energy** Many electricity retailers have an option to use green-generated power. While it does usually cost slightly more, not only is your polluting contribution reduced, you are also actively supporting the development of more environmentally friendly sources of power.
- **Compost your waste** In landfills and poorly managed compost heaps where there is no fresh air, food scraps break down anaerobically (without oxygen), producing the greenhouse gas methane.

See 'The outdoors', pages 309–11, for tips on constructing a compost heap.

Clean and green

If you are interested in making your house a more environmentally friendly place, there is no easier way to start than in considering the chemicals that you use in it. And no better place to begin doing this than by reviewing your cleaning and pest control regimens — what is their impact on health and the environment? It's up to you to choose the types of materials you wish to use — whether traditional, green or commercial products, your own combination of them all, or even your own home-made cleaning brews.

Everyone needs to wash dishes by hand, at least occasionally. This calls for dishwashing liquid, which doubles as a gentle cleaner for light jobs, such as wiping down windowsills or mopping up a small spill on the sofa. You need an all-purpose cleaner for greasy kitchen benchtops and stove-top spills. You also need to be able to clean your oven, wash hard flooring and bathroom surfaces, clean the toilet and wash your clothes.

Commercial cleaning products can contain solvents, surfactants and many other chemicals with potential to harm skin, mucous membranes and the respiratory tract.

If you wish to avoid harsh chemicals, there are alternatives. With a few basic ingredients, including several from the kitchen cupboard — items you probably already have as they are frequently used in cooking — you can make a range of low-toxic cleaners suitable for every job in the house.

However, using basic household aids may require a little adjustment. Some people, for instance, dislike the smell of vinegar and find it quite overpowering. And sometimes, you may need to apply a little more 'elbow grease' with green products.

Innovation on the home cleaning front

The search for technologies that produce gleam without compromising the environment or people's health continues to produce new products.

- **Plant-based solvents, such as D-Limonene from orange and lemon skins, form a key ingredient of a range of cleaning solutions that manufacturers claim are very low in toxicity.**

- **According to the manufacturers, micro fibre cleaning cloths clean without using any chemicals, only water: each cloth contains more than a million tiny fibres which are said to grind away at dirt.**

ARE YOU A CLEANING PRODUCTS JUNKIE?

It's surprising how few items you really need to clean your house, and yet — take a look at your household cleaning armoury and what do you find? A mould cure, pre-wash treatment and stain remover (probably a few types including a soap bar and a spray), lime scale remover, carpet stain mousse, dishwasher powder, finishing rinse, silver polish, fabric softener, oven cleaner, window cleaners (one with white vinegar and one with an insect remover), bleach, toilet gel, laundry powder, laundry liquid, wool wash, all-purpose cream cleanser and several types of bathroom cleaner!

Does this reveal a hygiene mentality deserving prizes, a soft spot for marketing jingles or a distinct lack of understanding of how cleaning works? More to the point, do you *really* need all these products to keep a clean and pleasant home? The short answer is 'no'.

(See 'What's in a name?', page 338, for a full list of the chemical ingredients in your cleaning products.)

YOUR BASIC GREEN INGREDIENTS

■ **Bicarbonate of soda** Also known as sodium bicarbonate and baking soda, bicarbonate of soda is used in baking to aerate cakes and bread, but it has many other household uses. A gentle, moderately alkaline, non-toxic abrasive, bicarbonate of soda cuts through grease and oil because it reacts with the fatty acids to form mild detergents. Use baking soda to clean, deodorize and buffer, and to extinguish fires. You can even use it to clean your teeth!

■ **Lemon juice** This is a natural bleach which can be used for many purposes, including stain removal, deodorizing and mould inhibiting.

■ **Salt** A natural gentle abrasive and disinfectant, salt is useful for clearing drains and scouring kitchen utensils.

■ **White vinegar** This type of vinegar has a key role in alternative home cleaning because of its acidic properties, although it is not a general cleaner. It is a moderately strong acid, which can remove bathroom scum and hard water deposits as well as discolouration from metals such as aluminium, brass, bronze and copper. It can also remove rust stains and rust on iron. White vinegar makes an ideal cleanser for the bathroom.

For recipes and details on cleaning with these natural products, see 'The kitchen', page 84; 'The laundry', page 126; 'The bathroom', page 191; and 'The living room', pages 228, 229, 237, 239 and 252.

The right tools for the job

With the appropriate tools, a job becomes, if not easy, then at least not infuriatingly tedious. Modern cleaning equipment has become a lot more sophisticated, with washing machines to agitate, wash, rinse and spin your laundry; vacuum cleaners to suck dirt out of carpets and upholstery; and dishwashers that even detect how dirty your plates are and what washing program they need. But you can't go far in cleaning your house without some very humble, simple, 'green' equipment such as buckets, rags and cleaning cloths — plus as much elbow grease as you can muster.

■ Brushes and brooms **These come in many useful forms: dish brushes; scrubbing brushes; toilet brushes; old toothbrushes for hard to reach areas around taps or along the edge of a bath; soft-bristled dustpan brushes for picking up dust and small solid spills; hard-bristled brooms for sweeping outdoors; relatively short-bristled shoe brushes for** applying polish and shining leather; and bottlebrushes for bottles and other narrow-necked containers. Keep brushes clean so they can do their job properly. Wash them in detergent, rinse and then hang outside to dry.

Buckets Use buckets for soaking dirty laundry and for making up cleaning solutions.

Cleaning caddy A box or basket is useful for carrying the cleaning kit of rags, brushes and cleaning products from room to room.

Cleaning cloths Wiping, dusting and rubbing all require a cloth, rag or sponge. Soak up a big spill with an old bath towel. It deals with the job immediately and then you can wash it. For many other jobs, rags are ideal. Rags and cloths, cut from old t-shirts and towels or dusters and sponges, need to be kept separate according to the job they do: kitchen ones in one place, floor cloths in another, and general household dusting and wiping ones in another place. To clean rags, soak them in hot water and bleach, then wash them as usual.

Dust mask For very dusty jobs – such as cleaning out a rarely used shed or attic – wear a dust mask to protect your respiratory tract. If you're prone to hay fever-like allergies, then a dust mask is an essential item for your cleaning caddy.

Gloves A great help with a dirty job, gloves also protect the skin on your hands when you use strong chemicals. Any detergent strips the oily

DRESS FOR ACTION

You'll be more likely to throw yourself into cleaning jobs if you are dressed appropriately.

- Old outsized t-shirts over your clothes
- Workman's overalls
- Baggy shirts for a protective layer
- Apron with plenty of pockets
- Sports gear (tracksuits, leggings, sweatshirts) for ease of movement and comfort

protection from the skin's surface, making your hands prone to drying and cracking, and other chemicals can irritate the skin further. Gloves also reduce the possibility of contact allergic reactions, unless you are allergic to rubber, in which case you need to wear cotton-lined rubber gloves, or separate cotton gloves under the waterproof ones. Disposable plastic gloves are great for dirty jobs but very wasteful.

- Mop Refillable sponge mops, which come in many types and brands, are usually self-wringing. The main issue is the continued availability of refills. A cotton mop may last longer but you'll need to use it with a wringing bucket to avoid flooding the floor.

- Scourers These are useful for tough dishwashing jobs such as cleaning saucepans and roasting trays. Sometimes impregnated with cleaning materials, they come in metal, plastic or nylon.

- Sponges Use these for washing up, mopping up spills and wiping down benchtops and other surfaces.

- Vacuum cleaner Inefficient carpet sweepers were replaced by vacuum cleaners around the beginning of the 20th century. There are two main types of vacuum cleaner — upright and cylinder, each varying in suction power, manoeuvrability and number of accessories. More recent technologies have come up with steam cleaners, better suction, and Hepa filters which capture microscopic particles that can cause allergic reactions. 'Robotic' vacuum cleaners that work their way round a room in an optical motion, steering around walls, are also available.

No poison — no pests

Pesticides are designed to kill plant or animal life, so of course many of them are highly toxic. You can make your home a friendlier, greener place by choosing non-toxic or low-toxicity pesticides and pest control methods both indoors and out. For instance, pyrethroids, based on the naturally occurring pyrethrins, are highly toxic to insects, but only slightly toxic to humans; traps such as beer traps for slugs, or glue traps for cockroaches, do not introduce any chemicals into the living environment.

For more friendly ideas on dealing with pests, see 'The kitchen', page 109, and 'The outdoors', page 323.

Clever shopping

Buying in bulk cuts down your petrol use as well as often saving you money. If you can arrange it, you may be able to obtain wholesale prices at fruit and vegetable markets if you shop with other households. To reduce the use of packaging, take your own reusable shopping bag and buy products with less packaging. Where possible, buy local produce, reducing transport costs and the fuel that goes with it. Consider buying organic produce to support farmers who are not using pesticides.

Organic produce and recycled products were once the domain of the funny little alternative shop in the back streets. Now even supermarkets are waking up to the fact that some consumers like to choose products that are produced and marketed in ways they are comfortable with.

Find further uses for packaging and other items wherever possible. Cereal and egg boxes can become children's craft supplies, paper can be reused for telephone message pads, drawing and painting. Old clothing can be cut up for rags or taken to the local charity shop.

USE IT AGAIN, SAM

Recycling saves energy in manufacture and also in landfill. Find out about active recycling schemes in your area. Paper, glass, steel, aluminium and some plastics are commonly collected by local authorities, but tyres, batteries and all sorts of household items can also be reused again. Check with your local authority as they may be handled by reverse garbage depots.

Sort and separate your household waste according to what can be done with it: glass in one container, newspapers and other items for recycling in others; toxic substances, such as old pesticide containers, should be collected by the local authority; vegetable peelings and other biodegradable waste can be composted.

RENOVATIONS AND EXTENSIONS Use recycled building materials where possible and timber from sustainable sources. Many materials can be used again — wooden flooring, beams, staircases and posts; basins, laundry tubs and baths; fireplaces, windows and doors; roof tiles, security grilles and garden gates. Where used timber is unavailable or unsuitable for the job, using plantation timbers rather than native forest woods places one less burden on the environment.

THE GREEN SHOPPER

Making 'green' choices when you shop can have far-reaching benefits.

Packaging

In industrialized countries, around 30 per cent of plastics are used for packaging, which is used once then thrown away. While some packaging is clearly useful as protection, some is nothing other than wasteful. Put your money where your beliefs are and buy products with less packaging. Let manufacturers know you disapprove of excess packaging by writing to them.

Eco-labelling

As companies vie for the green consumer's dollar, in some countries there are labelling schemes to help you evaluate claims such as 'recyclable' or 'made from recycled materials'. Consumer groups and government fair trading or consumer affairs departments should be able to give you local information.

Ethical purchases

An increasing number of retailers and direct mail companies are offering textiles, crafts and food products made by people in developing countries, often in co-ops, who will directly benefit from your purchases. In many cases middle men have been eliminated from the buying and selling chain so that more profit ends up with the makers of the products.

Organic produce

Organic fruit, vegetables, dairy foods and meat are part of a growing market that offers consumers foods produced without pesticides. Organic meat comes from animals that spend a certain proportion of their time outside in a non-intensive farming fashion. There are also regulations about the drugs and feed they may be given. Most countries have official organic inspecting bodies. Look for their labels when buying organic products.

Energy-efficient rating

Appliances such as fridges and washing machines now often carry efficiency ratings. These offer valuable information as to how efficiently an appliance uses energy and how economical it is to run.

Economy shopping

If you put your mind to it, you need never buy full price mainstream products again. Numerous outlets offer end of line or sales goods at discounted prices — surplus stores, factory outlets, all stores at seasonal sales. In addition, home brands at major supermarkets and department stores are usually a cheaper option. Buying in bulk, whether at wholesale markets or at the supermarket, can often save money. So too can the purchase of concentrated products.

Efficient and safe house

Your household can become a less wasteful, more efficient and more comfortable place to live in if you make some small changes.

- **Organize your spaces so they work optimally for their particular use. Clear space for exercises and relaxation like yoga.**

- **Designate surfaces and storage areas for hobbies, mementoes and household activities.**

- **When you are short of space, make each room as versatile as possible by doubling up on purposes. For instance, with a folding dining room table and a sofa bed, a room can double up as the dining room as well as an occasional guest room. Use a screen to divide a room for home office use and a sewing room, and so on.**

- **If you have a clutter problem, get ruthless and attack the house room by room, cupboard by cupboard, sorting duplicates, unused and unwanted items. Then offload your excess by giving it away to friends, schools and charity shops.**

MEMO TO MUDDLERS *This section is devoted to muddlers — the housewives who, no matter how hard they try, just cannot keep organized. For example there is the housewife who, instead of getting the house clean and straight in the morning and having the afternoon free for sewing, visiting or playing with the children, works on and off all day, often dropping into bed late at night after ironing all evening, or washing, or cleaning the cooker. Yet the house still looks a mess. It isn't that she's lazy — it's just that as fast as she cleans and tidies, she creates more muddle, aided and abetted by her family.*

Jane Harvey, *Hoover Book of Management* (1963)

Sound familiar? 'If you are a muddler, you must just make things easier for yourself,' continues Ms Harvey. Then as now, the advice for salvaging this all too common scenario starts with war on clutter.

THE GOLDEN RULES OF CLUTTER CONTROL

1   When in doubt, throw it out
   - Clothes that don't fit.
   - Gifts you don't like and never intend using.
   - Broken things you don't miss and are unlikely to ever get round to mending.
   - Books you don't value.
   - Appliances you never use.

2   Do it now
   - Take things upstairs when you're going anyway.
   - Take things downstairs when you're going anyway.
   - Pick up things when they drop.
   - Wipe spills when they happen.
   - Vacuum messes when they occur.
   - File bills and correspondence immediately.
   - Dump junk mail the minute you receive it.

3   Set limits
   - Allow yourself a set number of bags, food containers and boxes that you keep because they 'might come in handy one day'.
   - Pare down on mementoes. When the cupboards are bursting, clear and sort them, fill them in an orderly fashion, and find another home for the excess, whether it's the garbage bin, shed or school fete.
   - One in, one out. In other words, throw/give away one item each time you acquire another. This may be worth trying if you are constantly acquiring new things, be it from friends, charity shops or boot sales.

Clutter control

Clutter makes it harder to clean and harder to find things when you want them. Whether it's piles of paper hiding the dining room table, dozens of empty jars that you think you might need one day, or stashes of pens that don't work, clutter of one sort or another is very often the root of a feeling of mildly unnerving chaos in the home. If you feel like this you most certainly are not alone. There are even people who earn a living by helping people declutter their lives — either as a personal service or in a workshop. A few time-tested principles may help you gradually clear your home and regain a sense of control.

Getting organized: The box method

Take six boxes or containers and sort your junk and treasures.

Box 1: Throw away

Box 2: Give away or sell
Charity shops need goods for raising money. Yard sales (or garage sales) and classified ads are ways you can sell it yourself.

Box 3: Put away
Things to put away later, sorted by room if that's easy enough to do quickly.

Box 4: Storage
This box is for seasonal clothing and items you only use occasionally such as camping equipment, decorating tools and archive documents.

Box 5: Limbo (or the 'One year box')
This is the 'not sure' box where anything you're not sure about goes. It gets packed away for one year and if you never use it within that time, it's time to throw it out.

Box 6: Needs repairs
Be realistic — will you actually fix it? Otherwise, it's into Box 1.

When it's overwhelming

When you feel as if you are never going to make progress:

Use the timer
Give yourself 5/10/30 minutes to tidy a room or put away things.

Count
Put away a set number of items — say, five or ten.

Start small
Go through one drawer or one shelf per session.

Get ruthless
Dump everything on the floor, then take back what you want to keep. To stay, an item needs to pass the clutter test.

- **Is it in good shape?**

- **If it's broken, can it be fixed?**

- Do you really need it?
- Have you used it in the past year?
- Would it be hard to replace if you ever need it again?
- Would you pay money to store it?
- Does it have sentimental value?

The paper chase

We have not achieved the paper-free home any more than the paperless office. Letters from school, invitations, newspaper clippings, bills, junk mail...There are times when you need a radical paper sort. Here is one way to go about it.

1   Put all your papers into a box. As you go, bin the items you don't need.

2   Sort the papers into the following categories. They may need halfway houses, such as boxes, till you find them more permanent homes.

- Act on Have a special spot for things you need to act on, such as bills — perhaps a special noticeboard or a folder that you go through regularly.
- Personal This is where letters, anniversary cards and the like are kept.
- Banking Statements, letters from the bank, spare cheque book.
- House maintenance The instructions for the air-conditioning or water heater, guarantees for appliances.
- Expenses Your dockets and invoices.
- Tax Anything that will be relevant when tax time comes around.
- School Sporting dates, school calendars, permission notes, timetables.

Finally, create an 'in' box which you empty and file once a week.

Staying uncluttered

- Spend ten minutes each morning or evening picking things up and putting them back where they belong.
- Institute family or household rules for clearing up after one activity and before starting another.
- Deal with things as they arise.

Safe and sound

A few general safety principles will go a long way towards making your home a safer one to live in, especially if you have children.

Electricity

Adults sustain most electrical injuries at home during DIY activities, while children are more at risk from 'mending' electrical equipment and pushing objects such as pins into sockets. Safety switches, or circuit breakers, can save lives and prevent injuries by turning off the electricity when they detect current passing out of the circuit. To minimize risks, keep the following in mind.

- Keep wiring and appliances in good order and do not use them if you suspect they are faulty.
- Keep all electrical appliances out of reach of children.
- Consider fitting power point covers.
- Never use electrical appliances in wet areas.
- Always turn off the power before removing a plug from a power point.
- Do not attempt electrical repairs if you are not qualified.

Smoke alarms

Smoke alarms give an early warning of fire, the chance to escape and an earlier opportunity to call the fire brigade. They are inexpensive and very easy to install. One, preferably two, smoke alarms per household is the minimum recommended by fire safety experts. Research shows that 10 to 15 per cent of smoke alarms in homes don't work properly, so it's important to change the battery regularly and check monthly that smoke alarms are working.

DANGEROUS DIY

House repairs and renovations are the occasion of many an accident, particularly when they involve climbing ladders. Make sure you keep ladders in good repair, and only use them when they are well secured. Step ladders should be fully extended with the crossbar in place. Use ear protection for noisy jobs and goggles for tasks that produce lots of dust, sparks or UV light. Wear protective clothing when handling toxic chemicals.

Out of reach

Keep all dangerous items such as matches, knives, kettles and their cords out of reach of young children. Keep all cleaners and other chemicals either high up or in a locked cupboard. Store medicines well out of reach.

Scalds

Hot water burns like fire. The main risks are from hot drinks, kettles and saucepans being knocked over or pulled down and from tap water. Reducing the temperature of your hot water to 50°C (122°F) greatly lowers the risk of scalds: it takes only one second for a major burn at 60°C (140°F), ten seconds at 55°C (131°F), yet five minutes at 50°C (122°F). If it's impossible to alter the temperature of your hot water, consider installing mixing valves or other devices that limit the temperature of water at the tap.

Prevent falls

Consider areas where babies and toddlers could fall. Install stair gates top and bottom, and closely examine balcony areas for safety. Effective gates and barriers are ones that can't be climbed.

Elderly or infirm family members can fall in slippery bathrooms. If appropriate, install non-slip flooring and safety rails in your bathroom.

Fire exits

Make sure you have an alternative route of escape in the case of fire and keep it clear of obstacles. If your windows are barred, make sure that at least one can be opened with a key. If you dead-lock your doors at night, keep the key by your bedside.

A rehearsed fire exit plan can really help children survive a fire as they are at high risk of smoke inhalation and asphyxiation. Use phrases like 'Stop, drop and roll' and 'Get down low and go go go' to help them remember the drill.

Outdoor lighting

Lamps that light up driveways, paths and front doors help young and old alike to avoid falls, and deter intruders from lurking in the shadows.

In an emergency

A little forethought saves time and hassle later. Stick a list of emergency phone numbers somewhere prominent so that all mehbers of the household can find them easily if they need them. Make sure the medicine cabinet and first aid kit are well stocked at all times.

EMERGENCY PHONE NUMBERS

- Family doctor
- Nearest hospital with accident and emergency unit
- Local police station
- Local fire brigade
- Plumber
- Locksmith
- Glazier
- Electrician
- Electricity company's emergency phone number
- Local gas emergency number
- Local builder
- Vet
- Work numbers of the adults in the household
- School/day care numbers (as appropriate)
- Relatives or friends whom children can ring in an emergency

The medicine cabinet

A well stocked medicine cabinet and first aid kit are blessings, as it seems you need them most in an emergency or when it is difficult to get to a chemist. Remember that your cabinet should be child-proof, either locked or well up out of reach. If you are starting one from scratch, this list will help.

- Pain relievers and medicines to bring down fever (adult and junior versions if you have children in the house)
- Antiseptic cream
- Cotton buds
- Cotton balls, including a sterile pack
- Antacids for heartburn, stomach aches
- Anti-diarrhoea medicine
- Anti-itch cream
- Mild laxative
- Hydrocortisone cream for insect bites and eczema
- Bicarbonate of soda
- Petroleum jelly
- Cold/allergy remedy
- Antihistamine and decongestant
- Expectorant cough medicine
- Methylated spirits
- Metric teaspoon or other dose measure, such as syringe, for children
- Hydrogen peroxide
- Syrup of ipecac
- Sunscreen
- Thermometer
- Family medical guide
- Hot water bottle
- Heat pack
- Ice pack (stored in your freezer)

First aid kit

A first aid kit comes in handy when you least expect to need it. Keep a kit in your car, as well as in the house. Pharmacists sell ready assembled kits; check against the following list and supplement where necessary.

- 1 small roller bandage
- 1 large roller bandage
- 1 small conforming bandage
- 1 large conforming bandage
- 2 eye pads with bandages
- Scissors
- Safety pins
- Calamine cream
- Pack of gauze swabs
- 2 triangular bandages
- Hypoallergenic tape
- 2 sterile pads
- Waterproof plasters or bandaids
- 1 finger bandage
- Tweezers
- 1 sterile dressing with bandage

Other useful items

- Face washer or flannel (to use as a cold compress)
- Sheet and pillowcase (covering for burns)
- Clean plastic bags (to put over burned foot and secured with bandages)
- Plastic wrap (to dress burns and seal chest wounds)

the kitchen

The kitchen is the hub of most households. This is the room where you prepare your meals, make morning tea and nightcaps. Try to have kitchen surfaces that are durable and easy to clean: floors that can be swept and mopped or wiped frequently; tile splashbacks behind stoves and sinks to protect against moisture; walls painted with washable paint; and worktop surfaces that will not show every little spill as a stain.

A DIRTY KITCHEN IS A DISGRACE. *It takes no longer to keep a kitchen clean and orderly than untidy and dirty. For the time spent in keeping it in good order is saved when culinary operations are going on and everything is clean and in its place. Personal cleanliness is most necessary, particularly with regard to the hands.*

Mrs Beeton's Book of Household Management (1861)

the kitchen

The clever kitchen

The clever kitchen is kept clean — with low-toxic cleaners — and well ventilated to reduce bacteria. It uses energy-efficient appliances and has water-saving features.

- Ventilation **The clever kitchen is well ventilated to counteract the mould-encouraging effect of steam and to dissipate combustion by-products — both produced by cooking. This helps make the kitchen a healthier place for all household members, especially those who may be prone to mould- and mildew-induced allergies, or to respiratory allergies and irritations made worse by pollutant gases. Managing moisture in the kitchen has a knock-on effect throughout the house: keep the door closed when it's hot and steamy.**

- Energy-efficient appliances **The clever kitchen uses a top-rating efficient fridge, freezer and stove which are run on a combination of solar power and natural gas back-up.**

- Tap water **This is rainwater which is hygienically collected and regularly tested to check it conforms to drinking water standards.**

- Waste water **This passes into the household water-recycling system, which has good quality filter systems. Once treated, this water is used on the garden, to flush the household toilets and to wash clothes.**

- Detergent **Dishwashing liquids and other cleaners are phosphate-free and low in toxic additives.**

- Recycling corner **All items recycled by the local authority — glass, paper, steel, plastic, aluminium — are stored for recycling and regular pick-up. Other items, such as batteries and tyres, are periodically removed to a local recycling depot. Some items are kept for recycling in the house.**

- Biodegradable scraps **All compost items are placed in a mini kitchen bin and regularly taken out to the compost heap.**

- Safety **Dangerous items such as knives and chemicals are kept out of reach.**

- Kitchen pests **These are controlled with natural methods.**

Saving energy in the kitchen

There are many ways to use less energy when cooking and storing food, and clearing up afterwards. It needn't be harder or take more time.

The dishwasher

- An energy-efficient dishwasher can actually use less water and energy than doing the dishes by hand, but only if you use it efficiently.

- Choose a dishwasher that allows you to eliminate the heated drying cycle and dry by air instead, or turn your machine off before that phase.

- Save water by using the dishwasher's rinse and hold function instead of rinsing dishes before you load them into the machine.

- Wash only full loads.

- Use hot water from your hot water system if it's gas or solar, and run the dishwasher at its lower temperature settings.

- Use a detergent with low environmental impact. Alternatively, replace up to 50 per cent of a standard detergent with washing soda.

Saving energy when cooking

- Allow frozen food to defrost in the fridge overnight.

- Where appropriate, use small appliances, such as pressure cookers, toasters and electric kettles.

- Match the size of pots to the size of a hot plate or burner – turn down the burner if flames are lapping up the side of the pan.

ON DISHWASHING MACHINES *A dishwasher saves barely one minute in clean up time. According to the industry, this is because people needlessly scour the dishes before placing them in the machine. Or they take advantage of the convenience to use more dishes.*

James Gleick, *Faster* (1999)

- Keep reflectors under burners clean.

- Use the minimum amount of water when boiling or steaming.

- Where possible, cook more than one item in the oven at the same time.

- Leave the oven door shut. When you open the oven door the temperature can drop by as much as 15°C (59°F). It takes more energy to restore the correct temperature.

- Microwave ovens use less energy than conventional ovens. Fan ovens use less than conventional ones, but more than microwave ovens.

The fridge

- Locate fridges in cool spots — not in the sun, nor next to the oven.

- Ensure good circulation around the coils and dust them regularly.

- Keep the fridge defrosted to enable maximum efficiency.

- Keep the door seals clean and in good condition. (To test your seal, try closing the door on a sheet of paper. If you can pull it out easily, the seal is not working properly.)

- Run the fridge between 3°C and 5°C (37.4°F and 41°F). Freezers should run at a temperature of between −15°C and −18°C (5°F and 0.4°F). Every degree lower costs 5 per cent more in running costs and greenhouse gas pollution.

- Shut that door! Be quick when you open the fridge door as the longer it is open, the more it will warm up.

- Cut the chances of ice forming inside the fridge by covering all liquids.

General care and cleaning in the kitchen

Even if you don't care for cleaning any other part of the house, you should always keep the kitchen spotless and follow the rules of hygiene when storing and preparing food.

Work surfaces

The rule is to clean as you go – before food preparation and afterwards. Most surfaces can be cleaned with a cloth dipped in mild detergent and hot water. These surfaces include Corian, laminate, marble, slate and tiles. Some may be lightly scoured, while others may need oil.

- Corian **Use a gentle scourer for stains on Corian, which is a blend of natural materials and pure acrylic polymer. Treat stubborn ones with very fine abrasive paper, then polish with a soft cloth.**

- Granite **Wipe regularly with a hot cloth. Clean greasy marks with a few drops of household ammonia in water.**

- Laminate **Use a few drops of eucalyptus oil to disinfect. For tough marks, use neat detergent, leave for a few minutes then rinse. Do not scour. Take care with hot saucepans. Although laminate can take heat from pans and cooking utensils, it will become damaged if they are left to stand.**

- Slate **To shine, wipe with a few drops of lemon oil then polish with a soft dry cloth.**

- Tiles **To remove stains, try rubbing on salt with a cut lemon.**

- Sealed wood **Pots and pans should go on a tile or board to prevent burns to the bench surface.**

- Unsealed wood **Rub with boiled linseed oil and wipe excess off with a soft cloth. Try salt and lemon on stains and scorch marks.**

MAKE CLEANING EASIER

- Reduce the likelihood of spills by covering food in the microwave.
- Use splatter guards on hot frying pans.
- Don't overfill saucepans.

Chopping boards

■ Plastic **Scrub with a small brush with hot water and detergent. Most are also fine in the dishwasher. To kill bacteria, wipe over with a mild solution of household bleach.**

■ Wood **Rub with a little vegetable oil to protect from splitting and warping. Scrub well with a stiff brush and hot water to remove stains. Clear food odours by rubbing with salt – a natural disinfectant – and cut lemon. Store where plenty of air can circulate.**

CHOPPING BOARD HYGIENE The hygienic kitchen needs two chopping boards – one for vegetables, one for meat. If chopping raw and cooked meat, scrub the board well after chopping the raw meat.

The kitchen sink

Although these days many households have a dishwasher, the sink is still an essential part of the kitchen. Wipe the sink down each time you wash up, and scrub it at least weekly. If it needs a little more attention, check these tips.

■ Acrylic **Remove water marks with white vinegar. Never use an abrasive cleaner such as an abrasive cleansing cream or a scourer, as you will risk scratching the surface. Remove scratches with metal polish.**

■ Corian **Clean as for a Corian work surface (see page 75). To restore colour to a stained sink, fill the sink with a solution of 1 part household bleach to 4 parts water. Leave for half an hour, then drain and rinse.**

■ Enamel **Do not use bleach or scourers on enamel. Remove stains with borax and a cut lemon or a paste of bicarbonate of soda and hydrogen peroxide (a gentle bleach). Start with bicarb and add just enough hydrogen peroxide to make a paste. Rub, allow to dry, then rinse off.**

■ Stainless steel **If you are concerned about scratches, do not use abrasive cleaners or scourers. Use neat detergent on stains. For a shiny look, polish with methylated spirits and a dry cloth.**

WHAT'S IN THE KITCHEN SINK?

- A kitchen sink uses 5–15 L (1–4 gal) of water, depending on its size and how much you put in it.
- A dishwasher cycle uses 15–60 L (4–16 gal) of water.
- Waste kitchen water contains any amount of the following: soap, detergent, food scraps, grease and oils, but it can be recycled as 'grey water' by passing it through simple filters.

See 'The outdoors', page 315, for more details on recycling grey water.

KITCHEN SPONGES To freshen and revitalize kitchen sponges and cloths, dissolve a generous handful of salt and 1 tablespoon of washing soda in 1 L (2 pt) of warm water. Dunk the cloths, leave for a couple of minutes, rinse in cold water and allow to dry.

Keeping the drain clear

A little attention now and then can prevent serious blockages developing.

- Selective disposal **The first step in trying to keep drains clear is to put as little as possible down the drain in the first place. Catch food debris and prevent it clogging the drain pipes by using a sink strainer before disposing of the scraps in the compost. Use the compost bin for biodegradable matter, including tea leaves and coffee grounds, and scrape fat and oil into the garbage rather than wash up dishes and pans caked with fat.**

- Boiling water **Pour boiling water down the kitchen sink to melt grease and wash it away.**

- Drain cleaners **Keep the kitchen drain clear by regularly using a drain cleaner. It's much less time-consuming than clearing an already blocked drain. Commercial drain cleaners often use sodium hydroxide and aluminium. These rely on bubbling from aluminium and heat formed when the sodium hydroxide dissolves, to agitate and melt grease. Or try one of the home remedies listed on the next page.**

UNDOING YOUR BLOCK: NATURAL DRAIN CLEANERS

When the water won't drain and you are faced with a sink full of water, try one of these natural drain cleaners, then use a plunger. Place the plunger tightly over the drain hole, push down then pull up rapidly, keeping the plunger over the hole. If your seal is tight, the air and water inside the pipe is forced back and forth, with any luck sloshing and sucking the blockage away. If you are unsuccessful, try a different drain cleaner and leave overnight.

1 Sodium bicarbonate and vinegar

INGREDIENTS

1/2–1 cup sodium bicarbonate

1 cup white vinegar

METHOD

Pour the sodium bicarbonate down the drain, then slowly pour in the white vinegar. The sizzling sound is the reaction between the two. Follow with water and repeat the whole process if necessary.

2 Ammonia in boiling water

INGREDIENTS

2 teaspoons household ammonia

Kettle of boiling water

METHOD

For moderate blocks, try household ammonia chased with a kettle of boiling water. Then use the plunger to loosen the blockage.

3 Washing soda and boiling water

INGREDIENTS

2 cups washing soda crystals

Kettle of boiling water

METHOD

Pile the washing soda at the drain then slowly pour on a kettle of boiling water.

Caring for taps

To remove caked dirt from kitchen taps, use a toothbrush dipped in detergent or bicarbonate of soda. Most taps can be washed in a hot detergent solution or a solution of bicarbonate of soda.

- **Brass and copper** Wipe a lacquered finish on brass or copper taps with a damp cloth. Use metal polish on unlacquered surfaces. To remove verdigris or other tarnishes, rub gently with a paste of salt and lemon juice. Alternatively, wipe with household ammonia, rinse and dry with a soft cloth.

- **Chrome** Polish chrome taps with a cloth soaked in white vinegar or a weak solution of household ammonia in water.

The stove

Cleaning a dirt-encrusted stove once in a while is a very time-consuming and labour intensive job. It's certainly one of those jobs where a little prevention is very much better than hours of unpleasant cure, so try to get in the habit of cleaning as you go and encourage anyone else who uses the stove to do the same thing.

The stove top

Every time you use the stove top, wipe it with hot water to prevent a build-up of spillages. Avoid abrasive cleaners on stainless steel and enamel tops. For encrusted stains, try a poultice made from a cloth soaked in a cleaning solution, leave for a few hours then wipe away. Alternatively, apply a caustic cleaner with a toothbrush, leave for a few hours, then scrub off with hot water.

The grill pan

It's best to wash the grill pan in hot water and detergent after each use. But if your domestic routine slips up and you find yourself with a build-up of grease, scrape out the solids with a spatula, wipe the pan with balls of newspaper, then wash it.

The oven

Commercial oven cleaners contain highly caustic, unpleasant substances. To avoid these, don't let the oven get too dirty before getting round to cleaning it. Wipe the surfaces with a hot damp cloth after each use and clean up spills on the oven floor.

When you do have to clean the oven, try one of these alternatives to strong cleaners.

- Preheat the oven to warm, or proceed immediately after cooking in the oven. Place 1/2 cup of cloudy ammonia inside, shut the door and switch off the oven. Leave overnight if possible, or for at least a few hours. Wipe thoroughly with hot water and detergent.

- Wet the surface and sprinkle it with bicarbonate of soda. Rub with fine steel wool then wipe off the residue with a damp cloth. Repeat if necessary. Rinse well and dry.

- To clean very dirty shelves, soak them in a mixture of 1 part washing soda to 4 parts hot water. If the shelves are too large to submerge fully in the sink, turn them around every 20 minutes, or use the bath or laundry sink.

Large kitchen appliances

Most kitchen appliances can be wiped and washed with hot water and detergent or another general purpose cleanser of your choice, such as bicarbonate of soda mixed with water, which is mild, non-toxic and environmentally friendly. Here are some specific tips.

- Microwaves **For stubborn stains, place a bowl of hot water in the microwave and switch on to high for about five minutes. Allow to stand for a few minutes and remove. Wipe inside with a soft cloth.**

- Dishwasher **Clean the filters and seals on your dishwasher regularly. To restore a dull interior, run the machine empty on a short cycle with 2 cups vinegar in the detergent receptacle.**

- Fridge **Use a solution of 1 part bicarbonate of soda to 7 parts water to wipe down the inside of the fridge.**

  - Wash any removable parts in hot water and detergent.
  - To prevent mould forming on the door seals, wipe over them with white vinegar.
  - If you can reach them, vacuum the coils behind the fridge using your vacuum cleaner's brush attachment.
  - To absorb odours, place a small open bowl of bicarbonate of soda on one of the shelves. Change it regularly.

Small appliances

Here is some general advice on caring for and cleaning small kitchen appliances. Always remember to turn off the power and remove the plug from the socket before cleaning any electrical item, and also be sure to check the manufacturer's instructions on cleaning.

SWEET AND FRESH To leave the fridge smelling fresh, wipe over the inside with a damp cloth and a few drops of vanilla essence.

- Wipe over chrome appliances with a paste made from bicarb and water.
- Wipe over an appliance with a damp cloth immediately after using it.
- Once washable parts, such as a processor bowl, are disassembled, rinse them in hot water, removing food debris with a soft brush.
- Do not immerse electrical components in water unless advised to by the manufacturer.
- Dry each part carefully before storing.

MOULD-FREE To prevent mould growing when your fridge and freezer are empty and switched off for more than a few days, wipe the inside with vinegar and leave the doors propped open.

A CLEAN CAN OPENER To clean your can opener, use a toothbrush and warm water with detergent in it. After drying, rub a little cooking oil over the teeth.

NATURAL WAYS TO DE-SCALE YOUR KETTLE

- Cover the element with vinegar then top up with water. Bring to the boil and leave overnight, preferably for about 12 hours. Pour liquid away.
- Fill the kettle with water and place it in the fridge overnight. The build-up comes loose in the cold. Next, boil the water; the lime will dissolve in it and can be poured away.

Kitchen cupboard cleaners

Why use dangerous chemicals when almost everything you need to keep your kitchen clean — and much less toxic — is probably in your cupboard?

The raw ingredients

Here's a list of basic ingredients for making all the cleaners you need.

- Bicarbonate of soda
- White vinegar
- Washing up liquid
- Ammonia
- Washing soda
- Bleach
- Laundry detergent

All-purpose cleaner 1

INGREDIENTS

2 heaped tablespoons bicarbonate of soda

1 tablespoon white vinegar

METHOD

Mix the bicarbonate of soda and white vinegar together and store the cleaner in an airtight container.

All-purpose cleaner 2

This recipe makes a mild cleaner and deodorizer suitable for light soiling on the fridge, oven and any other surfaces.

INGREDIENTS

4 tablespoons bicarbonate of soda

1140 mL (2½ pt) warm water

METHOD

Mix the ingredients together. Wipe surfaces with a soft cloth dipped in the solution. Rinse with clean water.

Strong all-purpose cleaner 1

This cleaner can be used in kitchens and bathrooms, on floors, tiles, cupboards, appliances, ovens and so on, but not on fibreglass or aluminium.

INGREDIENTS

1/2 cup washing soda

4.5 L (9 1/2 pt) warm water

METHOD

Mix the ingredients together.

Strong all-purpose cleaner 2

This is a good all-round cleaner for many surfaces and materials including appliances, glass and silver. It will also strip floor wax and dissolve resinous matter.

INGREDIENTS

4 L (8 1/2 pt) hot water

100 mL (3 1/2 fl oz) household ammonia

100 mL (3 1/2 fl oz) white vinegar

200 g (7 oz) bicarbonate of soda

METHOD

Mix the ingredients together and store in a tightly sealed bottle.

Mild abrasive cleaner

Use this cleaner on plastic and on painted walls.

INGREDIENTS

Few drops of water

Bicarbonate of soda

METHOD

Add a few drops of water to baking soda to form a paste. Apply it with a stiff bristled brush on hard surfaces, and with an old toothbrush between tiles.

Scouring cleaner 1

INGREDIENTS

1 teaspoon borax

2 tablespoons white vinegar

2 cups hot water

METHOD

Combine the ingredients together and pour the mixture into a spray bottle.

Scouring cleaner 2

INGREDIENTS

1/2 cup bicarbonate of soda

3 tablespoons sodium perborate

METHOD

Mix the bicarbonate of soda with the sodium perborate. Use a wet sponge to rub the mixture onto areas that need whitening. Leave for 10–15 minutes before rinsing.

Disinfectant 1

This disinfectant can be used in the kitchen, bathroom and around the house on various surfaces, including marble, plastic, fibreglass, fridges, nursery furniture such as cots and high chairs, plastic mattress covers and ceramic tiles (although you should test first on dark colours or coloured grout).

INGREDIENTS

3/4 cup bleach

1.5 L (3 pt) warm water

1 tablespoon powdered laundry detergent

METHOD

Mix the ingredients together. Wash the surface and keep it wet for five minutes before rinsing and allowing it to dry.

Disinfectant 2

INGREDIENTS

1 teaspoon borax

2 tablespoons distilled white vinegar

1/4 cup liquid soap

2 cups hot water

METHOD

Mix the ingredients together. Use this disinfectant in the same way as 'Disinfectant 1' above, or store it in a spray bottle and spray it on.

Disinfectant 3

Use this disinfectant for hairbrushes and combs, mopping vinyl, and sanitizing and deodorizing garbage bins.

INGREDIENTS

3/4 cup bleach

1.5 L (3 pt) water

METHOD

Mix the ingredients together. Keep the surfaces wet for five minutes, rinse and allow to dry.

Disinfectant 4

INGREDIENTS

2 teaspoons borax

4 tablespoons white vinegar

3 cups hot water

METHOD

Mix together all the ingredients. Pour the mixture into a spray bottle. For greater cleaning power, add 1/4 teaspoon liquid soap.

Basic dishwashing liquid

Use 1 teaspoon to 5 L (10½ pt) water when washing up, or use 1 cup per load in a dishwasher. (*Note:* It doesn't remove coffee and tea stains.)

INGREDIENTS

50 g pure soap

½ cup washing soda crystals

½ cup white vinegar

1½ teaspoons eucalyptus oil or tea-tree oil

Few drops lemon or lavender pure essential oil for fragrance

5 L (10½ pt) cold water

4.5 L (9½ pt) hot water

METHOD

1 **Grate the soap into a large saucepan and cover with 1 L (2 pt) of the cold water. Bring to the boil, add the washing soda and stir until it is completely dissolved.**

2 **Stir in the eucalyptus oil, vinegar and essential oil.**

3 **Pour into a bucket, add the hot water then stir in the remaining cold water.**

4 **When cool, transfer to smaller containers and label.**

All-purpose spray cleaner

This all-purpose cleaner is suitable for the kitchen and bathroom.

INGREDIENTS

4 L (8½ pt) hot water

2 tablespoons cloudy ammonia

125 mL (4 fl oz) white vinegar

2 tablespoons bicarbonate of soda

2 drops lavender or lemon oil

2 tablespoons basic household soap cleaner

METHOD

In a bucket, mix all the ingredients into the water. Cool, then fill spray bottles.

Wall and paint cleaner

INGREDIENTS

1 L (2 pt) hot water

1/4 cup washing soda crystals

4 L (81/2 pt) cold water

125 mL (4 fl oz) cloudy ammonia

125 mL (4 fl oz) white vinegar

METHOD

Mix the hot water and washing soda crystals together in a bucket. Add the cold water, then the cloudy ammonia and the white vinegar.

Disinfecting floor cleaner

INGREDIENTS

1/2 cup borax

3 L (61/2 pt) hot water

METHOD

Mix the borax and hot water together. Use the cleaner with a cloth or mop as usual.

Strong floor cleaner

Wear protective gloves when using this cleaner.

INGREDIENTS

1/4 cup washing soda

1 tablespoon liquid soap

1/4 cup white vinegar

3 L (61/2 pt) hot water

METHOD

1   Mix the ingredients together. Use the cleaner with a cloth or mop as usual, but do not use it on wax floors.

2   For a floor cleaner especially formulated for timber floors, see 'The living room', page 230.

WASHING UP SKILLS *Among the many families who continue to wash-up by hand, there are many many ways of tackling the job. Some have it down to a fine art, some still muddle through after twenty years of washing up three times a day.*

Jane Harvey, *Hoover Book of Home Management* (1963)

Washing up

It's not a hi-tech task but it's one that takes up a lot of time — you've no sooner finished one lot than it's time to do another.

THE IDIOT'S GUIDE TO WASHING UP

The right tools ease the burden of the daily drudgery. If you don't have a dishwasher, it's helpful to have plate racks, draining board, bottle brushes, hand mop, wire brush, plastic and metal scouring pads — and lots of clean tea towels.

- Stack dishes and pans in like piles — plates in one pile, glasses grouped together, pans and sticky utensils in another.
- Scrape all food scraps into the compost bin (using a spatula on surfaces that might be damaged by scratching).
- Start with very hot water and a squeeze of washing up liquid or cleaning aid of your choice. A bowl inside the sink means you can still tip liquids into the sink while washing up. It's kinder on crockery and glass at the same time.
- Wash glasses first and rinse before resting on a draining rack to dry.
- Rinsing can be in a second sink, if you have one, under a slow running tap (turn it off when you tackle dirty saucepans or shift a new stack into the bowl) or a plastic bowl or bucket placed on a stool near the sink.
- The rest of the washing up should be in order of cleanliness: cleanest first, dirtiest last.
- Change the water when it gets dirtier than the next bowl of dishes!

TEA AND SALT To remove tea stains from china cups, rub crushed salt on with a dish cloth.

Washing cutlery

- Cutlery stains **Dissolve a little salt in lemon juice. Dip a soft cloth into the solution and rub the cutlery. Rinse in warm water and rub with a chamois.**
- Bone and wood handles **Never leave handles of ivory, wood, horn or bone lying in the water. Stand the metal parts in a jar of hot washing up water, wipe the handles with a hot damp cloth and dry.**
- Silver and silver plate **Wash silver cutlery as soon as possible: some foods leave stains that are hard to remove the longer you leave them.**
- Stainless steel **Do not use steel wool. Rinse soon after using as acidic or salty foods may cause pit marks.**
- Bronze **Thai bronze cutlery can be treated like stainless steel. Remove green spots by rubbing with a soft cloth dipped in turpentine, then wash.**

BONE CHINA AND PORCELAIN Check the manufacturer's instructions as to the suitability of bone china and porcelain for the dishwasher. The harsh detergents used in dishwashers can spoil some glazes, especially metallic ones.

LESS WASHING UP

You can cut down on the volume of messy washing up by taking just a few precautionary measures.

- Put a sheet of kitchen paper on the turntable in the microwave. It will catch spills.
- Put foil inside the grill pan.
- When reheating food, especially for solo diners, consider using a single bowl in the microwave rather than a saucepan and a bowl.

KITCHEN LINEN *In the kitchen six tea towels and cloths for drying the china will be sufficient, and the young housekeeper should have a couple of kettle-holders and an iron-holder.*

Mrs Lance Rawson, *The Australian Enquiry Book* (1894)

Kitchen lore and order

Here are a few tried and true tips, both old and new, to keep everything in your kitchen sparkling clean.

Lemon fresh

To wash and deodorize the fridge, garbage bin or kitchen compost container, use a solution of 1 teaspoon lemon juice to 1 L (2 pt) water.

Tarnished silver cutlery

A quick fix is to place a piece of aluminium foil into a plastic bucket and sprinkle over 3 tablespoons bicarbonate of soda. Lay silver on top. Cover with hot water. Leave until bubbles stop, rinse and polish with a dry soft.

For sparkling crystal

Dip crystal in a solution of 1 part vinegar to 3 parts water. Polish with a dry, lint-free cloth.

Washing glass

Wash glass water bottles and flower vases with 1 tablespoon vinegar and 1 tablespoon salt in warm water. Allow to stand for several hours and shake occasionally.

Wash very dirty cut glass in warm soapy water to which a few drops of ammonia have been added, and scrub gently with a small brush. (Do not use ammonia on glass decorated with gilt or enamel.)

DECANTERS *Stained decanters may be cleaned by filling them half full of warm soapy water to which some tea leaves have been added. Allow them to soak, shaking well at intervals, then empty them and rinse thoroughly.*

Mrs Beeton's Hints to Housewives (1928)

Removing wax from candlesticks

- **Hot method** Re-melt wax with a hair dryer on the hot setting, and wipe the wax as it softens.
- **Cold method** Place candlesticks in the freezer for about an hour. This makes it easy to peel the wax off.

Burnt pans

- To clean a badly burnt saucepan, pour in a little olive oil, heat gently and leave to stand for one or two hours. Pour off the oil into a container, ready to use for the next burnt pan, and wash the pan as usual.
- To clean burnt food from a pie dish, dip it in very hot water then quickly turn it upside down onto a flat surface. This traps steam which loosens the residue.
- To restore an enamel baking dish that seems burnt beyond use, soak it in a mixture of water and strong soap powder. After a couple of hours, pour off the water and rub the dish with a soft cloth.

Greasy grill pans

When you've scraped off as much grease as you can with a spatula or newspaper, sprinkle with washing soda crystals and pour on boiling water. Leave it to soak for at least ten minutes, then clean up. The grease and debris just lift off.

Stained enamel

To whiten enamel lined pans: finely crush egg shells and rub with a cloth dipped in salt if stained.

Delicate china

When hand washing the heirloom china, place a towel at the bottom of the washing up bowl to help prevent chips and breakages.

Gilt china

Do not use washing soda or soap powder containing soda on gilt as it may damage it. Use a few drops of borax instead.

Cleaning coffee and teapots

- ▣ Wash all coffee-making equipment thoroughly after using.

- ▣ To de-scale a drip coffee maker, run a water and vinegar solution through the machine or use a shop-bought product.

- ▣ To remove stains, fill the pot with 1 part bicarbonate of soda to 2 parts hot water and leave to stand overnight. Rinse thoroughly and dry.

- ▣ A patina of tea inside the pot may add depth of flavour to the brew, but it can look ugly on the spout tip. Wrap a piece of nylon stocking around a pipe cleaner and dampen it with salty water. Use it to clean the spout.

- ▣ If you wish to remove tannin stains inside pottery and enamel teapots, fill with a salty solution made of 1 cup salt to 2 cups water, leave to soak overnight and rinse with hot water.

- ▣ To remove tannin stains from silver teapots, drop in 6 pieces of aluminium foil, add 1 tablespoon bicarbonate of soda and pour on boiling water. Leave to cool, then rinse out with hot water and dry with a soft cloth.

Premium care for pots and pans

Fill pots and pans with hot water as soon as they are emptied. For greasy pots, wash with a solution of washing soda and hot water. Saucepans that have contained rice, potato and porridge are better off soaked in cold water. Wipe out excess grease with newspaper. However, stains, burnt on food and tough cleaning jobs require a different approach.

- ▣ Aluminium To clean stained aluminium saucepans, boil up 2 teaspoons of cream of tartar with 1 L (2 pt) of water. Apple peelings or citrus skin will also clean aluminium saucepans. Boil in the pan with water.

- ▣ Cast iron Season new pans by brushing the bottom of the pan with vegetable oil. Gently heat over a low flame or in the oven for an hour. Remove from the heat and allow to cool. Pour out the oil and discard, then wipe out the pan with kitchen paper. After using the pan, wash it in hot water and detergent, then dry. Brush on a little oil before storing.

- ▣ Copper Do not scour. Soak encrusted food in warm water. Clean off poisonous green stains. Clean the outside with a solution of 1 part salt and 2 parts white vinegar, rinse, then dry and polish.

■ Glazed earthenware Soak in hot water and use a plastic scourer to remove food remains.

■ Unglazed earthenware To season before first use, soak in water. Use hot water only, no detergent, to clean. Soak difficult stains but do not scour.

■ Enamel Season as for cast iron. To clean, use a very gentle scouring pad. Bleach discoloured enamelware with a mixture of coarse salt and vinegar.

■ Glass Heatproof glass baking ware and saucepans can go in the dishwasher. Use a plastic scourer when necessary.

■ Non-stick finishes Soak to remove food; never use a scourer as it will scratch and remove the surface.

■ Plastic Do not scratch by scouring as the scratches may harbour bacteria. Hand-hot water is fine, but dishwashers may get too hot.

■ Stainless steel Scourers will scratch, but you may not be bothered by a patina of small scratches. Usually dishwasher safe. To remove calcium deposits, boil water and vinegar together.

■ Tinware Baking trays and cake tins need to be seasoned like cast iron to prevent rusting. Do not scour. Check the manufacturer's instructions after purchase. After turning out biscuits or cakes, fill tinware with cold water, add a handful of washing soda and let it stand on a warm stove until the crust is loose and can be removed without scratching.

CARING FOR KNIVES

■ **Blunt knives** Sharpening stones are best. Wash individually by hand in cold or lukewarm water, as hot water can warp blades. Dry thoroughly and store in a wooden knife block.

■ **Rusty knives** Soak in raw linseed oil for a few hours then wipe off the rust. Polish the knife with emery paper.

■ **Stained blades** Clean with emery paper rubbed with a slice of raw potato or salt and cut lemon. Alternatively, use a scouring pad.

■ **Stained knife handles** Restore ivory handles by rubbing them with salt moistened with lemon juice.

Caring for metal

As a general rule, metal can be dusted and, if necessary, wiped with a cloth dampened in water or a mixture of water and an all-purpose cleanser such as detergent. Rinse and dry it at once, especially if it's a metal that is prone to rust.

- Iron, silver, copper and brass are prone to tarnish: that's when the surface of the metal reacts with a substance in the surrounding air, forming a discolouring compound. The process is accelerated by humidity and temperature.

- Gold, platinum, pewter, bronze, aluminium, stainless steel and chrome do not tarnish, although they can stain.

- Metal polishes may be all-purpose or specific for a particular metal. They contain abrasives or solvents, sometimes both. The more valuable a piece of metal, the more care you need to take when cleaning it, and the less eager you should be to use all-purpose 'all metals' cleaners. If you use solvents and abrasives that are too strong, you run the risk of losing detail on raised designs and etching as the top surface is likely to be removed.

Aluminium

- To brighten dull aluminium, boil 1 L (2 pt) water with 4 tablespoons white vinegar.

- Harmful substances that will damage the metal include chlorine bleach, strong bicarbonate of soda solutions, and alkaline cleansers, including oven cleaners.

Brass

- Rub briskly with a cotton wool pad wrung out in vinegar, then wash thoroughly in hot soapy water. Rub dry with a soft towel.

- For mild tarnish, clean with a mixture of salt and lemon juice, then rinse. Use an old toothbrush to clean patterned areas.

- Try removing stubborn marks with Worcestershire sauce and salt; apply with a toothbrush, wash in warm water, dry well and rub with a clean cloth. If that doesn't work, try toothpaste on the toothbrush. Leave on for a while, rinse off with warm water and polish dry. Alternatively, try lemon juice and bicarbonate of soda or a paste of equal parts salt, white flour and vinegar. Rub on, leave for an hour and rinse off. Dry with a soft cloth then buff. Last but not necessarily least, a simple piece without trimming and decoration can be boiled in a solution made from 1 tablespoon vinegar, 2 cups water and 1 tablespoon salt. Rinse and dry.

TO LACQUER OR NOT TO LACQUER?

Bronze, brass and copper readily tarnish and need regular polishing unless lacquered. Once thoroughly cleaned and lacquered they will stay bright and tarnish-free.

However, if cracks begin to appear in the lacquer it must be removed with acetone, the metal cleaned and lacquer reapplied.

Paste wax and mineral oil both inhibit tarnishing, if you decide against lacquer.

■ To clean brass fireplace screens and tools, dust the soot off first, then wash in detergent and warm water. Rinse and dry with a soft cloth.

■ A number of substances – including chlorine bleach, oven cleaners and some window cleaners – corrode and discolour brass.

Bronze

■ Do not wash bronze. Dust regularly with a soft cloth. Polish from time to time with a cloth dipped in boiled linseed oil. Buff with a soft dry cloth.

Cast iron

■ Items not used for cooking can be protected with paste wax. Hinges and locks should be oiled with machine oil to prevent rust.

■ Wash by hand and dry thoroughly after washing to prevent rusting: a few seconds on the stove top ensures all moisture evaporates.

■ To remove rust, scour off and dry.

■ To season cast iron pans, see page 94.

Copper

■ Rub in a mixture of 2 tablespoons vinegar to 1 tablespoon salt. Plunge into hot water and rinse. Dry thoroughly with a soft cloth.

■ Remove mild tarnish with salt and lemon juice, as for bronze, above.

■ Never let copper stand in chlorine bleach for more than a few hours or the metal will become discoloured.

Iron

■ Wrought iron merely needs dusting, but it can be washed if necessary. Rub stubborn marks
with steel wool. Paste wax gives extra shine and protection against rust. Apply to a thoroughly
clean iron with a cloth, allow wax to dry, then buff with a clean cloth.

■ To remove rust, wipe with a solution of white vinegar and water.

Pewter

■ Wash in warm soapy water. To help keep pewter bright, add 2 tablespoons ammonia per 1 L
(2 pt) water.

■ For stubborn marks, try mixing finely powdered artists' whiting (sold in art supply stores) with
a little oil and apply with a soft cloth. Rub in well, then polish with a clean cloth and finally a
chamois. Rinse in warm water. Wipe dry with a clean towel.

■ Remove grease marks by rubbing with a cloth moistened with methylated spirits.

■ Pewter is vulnerable to damage by acids, including those in oak and unseasoned wood, and
in some food. If necessary, polish it with silver polish.

Silver

■ Using silver is the best way to keep it looking bright; too much polishing can wear it out.

■ Some foods tarnish silver, so wash silver or silver plate quickly after a meal. Items that contain
sulphur tarnish silver. These include felt and chamois leather, as well as a number of foods.

■ To wash silver, wash in very hot water and detergent. Rinse carefully (as soap residue can
make it tarnish) and dry with a cloth rather than let it air dry, as water standing on silver
causes tarnish.

■ Rub egg stains on silver with wet salt.

■ For other stains, use fine whiting moistened with ammonia or alcohol then wash and polish.

■ Clean tarnished silver plate with starch mixed with methylated spirits to form a paste. Let it dry
on the silver then rub off with a soft cloth.

■ To remove wax on silver candlesticks, warm gently in the oven or with a hair dryer. Peel it off.

■ To prevent silver tarnishing after cleaning, smear lightly with petroleum jelly – but remember,
this must be washed off before the silver is used with food again.

■ To clean the old-fashioned way, cover with sour milk for half an hour, wash and rinse.

- Remember to clean all silver thoroughly before polishing.

- To polish silver, use a commercial silver polish. Apply polish gently with a soft clean cloth in a circular motion, polishing bit by bit for larger objects. Don't rub with a dirty cloth as the dirt can scratch – keep moving to a clean part of the cloth. Rinse polish off thoroughly with hot water as it can sometimes corrode silver, then buff with a soft cloth. (Don't leave to air dry.)

- Don't polish silver plate too vigorously – you may remove it altogether.

- For valuable antiques, commercial silver polish may be too harsh. Instead, use a paste of distilled water and artists' whiting.

- To store silver, you can buy cloths, bags and drawer liners that have been treated with silver nitrate or other chemicals to retard tarnish. (It is not necessary to clean tarnish before storing; polishing up silver so that it is ready just before use will save time.)

- Plastic wrap can help retard tarnish too. The silver must be absolutely dry. It needs to be wrapped in archival quality, sulphur-free tissue paper before being packed in plastic. Place moisture-absorbing silica gel packets in the packaging and store out of direct sunlight.

Stainless steel

- Stainless steel may be damaged by salty or acidic substances such as vinegar and citrus juices as well as some dishwasher detergents and denture cleaners.

- Brown and blue streaks can occur with overheating; stainless steel cleaners will remove them.

- Small white dots or pits are produced by salted liquids. White dots will come off with a scouring pad or a soaped steel wool pad. Pits, however, are permanent. Prevent them by always bringing liquids to the boil before adding salt.

ACID DIPS AND ELECTROLYTIC CLEANERS

Acid dips can be rough on silver and are best used only for black tarnish that resists all other polishes. In addition, many experts advise wiping with the solution rather than immersing an object. Cracks and crevices filled with acid may continue to corrode, so wash a piece after using it.

Pieces cleaned by electrolytic cleansing are prone to tarnishing more quickly because they more readily absorb substances that tarnish. If you are tempted to use this method, ensure you wash the piece thoroughly afterwards to prevent solution being trapped in cracks.

Food fundamentals

Keeping a clean kitchen and taking care to wash the dishes properly is one defence against illness. Hygienic handling of food is another. Most cases of food poisoning are the result of eating food that has been left to stand, either cooked or uncooked, at temperatures that are conducive to bacteria growth.

DANGER ZONE

The range of temperatures that are conducive to bacterial growth is broad – between 4°C and 60°C (39.2°F and 140°F). Bacteria are an omnipresent fact of life. They are present in most foods at harmless levels, and on your hands, arms, face and inside your body too. In addition, many bacteria are harmless. But high levels of harmful bacteria can make you ill and may even kill you. The danger comes when harmful bacteria are transferred to foods where they can multiply quickly and reach a hazardously high concentration. Transfer of bacteria from uncooked foods to cooked foods is particularly dangerous, as the cooked foods may not be heated again to destroy bacteria.

The most important principles of food hygiene are aimed at minimizing the time food spends in the danger zone.

- Keep food hot – above 60°C (140°F) – if it's to be served hot.
- Refrigerate food after cooking if it is not going to be eaten immediately.
- When reheating, ensure the centre of the food reaches 75°C (167°F) to kill any bacteria present.

Take extra care with cooked meat

One of the most common sources of food poisoning is cold cooked meat – often by cross-contamination from knives, hands and chopping boards.

- Never handle cooked and uncooked meats together.
- When preparing cooked and uncooked meats, either use different chopping boards and utensils, or thoroughly wash and dry them before switching foods.

Using the fridge

The refrigeration of food inhibits the growth of spoiling micro-organisms and chemical changes in food. Most care is needed with foods of the flesh: meat, especially minced meat – liver, kidney, poultry and seafood. This is because these foods always contain large numbers of micro-organisms that can cause spoilage and food poisoning.

When buying chilled (or frozen) foods, wrap them in newspaper to keep temperature changes to a minimum while you're on your way home. Pack them in an insulated container if putting them away is likely to be delayed. Put chilled foods away immediately on returning home.

Wrapped and unwrapped meats

Meats wrapped in plastic do not last as well as unwrapped meat because they contain more water and the wrapping encourages bacterial growth at the surface, which can become slimy after about three days. Throw it out if this happens.

The surface of unwrapped meat dries out, discouraging bacterial growth, although it is less attractive looking and may lose some flavour. To keep meat covered without letting anything come into contact with the surface, place it in a ceramic bowl covered with greaseproof paper, plastic film or a plate.

LIFE IN THE DANGER ZONE

TEMPERATURE	COMMENT
100°C (212°F)	Boiling point cooking temperatures destroy most bacteria
60–74°C (140–165.2°F)	Warming temperatures prevent growth but allow survival of some bacteria
4–60°C (39.2–140°F)	Danger zone: temperatures in this zone allow rapid growth of bacteria, including food-poisoning bacteria
0–4°C (32–39.2°F)	Chilling temperatures restrict growth. Some food-poisoning bacteria may grow very slowly
0°C (32°F)	Freezing point
-12°C (10.4°F)	Freezing temperatures stop the growth of bacteria

RECOMMENDED STORAGE TIMES AND TEMPERATURES FOR REFRIGERATED FOODS

FOOD	TEMPERATURE	KEEP FOR
Seafood	0–3°C (32–37.4°F)	3 days
Crustaceans and molluscs	0–3°C (32–37.4°F)	2 days
Meat	0–3°C (32–37.4°F)	3–5 days
Minced meat and offal	0–3°C (32–37.4°F)	2–3 days
Cured meat	0–3°C (32–37.4°F)	2–3 weeks
Poultry	0–3°C (32–37.4°F)	3 days
Fruit juices	0–7°C (32–44.6°F)	1–2 weeks
Milk	1–7°C (33.8–44.6°F)	5–7 days
Cream	1–7°C (33.8–44.6°F)	5–7 days
Butter	0–7°C (32–44.6°F)	8 weeks
Oil and fat	2–7°C (35.6–44.6°F)	Approx. 6 months
Chilled meats and meals	0–3°C (32–37.4°F)	Up to use-by date
Leftovers	0–3°C (32–37.4°F)	3–5 days

Source: CSIRO and AFSIC, 'Handling food: The home', *Food Science Australia*, March 2000.

PUTTING HOT FOOD STRAIGHT INTO THE FRIDGE

Q. Is it OK to put piping hot food straight into the fridge? Or do you need to cool the food first?

A. Modern fridges can cope with large quantities of hot food without heating up other fridge contents. Cover the container, and if you are concerned the food will not cool quickly enough, you can always divide a large quantity into smaller amounts in shallow dishes.

FRIDGE HYGIENE

Here are some tips on storing food in your fridge.

- Store food you want to keep for a long time and foods such as seafood in the coldest part of the fridge.
- Store cooked foods above uncooked ones: this minimizes the risk of food poisoning by drips from the uncooked foods.
- Wrap foods with strong odours, such as seafood and cheese, and avoid storing them close to milk and cream, which are susceptible to tainting.
- Throw out food going off: the slimy lettuce at the back of the fridge can taint other food.

HOARDING IN THE FREEZER While a well stocked freezer may be highly convenient, long-term hoarding of packaged frozen goods does not make sense. It's better to stock less and buy more often, as a shop's freezing cabinets hold food at a much lower temperature than home freezers can offer.

Using the freezer

Freezers run at around −18°C (0.4°F), a temperature which almost, but not quite, prevents foods from deteriorating.

- Cook immediately **If you defrost meat out of the fridge, don't be tempted to put it in the fridge once you have defrosted it: you must cook it immediately to avoid food poisoning.**
- Don't refreeze **Once thawed correctly (in the fridge), food can be kept another 48 hours in the fridge, but it should never be refrozen.**

FAST DEFROST If you don't have time to defrost meat in the fridge, the next safest method is under cool running water or in the microwave oven. If you are not sure that all portions of the meat have defrosted, use a meat thermometer when cooking to check that the interior reaches 75°C (167°F).

FREEZE FAST AND OTHER RULES

■ **Freeze fast** Put frozen foods away as soon as you get home from the shops.
■ **To thaw or not to thaw?** Vegetables can be cooked from the frozen state. Many have been blanched before freezing and need only light cooking. Always completely thaw meat and poultry to avoid the possibility of starting cooking with a frozen patch which then does not reach a bacteria-killing temperature.
■ **Defrost in the fridge** Food hygiene experts say the general rule is never defrost meat out of the fridge because it may reach 4°C (39.2°F) — the temperature at which bacteria starts to breed, potentially causing spoilage and food poisoning. This means allowing 24 to 48 hours for a large piece of meat, or a whole chicken, to defrost in the fridge.

Storing dried goods

Dehydration slows down deterioration of food, but once the foods are exposed to water again — even when packets are open to the air — the microbes present in the food become active again. Dried food keeps in an unopened container for about six months when stored at 21–24°C (69.8–75.2°F).

■ **Store dried goods in a cool place away from sources of heat or direct sunlight. Inspect regularly for contamination.**

■ **Opened packages of dried fruit will keep for longer in the fridge.**

■ **Once dehydrated foods, such as dips, are reconstituted, treat them as fresh food and refrigerate them.**

How long can you keep cans?

Most canned food can be safely kept for 12 months, if not longer, when stored at 21–24°C (69.8–75.2°F). Exceptions are rhubarb, fruit juices, soft drinks and some baby foods, which have a maximum storage life of six months. Keep an eye on the use-by dates and remember to rotate pantry items so that you use the oldest first.

TESTING FOR FRESH EGGS A fresh egg is dull, while a stale egg has a glassy smooth shell. If in doubt, place the egg in a bowl of water. If it sinks to the bottom, it's fresh — if it floats, it's bad.

THE CLEVER SHOPPING BASKET

When shopping for food, always avoid the following.

- **Swollen chilled food packages** This occurs in fruit juices, yoghurts and unprocessed cheese, and is a sign that the food is going off, being overpopulated with micro-organisms which are producing gas.
- **Swollen and severely dented cans** Swollen cans can indicate the same problem as swollen chilled food packages — a fault in the original processing has allowed bacteria to multiply. Badly damaged cans could indicate that the can is no longer properly sealed.
- **Dairy produce or delicatessen items not kept under refrigeration** These items should always be cold on purchase.
- **Refrigerated foods past their use-by date** This group of items presents a risk of food poisoning.
- **Frozen and refrigerated foods stored outside the load line of the display cabinet** Foods will keep to the correct storage temperature only below the 'load' line, usually about 5 cm (2 in) below the rim of the cabinet.
- **Frozen food packs with ice crystals or clumps of ice between them** This indicates refreezing, which usually means loss of quality.
- **Torn packaging or imperfect seals** There is probably a deterioration of quality.

Which cooking methods are more likely to trigger allergy problems?

- Electricity produces fewer combustion by-products and less water vapour than cooking with gas or solid fuel, and is generally considered the better choice for allergy sufferers.

- Burning gas produces water vapour and chemicals such as carbon monoxide, carbon dioxide, nitrogen dioxide, sulphur dioxide and aldehydes. Ensure the kitchen is well ventilated for all the family.

- Ducted hoods are vented to the outside, removing combustion by-products and excess condensation. An open window or a window ventilator prevents air being sucked from the rest of the house. Recirculating hoods send air back into the kitchen after passing it through a filter. They remove grease and odours but not moisture.

Kitchen safety

Kitchen safety is largely a matter of commonsense. Unless you are prepared to be extra careful, the best rule is to keep young children out of the kitchen. Gates or barriers like those used on stairways can be a handy way of blocking the entrance while allowing young children to see you.

Proceed with caution

Carefully consider where to store or place the many dangerous items that are usually kept in the kitchen, and investigate the variety of inexpensive child-safe devices that make life easier — and safer — with a toddler.

- Keep glassware in above-bench cupboards or shelves.

- Sharp knives should be stored in a wooden block or in sheaths, not loose in a drawer.

- Items with blades or sharp points — such as blender blades, skewers and corkscrews — should be kept well out of reach.

- Cleaning products, especially dishwashing machine detergent which is very corrosive, should be stored in a child-proof cupboard.

- Stove guards prevent children pulling objects off the stove top.

- Turn saucepan handles away from the stove front and use rear plates whenever possible.

- Safety latches prevent small hands from opening cupboards.

- Carry plates to the pots rather than carry pots to the plates.

- Cordless kettles mean one less cord to be able to pull; empty kettles are one less source of hot water.

HOME-MADE ANTISEPTIC Dissolve salt in boiled water. Dip a cotton wool ball in the warm salty water and apply it to grazes and minor cuts.

FIRST AID FOR SCALDS

Hot water still scalds 30 minutes after if has boiled, so make sure hot water — whether it's in a cup, kettle or saucepan — is well out of reach of young children. If an accident does occur, follow these steps. Every second counts.

■ Immediately cool the scalded skin either in or under cool running tap water for at least 20 minutes.

■ Always remove clothing as it holds the heat and can cause a deeper scald.

■ Keep the child warm with a clean blanket and comfort him.

■ Seek medical advice. Call an ambulance if the scald is serious.

■ Do not use ice, oil or butter or anything else as these can damage the skin further.

■ Do not touch the affected area or burst any blisters.

■ Do not attempt to remove anything sticking to the burn.

Fire drill

■ Install a smoke detector. They are inexpensive and very easy to install.

■ Make sure every member of the household who is old enough to make a phone call knows the fire brigade number.

■ Keep a fire blanket or a bucket of sand handy in case you need to smother a fire.

■ Never leave a pan of oil unattended on the heat. If there is a fire in the frying pan, do not move the pan. Follow these steps.

1 Turn off the heat if it is safe for you to do so.
2 Smother the flames by covering the pan with a close-fitting lid, fire blanket, bucket of sand or damp cloth.
3 Do not touch the pan for another 30 minutes.

■ Never use water or an ordinary fire extinguisher to put out an oil fire.

Kitchen recycling

It's hard to avoid all the packaging that seems to come home with the shopping, but a great deal of it can be creatively recycled.

- Jars can be used as airtight containers for spices and grains.

- Plastic shopping bags can be reused for lining bins, especially bathroom ones, wrapping around disposable nappies, holding wet swimming gear – and shopping.

- Young children can build a play supermarket with cereal packets, toothpaste and tea boxes, egg cartons and empty plastic bottles.

- Collect bottle corks to make a cork board. Cut each cork in half lengthways and stick with strong glue to a piece of board. Corks also make good kindling for fires, but take care not to use plastic ones.

- Cardboard boxes can be called into service as storage boxes. Turn the flaps inside the box and fix them down with sticky tape for extra strength. Decorate the box by covering it in wrapping paper. They are also welcome – if temporary – toys for children to make into houses, boats and rockets.

- Tea leaves, onion skins and turmeric make safe natural dyes for crafts.

- Egg cartons are ideal seed propagation trays. The whole cup can be planted in the garden at the appropriate time – just cut out the bottom.

ALL HANDS ON DECK

Kitchen hands
To remove fruit stains from your hands, mix a little caster sugar into some olive oil to make a paste. Rub this well into the skin, leave for a few minutes then wash your hands in warm soapy water. Stubborn stains may require three goes.

Onion hands
To remove the smell of onions from your hands, rub well with celery or parsley.

Kitchen pests

Using toxic pesticides exposes not only you when you apply them, but also the whole household. Some groups of people are more prone to the side effects of pesticides: particularly vulnerable people include the elderly, children, babies, pregnant women, asthmatics and people with allergies. When used outside the home, pesticides may also kill beneficial insects and soil organisms in the garden. Many may also be toxic to birds, bees and fish.

Alternative methods of pest control focus on using mechanical means such as screens, traps and other practices that do not involve harsh chemicals. Often, prevention is a matter of commonsense, such as always putting away food in pest-proof containers and keeping your kitchen benches wiped clean.

As a last resort, some of the less toxic chemicals may be recommended.

Midnight munchers

Whether you're a human being or an insect, the best place for a midnight feast is the kitchen.

Grains and dried fruits, breakfast cereals, flour and spices are among the foods most vulnerable to pest attack in the pantry. Preventative measures are the most satisfactory: store these products in pest-proof jars and containers, bearing in mind that even the tiniest hole may be a large enough entry.

If you find an infested product, including eggs, dispose of it in an outside bin.

If an infestation is bad, you may be tempted to treat cupboards and other hiding places. If you are prepared to give it a go and try a less toxic cleanup first, empty the cupboard, clear it of all food debris and wash it down with a detergent solution. If the infestation returns and you want to try something harsher, first clear and clean the cupboard, then dust the cracks and corners with diatomaceous earth (this may be available in food grade, suitable for use near food preparation areas). Alternatively, pyrethrins or neem (a tree which is native to western Asia) could be used.

The use of persistent surface sprays in food areas is not recommended.

WHAT'S EATING YOUR FOOD?

Here's a list of the main culprits in the pantry.

- Rice weevil
- Lesser grain borer
- Rust red flour beetle
- Saw-toothed grain beetle
- Flat grain beetle
- Tobacco beetle

- Dried fruit beetle
- Cadelle
- Bean weevil
- Tropical warehouse moth
- Indian meal moth
- Angoumois grain moth

Ants

It is possible to deter ants without using harmful pesticides.

- One of the simplest, least toxic ways to kill ants is to put 1 teaspoon liquid dishwashing detergent in a spray bottle of water and use the solution to spray trails of ants as they trek into your kitchen.

- Follow the trail of ants and try to locate the nest. Pour a cup of water into the nest and spray the ants with a spray containing pyrethrin as they emerge from the hole.

- Alternatively, place a few borax and sugar baits around the trail and nest (see 'The outdoors', page 326, on making your own ant baits).

- Every few days, until they disappear, puff pyrethrin-containing powder down the holes where ants enter the house.

Cockroaches

In theory, keeping the house clean — clearing away food scraps, grease and dust — helps keep cockroach populations down, but as they have a remarkable ability to live on a few crumbs at a time, in practice it can be difficult to control their numbers. Here are some tips to try.

- Cockroaches need somewhere to hide. Seal as many cracks and crevices as you can and use screens on windows and doors.

- Use sticky traps near breeding areas.

- Use low-toxicity baits such as 5 per cent borax and sugar in a small lid.
- Use pyrethrum sprays in crevices and harbouring areas.
- As a last resort use a pyrethroid spray such as permethrin, or a misting bomb containing permethrin and hydropene. This has the disadvantage of covering every surface. You need to leave the house for two hours at least, but a weekend would be even better.

Flies

Deter flies with some simple old-fashioned remedies.

- Make your own fly papers. Take equal volumes of sugar, corn syrup and water. Mix together and boil for 30 minutes. Spread the mixture on paper strips, and once they set to a sticky consistency, hang them near doors and windows.
- A pot-pourri mixture of dried orange and lemon peel and cloves stored in open jars is said to deter flies.
- Burn eucalyptus, lavender, citronella or peppermint oil in an oil burner.

Rats and mice

Traditional rat and mice poisons are effective but contain quite powerful poisons which can also kill pets and even children if accidentally ingested.

If you wish to avoid chemical baits, you can try a baited spring trap — rats love pumpkin or brazil nuts, while mice are partial to dried fruit. You should never handle a dead rat or mouse with your bare hands.

If you do opt for poison, multi-dose rodenticides are considered safest for both the environment and humans, in the case of accidental ingestion, but poisoned animals should be buried deep in the ground where they will not be eaten by other creatures.

the laundry

Managing the household's laundry is a massive task: the average person generates over a tonne or ton of dirty clothes every year. Until the advent of easy-care fabrics and affordable automatic washing machines in the 1960s, a housewife would devote an entire day each week to washing her household's clothes and linen. In an affluent household there would be a room set aside for washing, starching, drying and ironing, with tub and dolly, mangle and washing board. Today's washing machine may be located in a purpose-designed laundry, but it is just as likely to be concealed behind folding doors in the bathroom or kitchen.

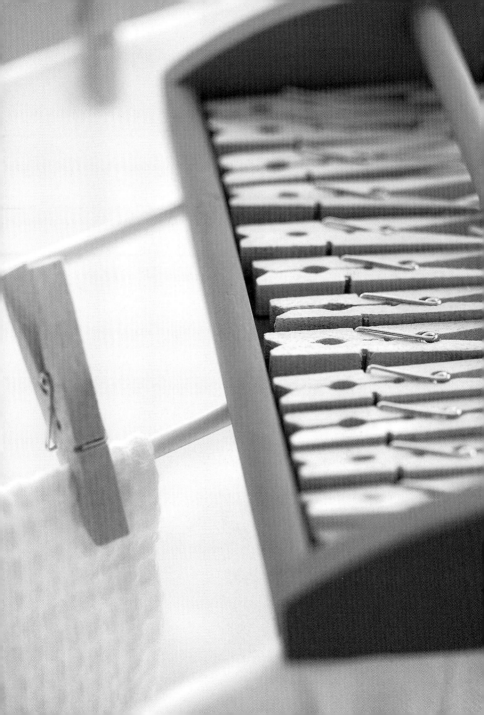

MY MOTHER MAINTAINED *an intricate hierarchy of cloths, buckets and dusters, to the Byzantine differentiations of which she alone was privy...And however rinsed and clean these utensils were they remained tainted by their awful function.*

Alan Bennett, *Writing Home* (1994)

the laundry

The clever laundry

An energy-efficient laundry does not waste water; it recycles as much as possible. It has an energy-efficient washing machine, and the tumbler dryer is used only as a last resort. The hot water comes from the solar heater, cold water from a rainwater tank and the grey or waste water produced is run into a holding tank which supplies the toilet cisterns in the house.

- **Water** **Mainly cold water washing reduces both heating costs and energy consumption.**
- **Soaking** **Presoaking of heavily soiled or stained garments minimizes the need for hot water and harsh chemicals.**
- **Washing machine** **Full loads or half-load settings waste less water and detergent. Fast spin reduces drying time.**
- **Detergent** **Using concentrates reduces the amount of chemicals released into the environment; the correct dosage cuts out waste. Non-biological powder can be used if a household member has sensitive skin.**
- **Clothes dryer** **Clothes are dried on a line outside whenever possible.**
- **Stain removal kit** **Using a range of stain removers keeps clothes looking good and cuts down on dry-cleaning costs.**

How energy-efficient is your washing machine?

If you analyze the environmental impact of a washing machine over its lifetime, you will see that the main areas of impact occur during the operating stage, in detergent manufacture and use, energy use and water consumption.

Front-loading units tend to have a lighter environmental impact because they use less water, detergent and energy for each wash. If you compare front and top loaders of a similar capacity, you'll find that front loaders use half the energy, 40 per cent less water and 30 per cent less detergent. The spin cycle also tends to be more efficient so clothes dry faster.

Consumer associations recommend dual connection front loaders as the best choice for the environment. A dual connection enables you to use hot water from your chosen heater rather than water that has been heated by your washing machine.

Programming your wash

Washing machines are now very sophisticated. Many models have computerized controls, enabling you to program each load in specific ways. If you organize each washing load to make the most of this facility on your machine, you will save energy, and therefore money, each time you wash. For example, wash heavily soiled garments together in one load.

Take these factors into consideration each time you sort out your washing. (See also 'Fabrics and their washing requirements', on pages 144–51.)

- **Temperature** **The hotter the water the greater its cleansing power, but you need to balance the temperature setting of your machine against the needs of each fabric type: only cotton and linen stand very hot temperatures, while silk may shrink and wool may felt. Hot water may result in a whiter wash, but it also uses more energy. To save energy, only use hot water for heavily soiled items. Alternatively, soak soiled items separately in a bowl of hot water before washing in a cooler load.**

- **Wash time** **Wash lightly soiled items and delicate fabrics, such as wool, for a shorter time. Dirty gardening gear, for example, may need longer.**

- **Agitation strength** **Regular agitation during the wash cycle may be too tough on lingerie or washable wool.**

- **Load size** **It is more energy-efficient to wash with the fullest load suitable for the fabric type. However, be careful not to overload the washing machine or the items will not move freely, making soil removal inefficient. Repeated overloading will also shorten the life of the machine itself. Use the half-load setting when washing small bundles of similar items; if you wash a small amount on the full load setting, you'll waste a lot of water.**

- **Spin cycle** **For delicate fabrics, set the machine to a slower spin cycle and a shorter spinning time.**

LINT TRAP To prevent lint from washing water blocking your drains, fit the end of the water outlet with a piece of pantyhose, and clean it regularly.

Washing aids

LAUNDRY AID *Usually, if all the washing is done at home, the mistress hires some one to assist at the wash-tub.*

Mrs Beeton's Book of *Household Management* (1861)

For those of you who have to do your own washing, here is a list of washing aids.

- ▪ Ammonia **A strong alkaline cleaner (the opposite of acidic), ammonia (NH$_3$) is also a mild bleach and grease solvent. It cuts through much of the grease, dirt and body debris which is acidic and finds its way onto laundry, but as it produces irritating fumes, make sure there is adequate ventilation when you use it.**

- ▪ Bleaches **These whiten, brighten and help to remove stains and mould; they are also used to disinfect. The two main types of bleach used in the house are oxygen (for instance, hydrogen peroxide, a mild bleach recommended for delicate fabrics) and chlorine (for example, sodium hypochlorite, a relatively strong bleach that can clean and kill micro-organisms). Lemon juice is a natural household bleach.**

- ▪ Blue **Containing a blue dye or pigment which absorbs the yellow part of the light spectrum, blue counteracts the yellowing that occurs with**

WASHING DAY BLUES

Before today's automatic washing machines reduced the housewife's burden, bluing was yet another stage in the long process of washing and drying the household's clothing and linen. Bluing came after rinsing and before mangling. *The Book of Hints and Wrinkles* suggests using enough blue to make the water 'deep azure in colour but not a strong blue' and to test with a white rag before starting to blue. In addition, it was advisable to avoid overcrowding or screwing up clothes, otherwise streaks or patches would occur. The book also recommends dipping household linen first, then 'body linen and handkerchiefs', delicate fabrics and, lastly, kitchen cloths. Then on to the mangling!

WHEN FABRIC SOFTENER STAINS

Fabric softener can stain clothes if the detergent has not been fully rinsed from an article. To remove stains caused by fabric softener, wash the garment in a strong laundry powder in warm to hot water, around 50°C (125°F), soak overnight in warm to hot water with a mild oxygen bleach, then wash again in laundry powder in warm to hot water.

You can prevent staining in the first place by following these steps.

- If you are using a concentrate, take extra care to dilute the softener. When you make it up, shake the bottle well.
- Do not allow detergent and softener to come into contact with each other. For instance, if you dissolve softener in a bucket, make sure this bucket is not used for dissolving detergent as well.
- Make sure the clothes are covered in water before adding the softener.
- Wash the machine drum according to the manufacturer's instructions.

some fabrics. This gives a blue tinge to white clothes which, by a trick of light, makes them appear whiter. To avoid staining, thoroughly dissolve the blue in water before bringing it into contact with fabric. Blue may be found in laundry detergents.

- Borax A strong alkali which softens water, borax allows a surfactant to act more effectively. It was a traditional laundry aid in Victorian times. Borax is also a disinfectant, stain remover, powerful grease remover and deodorizer. It may be used as a laundry booster when added to detergents. Use it for soaking nappies, but not delicate fabrics such as silk or wool. Borax is sold in powder form or as a colourless crystalline salt.

- Dry-cleaning fluids These are toxic solvents used for spot cleaning clothes and upholstery.

- Fabric softeners Containing waxy lubricants that coat the clothing fibres to make them feel soft and smell perfumed, fabric softeners work by decreasing static cling, wrinkling and drying time. They are added to the final rinse in a washing machine or straight into the dryer. (See 'When fabric softener stains', above, for information on correct usage.) There are

OLD-FASHIONED AIDS

- Add fragrance to a washing load by adding a few drops of lavender essential oil to a face cloth and dropping it into the machine. You could also try ylang-ylang, neroli, pine or eucalyptus oil.
- Clothes will be soft to the touch if you soak them overnight in a solution of 1 part vinegar to 3 parts water. Rinse well before washing.
- A cup of white vinegar in the final rinse water in a load of washing will help prevent lint from forming.

two types of fabric softener used in the dryer: the sheet type, where a sheet of synthetic fabric or polyurethane foam is impregnated with fabric softener; and the packet type, where a packet of softener is attached to the drum of the dryer. With both types, the heat of the dryer transfers the fabric softener to the clothes.

- Ironing aids The most basic ironing aid you can use is a damp cloth, preferably white cotton, as this won't result in colour run or leave behind fluff or lint. The cloth protects the fabric as you iron. Ironing aid products include sprays containing starch for extra body or silicone for extra glide. Silicone also leaves a protective layer on fabric. Some products are designed to be added to the washing machine — for instance, in the fabric softener compartment — while others are to be sprayed directly onto fabrics while you are ironing.

- Laundry detergents Available in tablet, powder or liquid form, laundry detergents often contain enzymes to attack stains and a range of other additives, including bulking agents, water softeners, bleach activators, perfumes, optical brightening agents and foam suppressants. The liquids are often concentrated; these contain fewer additives.

- Nappy soaks These sterilize and whiten laundry items such as soiled nappies, stained clothing and tea towels. They often contain sodium perborate (a mild bleach), water softeners and detergents.

- Prewash stain removers These are available as sprays or bars. Enzyme presoaks help remove difficult stains and heavy soiling. They often contain a combination of enzymes, builders, surfactants, solvents, fluorescent brighteners, bluing agents, fragrance and sometimes an oxygen bleach.

■ Soap As soap is 100 per cent biodegradable and does not pollute the environment, environmental groups recommend it for washing clothes in preference to washing detergents. Available in supermarkets, soap flakes are ideal for the gentle washing of clothes – for instance, silks and wools – that may be damaged by strong detergents. Laundry soap is also available in blocks and may contain additives such as borax, bleach, sodium phosphates and perfumes. Unlike synthetic detergent, soap does not dissolve well in cold water.

■ Washing soda Otherwise known as sodium carbonate, washing soda is a mild alkali available in a crystal or powder form. It is a good water softener and stain remover and is used as an additive in commercial laundry products. Use it with soap for laundry, as a tarnish remover on silver and to help unblock drains.

■ Wool washes A gentle surfactant mixture for washing wool, wool wash avoids alkalis, which can affect the dyes in wool, damaging the fibres, and causing running and fading.

THE TROUBLE WITH SOAP In hard water areas soap can leave scum on your washing. It's easily fixed if you add 1/4 cup washing soda to the wash cycle, or up to 3/4 cup if you live in an area with very hard water.

A world of detergents

When choosing a washing detergent, consider stain removal, skin sensitivity, the format of the detergent and the impact of your choice on the environment.

How green is your detergent?

'Biodegradability' refers to the degree to which a substance can be decomposed by the action of bacteria and other living organisms, such as fungi. Chemicals that do not biodegrade quickly can gradually accumulate in the environment and harm living organisms at several levels in the food chain.

Pure soaps stand out as the best choice environmentally, as they are 100 per cent biodegradable and contain no phosphates. (See 'How much phosphate?', below.) In addition, they can be extracted more easily at the sewage plant. However, they may not wash satisfactorily in hard water areas and may need to be combined with water softeners such as borax or washing soda. The grease emulsified by soap may be liberated when sewage is pumped into the sea, eventually forming scum on beaches.

These days even mainstream laundry detergents are designed to be more biodegradable. Many countries now have biodegradability standards, which may dictate, for instance, that 80 per cent of the detergent must biodegrade within 28 days. However, often these standards do not address the biodegradability of all the ingredients. Low-phosphate or phosphate-free detergents are also available, although the problem of phosphates in detergents is not a clear cut one.

Manufacturers of alternative brands offer detergents with plant surfactants (dirt-removing molecules) that they claim are 100 per cent biodegradable. These brands often omit a number of additives such as whiteners.

In many countries detergents are required to be biodegradable, but that is a qualified term. In Australia, the Standard says that surfactants classified as 'biologically soft' must be 80 per cent biodegraded in 21 days. 'Biologically hard' surfactants must biodegrade by 50 per cent in 21 days. Pure soap and soap flakes are considered to be 100 per cent biodegradable, and surfactants that are 100 per cent biodegradable in seven days have been developed.

How much phosphate?

Phosphates — compounds containing phosphorus — are found in detergents, laundry powders, liquids and shampoos (as well as in fertilizers, animal excrement, urban run-off and sewage). In detergent products, they are used as 'builders' to boost the cleaning power of the surfactant by softening water (they react with ions in hard water that interfere with cleaning), increasing alkalinity and helping suspend the dirt in water.

Phosphorus is a naturally occurring element found in all living things. In water systems it acts as a nutrient, encouraging the growth of plants. However, too much phosphorus in water systems encourages excessive growth of algae and weeds, robbing less aggressive plant life and animal life of oxygen, resulting, ultimately, in lifeless streams and rivers.

You can choose low-phosphate products, which contain less than 5 per cent phosphate, or ones without phosphate, although information about other ingredients in the product is often lacking.

Biological or non-biological?

Biological detergents contain stain-fighting enzymes that aid soil break-up. Non-biological laundry detergents may be less irritating to those with sensitive skins than ones containing enzymes. If you suspect the many additives in laundry detergents are the problem, it may be worth trying pure soap flakes. Soap-based powders may contain additives but are usually formulated to be milder than standard detergents.

Detergent format and quantity

- Concentrated powders omit the fillers that bulk out some powders. Obviously you need less, but try using less of any detergent, especially with lightly soiled items.
- Liquid detergents are easy to dissolve.
- Tablets make dose measurement foolproof.
- Soap is available in flakes and a solid bar.
- Some stains and types of soiling may call for more detergent, not less. For instance, thick creams and heavy perspiration decrease a detergent's action, as does hard water.

ALLERGY ALERT IN THE LAUNDRY

Ingredients in detergents, fabric softeners and soaps can cause skin irritations and other allergic reactions. Some people are allergic to the solvent 1,1,1-trichloroethane, which is used in stain removers. It has a strong odour and can cause sneezing or a tightening of the chest in people with respiratory allergies.

If you or someone in your household is prone to allergies, take these precautions.

- Consider using a non-biological detergent.
- Rinse clothes extra carefully, perhaps by using the rinse cycle twice.
- Before wearing new clothes wash them to remove excess factory finishes.
- Wear gloves when hand washing.

Alternative washing products

There's no need to use harsh chemicals in the laundry. With a few basic ingredients you can make a range of washing products yourself, many of which have been used traditionally for centuries.

See 'The kitchen', page 84, for more basic, low-toxic alternative cleaners.

Basic household soap cleaner

Use this cleaner in the following ways.

- **Laundry detergent** Suitable for machine washing or hand washing, for front loaders and top loaders. Use about 2 cups per load.

- **Prewash** Soak heavily soiled items in a solution before washing.

INGREDIENTS

50 g (1 3/4 oz) pure soap

1/2 cup washing soda crystals

1/2 cup white vinegar

1 1/2 teaspoons eucalyptus oil or tea-tree oil

Few drops lemon or lavender pure essential oil for fragrance

5 L (10 1/2 pt) cold water

4.5 L (9 1/2 pt) hot water

METHOD

1   Grate the soap into a large saucepan and cover with 1 L (2 pt) of the cold water. Bring to the boil, add washing soda and stir until completely dissolved.

2   Stir in eucalyptus oil, white vinegar and essential oil.

3   Pour into a bucket, add the hot water then stir in the remaining cold water.

4   When cool, transfer to smaller containers and label.

All-purpose laundry stain remover 1

Use this stain remover for soaking soiled clothing. Alternatively, apply it with a sponge and allow it to dry.

INGREDIENTS

¼ cup borax

2 cups cold water

METHOD

Mix the borax and water together.

All-purpose laundry stain remover 2

INGREDIENTS

3 tablespoons eucalyptus oil

1 cup methylated spirits

1 cup boiling water

METHOD

1   Mix the ingredients together in an enamel or stainless steel bowl.

2   Stand the bowl in a bigger saucepan of hot water on medium heat, stirring it until it turns transparent.

3   Pour into moulds such as empty milk or juice cartons.

4   When it has set, cut it into bars and leave for four weeks to harden.

HOUSEHOLD USES FOR ESSENTIAL OILS

ESSENTIAL OIL	PROBLEM	METHOD
Eucalyptus	Stains on clothing (e.g. perspiration marks, oil and soluble grease)	Add 2 teaspoons eucalyptus oil to a wash load or place an absorbent cloth under the stain. Moisten a clean rag with eucalyptus oil and gently but firmly brush the stain from its edge into the middle
	Stains on carpet	Put eucalyptus oil in a small spray atomiser and spray generously. Wipe with a clean absorbent cloth
	Ink (writing ink or printers' ink) on plastic or vinyl	Dip a cloth in eucalytpus oil. Test on a hidden patch first
	Glue, tar, chewing gum on fabric and other surfaces; adhesive tape on vinyl	Place a few drops on the stain, leave for two minutes and wash. Repeat a few times if necessary. Finish with a wipe of methylated spirits and eucalyptus oil
	Washing bathroom	Kill bacteria by adding a couple of drops of eucalyptus oil to the final rinsing water
	Washing vinyl or lino flooring	Add 1 teaspoon eucalyptus oil to the washing water
Lavender	Washing bathroom	Kill germs by adding a couple of drops of lavender oil to the final rinsing water
	Washing clothes	Add fragrance to a washing load by adding a few drops of lavender oil to a face cloth and dropping it into the machine
	Mosquito bite	Apply undiluted to the bite
Pennyroyal	Flea repellent	Mix 18 drops undiluted pennyroyal oil with 500 g (1 lb) bicarbonate of soda. Sprinkle over carpets and furniture, leave for one hour then vacuum
	For pets' bedding	Blend 20–30 drops pennyroyal oil with 10 mL (2 teaspoons) methylated spirits. Add to a pump spray bottle containing 500 mL (2 cups) water. Shake well then use on fine mist setting
	Fly repellent	Brush the oil onto woodwork surrounding doors and kitchen benches

Essential oils in the home

Essential oils have a variety of uses in the home – not just in the laundry – as disinfectants, fragrances, stain removers and insect repellents. Check the table opposite to see how you can put eucalyptus, lavender and pennyroyal oils to good use in your home.

Less is more

Whether you use 'green' or conventional chemicals, there are many ways to cut down on the amount you use.

- **Experiment with less and see if it works adequately.**

- **Give them more time to work. For example, soak stained clothes before washing them.**

- **Act quickly. Remove stains before they set and take more chemical power to remove.**

Fabric care

Nowadays there is an enormous range of fabrics and finishes – both natural and synthetic – from which we can choose our clothes and other household textiles. To prolong their life and keep them looking in optimum condition, it's worth taking the time to discover what they're made from, and how they should be cared for.

Sorting the washing

You can sort your washing in various ways. The obvious benefits of sorting are avoiding colour runs and saving on wear and tear, but it also makes your machine more energy efficient. How much time and trouble you take over it depends on the time you have available and your level of interest.

- By fabric type **Fabric type determines the maximum temperature at which an article can be washed without causing damage. In some cases it also determines spin speed and washing machine cycle length. Consult the care label of the garment for information. If you wash all your clothes in cold water regardless of fabric type, you may simply need to separate woollens and other delicate items that you wish to wash by** hand. It's usually best to separately wash items such as towels, especially new ones, to prevent lint spreading on to other garments.

- By colour Even when washing in cold water, you should separate loads of washing into coloureds and whites. You can break these groups down further into darks, mixed white and coloured patterns. Mainly white prints that are colourfast can be treated as 'white'. Always pay attention to the care label on each garment. Instructions to 'wash separately' mean just that: excess dye may bleed out of the fabric for at least the first few washes.

- By degree of soiling Pull out the items that will benefit from prewash treatment, whether they are stained or heavily soiled. Do not wash a single very dirty item with a load of lightly soiled clothes.

While sorting the clothes for washing, attend to these small jobs at the same time.

- Empty pockets of paper tissues, coins, keys and any other items that could harm the washing machine or ruin the wash.

- Close buttons, zips and other fasteners to reduce the risk of tearing.

- Tie tapes and strings to prevent tangling in the wash.

- Brush clothes free of loose dirt and fluff.

- Mend any tears and holes to reduce the chance of holes enlarging during the washing process.

Care labels

Care labels on textiles usually refer to four different care processes: washing, bleaching, drying and ironing. They may also give dry-cleaning advice and information. Most instructions have fairly obvious meanings. Care labels give the consumer information on the best way to wash a particular item. They tend to err on the side of caution. Many silk items that are labelled 'dry-clean only' may in fact be carefully hand washed. But if you do hand wash an item with such a label, and something goes wrong, you cannot complain to the manufacturer.

SCRATCHY LABELS If your skin is irritated by a care label detailing information you may need to refer to again, cut it off and reattach it to a side seam.

GUIDE TO CARE SYMBOLS

SYMBOL	MEANING
	Machine washable (normal cycle)
	Hand wash only
	Any bleach can be used
	Tumble dry after washing
	Tumble dry with high heat setting
	Tumble dry with low heat setting
	Hot iron
	Medium iron
	Cool iron
	Dry-cleaning
(A)	Any solvent
(P)	Any solvent except trichloroethylene
(F)	Petroleum solvent only

When there's no care label

If the care label on an item of clothing is faded, or if there just isn't one, you need to know how to treat each fabric type. These general guidelines, followed by a table specifying the care required for many different fabric types (page 144), will help.

- Synthetic fabrics in particular benefit from frequent washing as it prevents dirt from becoming absorbed into the fibres.

- To safeguard colour, finish and shape, and to minimize creasing, never wash hotter or longer, nor spin longer than recommended, unless you are absolutely confident of the results.

- Rinse thoroughly. Clothes and linen need at least two rinses to remove all traces of detergent and soil. Some finishes will not work effectively without proper rinsing – for example, showerproofing may not work as well, and towelling may become scratchy.

- Blends are made by spinning together different fibres to form a yarn, which is then spun and woven or knitted. Mixture fabrics are made by weaving or knitting together yarns made from different fibres. When washing blends and mixtures, determine which fibre needs the gentlest treatment before you choose a washing method. For instance, wash a blend of polyester and wool as if it were all wool, in warm water.

A–Z fabric guide

Consult this alphabetical listing for some general information on the most popular fabric types.

Acetate

Acetate (also called cellulose acetate) is made from wood cellulose that is treated with acetic acid. Fabrics made from acetate are smooth and silk-like. Triacetate is more versatile and is made into a greater range of fabrics. Both acetate and triacetate are relatively weak and are easily abraded. Acetate fibres become even weaker when washed, so it is usually recommended that they be dry-cleaned. Triacetate can usually be machine washed.

Both acetate and triacetate have little absorbency. They do not mildew and are generally not attacked by pests. They are damaged by concentrated acid or alkaline solutions and by solvents that contain acetone (such as nail polish remover and paint remover).

- ▦ **Dry-clean if this is recommended on the care label.**
- ▦ **Wash gently if the care label recommends it.**
- ▦ **Use lukewarm water.**
- ▦ **Use mild soaps and detergents.**
- ▦ **Use household bleach cautiously for stains. Mineral spirits (also known as petroleum spirits) may also be used with care on acetate and triacetate. However, the fibres in acetate are damaged by solvents such as those used in perfumes and by others that contain acetone, such as nail polish remover.**
- ▦ **Roll in a towel to dry after hand washing.**
- ▦ **Dry knits flat.**
- ▦ **Hang woven items to dry.**
- ▦ **Don't wring, twist or rub.**

Acrylic

Acrylic (short for polyacrylonitrile) and modacrylic (modified acrylic) are made from petroleum derivatives. They have soft, woolly, fluffy characteristics and are often used as a wool substitute. Modacrylics are also used in fake furs and in children's nightwear, because of their flame resistance.

Cotton

Cotton is made from the fluffy fibres that surround the seed of the cotton plant. Its quality depends on the closeness and regularity of the weave, the construction of the fabric and the cotton plant itself. Generally speaking, the longer the fibre (or staple), the better quality the cotton. Extra long staples include Sea Island cotton, Pima cotton and Egyptian cotton.

Cotton is strong, absorbent and cool, and is particularly suitable for dyeing. It tends to wrinkle, but many cotton fabrics have been anti-wrinkle-treated, and also preshrunk. Cotton is prone to mildew if left wet and, like all cellulosic fibres, it is also prone to damage by acid, including the acid found in perspiration.

YELLOWING COTTON In most cases, ordinary bleach treatment will rid cotton of yellowing caused by age or excessive sunlight. If you have the facilities, you can try boiling the fabric for 45 minutes to an hour with detergent.

Linen

Linen is made from flax plant fibres, which consist of cellulose polymers. It is strong and durable, and can be put to use in a variety of different fabric types – damask, towels, bandages, sheets, lace, clothing and upholstery. Flax fibres are separated into long and short fibres by a process called hackling. Long fibres, or staple, are used for fine linen, while short staple, or tow, is used for functional items such as tea towels.

Flax fibres range in colour from pale yellow to dark brown. Linen is bleached, a process which weakens it, to produce white linen, or in preparation for dyeing. As the fibres are smooth, linen is fairly resistant to staining; it is also cool next to the skin and highly absorbent. Unless it has been preshrunk, linen will shrink a little the first time it is washed, and it is prone to heavy wrinkling; resin treatments, which also weaken the fibres, are sometimes applied to make linen less wrinkle prone.

While some linen items are robust enough to bear tough laundering, even boiling, others, such as tailored jackets, are better off being dry-cleaned.

Nylon

Nylon is the name given to a group of polymers called polyamides derived from coal, petroleum, air, water and sometimes cereal waste products such as oat hulls or corn cobs. The characteristics of nylon fibres vary enormously and are sold under a variety of trade names. Generally, however, they are light, strong and highly resistant to abrasion. They are also highly elastic, and this is why they are such a suitable material for pantihose and stockings. The fibres are wrinkle resistant and have low absorbency. Nylon is not damaged by mildew, moths or other pests but it is prone to static build-up. It attracts dirt and holds oils.

- Wash white with white only as white nylon will pick up the slightest hint of colour in the washing water, rendering it dingy.

- Use a gentle machine cycle.

- Don't use chlorine bleach on nylon as it may yellow it. Use an oxygen bleach such as hydrogen peroxide instead.

Polyester

Polyester is produced from substances derived from coal, petroleum, air and water. A variety of polyester filaments are fabricated and these are made into a wide range of fabrics. Polyester is usually strong and wrinkle resistant. It is not absorbent, it dries quickly, and although prone to oil stains, is otherwise stain resistant. Polyester fibres are not damaged by acids and alkalis, nor by mildew, moths or other pests. This fabric tends to retain body odours.

Rayon

Rayon is made from cellulose in either cotton or wood pulp and can be fabricated into a wide variety of materials. These include the following.

- Viscose rayon **This constitutes the majority of rayon for sale, identified as 'viscose' or 'rayon'. It is soft and drapes well, with a feel a little like cotton. Highly absorbent but weaker than the natural fibres, viscose rayon becomes weaker and prone to stretching when wet and then tends to shrink on drying, so it needs gentle washing. It is prone to shrinking if not pretreated and may be wrinkle prone, depending on how it was treated during manufacture. Viscose rayon mildews if left damp and is vulnerable to attack by silverfish but not moths.**

- Cuprammonium rayon **Also known as Bemberg or cupra rayon, this fabric is soft, lustrous and silky, and is used for linings, dresses and blouses, even flags.**

- High-Wet-Modulus rayons **These rayons have better wet strength and are often treated to avoid further shrinkage. They may look and feel like good quality cotton and can usually be machine washed without trouble.**

- Lyocell **Sold under the trade name Tencel, and produced by dissolving wood pulp in a process considered environmentally favourable, lyocell is less prone to wrinkling and shrinking, and is stronger than viscose.**

Some rayon is best dry-cleaned as the fibres weaken when wet and also often shrink. In addition, they can go limp and wrinkle after washing. Viscose rayon is often treated with water-soluble finishes and stiffeners that can dissolve in washing.

Silk

Silk, the epitome of luxury, is made from the filament secreted by the silkworm, the larva of the Chinese moth *Bombyx mori*, which feeds on the leaves of the mulberry tree. It is smooth, soft, lightweight, lustrous, strong and resilient. Although silk dyes brilliantly, it also abrades easily, making it a poor choice for upholstery. Silk is highly absorbent, partially wrinkle resistant and prone to carpet beetles. Although it does not hold particles of dirt easily, because it is smooth, it does stain very easily.

- **Thrown silk Fine and sheer fabrics such as georgette, taffeta, voile, crepe de Chine, organza and grenadine are made from thrown silk, whereby filaments from several cocoons are combined and wound onto a reel, then twisted into threads.**
- **Spun silk Short lengths of filament are carded, combed and spun into threads, which tend to become fuzzy over time.**
- **Weighted silk When the gum that covers the filament is boiled off, the fabric loses a lot of its weight. Manufacturers sometimes replace the lost weight with metallic salts, which add body but also weaken the silk.**
- **Raw silk Raw silk still contains the gum, so it is bumpy and irregular.**

Many care labels advise dry-cleaning silk because its fibres become weaker when wet and because it is prone to damage by alkalis. If in doubt, dry-clean – especially expensive silks, which may have special finishes you will never see again if you try washing them yourself. It is often possible to wash silks if you do it carefully, especially if they have been treated to make them washable. Some washable silks should not be dry-cleaned, so it is important to refer to care labels.

As with wool, hand washing is the gentlest, safest option if you have decided to wash silk.

Velvet

Velvet is the name given to a type of fabric construction and not to the fibre it's made of. Velvet can be silk, cotton or an acetate/nylon blend. If the care instructions on a velvet garment are unclear, have it dry-cleaned.

Remove surface dust from soft furnishings upholstered in velvet with a vacuum cleaner or a soft brush.

Wool

The word 'wool' usually refers to sheep's wool, but can also mean the fibre that comes from the coats of Angora rabbits, cashmere goats, camel, alpaca, llama and vicuna. Wool is naturally warm, soft and absorbent. It provides cushioning and protects from dampness as it absorbs a great deal of moisture before becoming wet.

Wool fibres are used for a wide variety of textiles — woven clothing, knitting wool, upholstery and carpets. They vary in quality according to the type of sheep they come from — merino wool is the finest, softest and most elastic; Shetland and Botany wools are also good quality. The fleece type also varies: lamb's wool is the softest, while hogget wool comes from a yearling's first shearing and is also relatively soft compared to wool from more mature sheep.

Worsted yarns are made from long wool fibres that are spun to form a smooth, firm yarn. They make a flat, hard, smooth fabric commonly used in tailored suits. Fabrics made from worsted yarns are strong and relatively wrinkle resistant but they can develop shiny patches.

Short wool fibres are used to make woollen yarns that spin into fuzzier yarns. They are warm but less durable than worsted, and are commonly used in jumpers and blankets.

Oiled wool fibres have not been stripped of as much of their natural lanolin as other wool fibres and are used for heavy jumpers.

Wool shrinks and is stain resistant. You can often brush dust and dirt off the surface of wool; however, it can absorb and retain odours. Wool is highly vulnerable to moths but generally resists mildew unless it has been left damp for a long time.

WASHING WOOL

Washing wool takes care as this fabric is prone to felting and shrinking: the fibres swell and weaken when wet. For this reason, many care labels advise dry-cleaning only. There's little doubt this is the best option for tailored items and bulky jumpers that are either difficult to dry or too special to risk spoiling.

With gentle treatment, however, many woollen items are fine to wash, and it certainly is cheaper than regular dry-cleaning. In fact, textile technology has developed to such a degree that manufacturers have come up with various chemical and physical processes which make wool more washable — for example, finishes such as Teflon protect knitted wool. Alkaline detergents should be avoided as they harm the wool fibres.

If washing by hand, follow these tips.

- Use cool, tepid or lukewarm water for a heavily soiled item.
- Use soap flakes or a detergent especially formulated for wool.
- If in doubt about whether the fabric is machine washable, hand wash it.
- Gently squeeze the suds through the garment; rough agitation can damage the wool fibres.
- Rinse in cool clear water.
- Dry wool by wrapping it in a towel and rolling it gently. Never twist, pull or wring wool when it is wet. Dry it flat on a towel or other clean surface away from direct sunlight or heat.
- Don't soak a woollen garment for more than five minutes.

RECYCLING WOOL

Recycling wool from old, misshapen or unfashionable jumpers is an old craft. Recycled wool is also called 'shoddy', now a derogatory term that seems inappropriate since recycling has lost its negative image to some degree. As you unravel the wool, wind it round the back of a chair or a large piece of cardboard. To revive the wool, steam it by holding it over steaming water with two wooden spoons until it is evenly damp. Alternatively, hang it in the shower recess while you have a hot shower. Leave the wool until it is dry, then wind it into balls. Dye it or use it as is. Recycled wool is ideal for children's knitting experiments as well as more ambitious projects.

Where care labels advise it, or when you are prepared to risk it, woollens can be machine washed on a gentle cycle. Your washing machine may even have a special 'wool' cycle.

- **Use cool or lukewarm water.**
- **Use a gentle detergent suitable for wool.**
- **Use a fast spin to ensure the item is as dry as possible.**
- **Dry it flat.**
- **Don't tumble dry unless the care label advises it.**

STEAM TREATMENT To smooth out a wrinkly wool garment, hang it up in a steamy bathroom.

Allergies to different types of fibre

If you suffer from allergies or have very sensitive skin, your choice of fabric or fibre for clothes and other materials with which you come into close contact, such as bedding, can make a big difference.

- **Because of its tiny fibres, wool can trigger allergic reactions in the susceptible. Most other natural fibres such as cotton, silk and leather are not usually associated with allergic reactions.**
- **Cotton clothing and bedding is usually more comfortable for those people who are prone to allergies, such as eczema sufferers, probably because they do not induce sweating.**
- **Some people find the dyes used with polyesters irritating.**
- **The formaldehyde used on easy-care clothing can also be irritating.**

Finishing treatments

Fabric manufacturers have developed a range of finishes to alter the characteristics of a fabric. These affect the way we wash them and also the way they wear. Many treatments, such as permanent or durable press, weaken a fabric, so the washing process needs to be gentle if it is not to shorten the fabric's life.

- **Absorbent finishes** A variety of chemicals are used to enhance the natural absorbency of cotton, rayon and linen; sometimes they are used for underwear and towels. Absorbency is reduced by resin treatments, fabric softener and tight twisted weaves.

- **Antiseptic finish** This treatment is primarily used for mildew prevention and odour control in shoe linings, bedclothes, underwear and shoes.

- **Anti-static treatment** Used on synthetic fabrics such as polyester and nylon to reduce the static electricity that builds up with friction, this finish can make clothes hang badly and attract dirt; it may even cause minor shocks and sparks.

- **Anti-wrinkle treatments** During manufacture, resins are applied, and these react with cloth made from cellulosic fibres such as cotton, linen and rayon, thus forming cross links. The type of treatment is indicated by labels such as 'permanent press' or 'easy care'. Fabrics treated with this

FIRE RISKS

- Synthetic fibres such as nylon and polyester may be slow to ignite, but eventually they will burn and melt at a very high temperature.
- Light materials such as voile and muslin burn faster than the heavy types of fabric used in curtains.
- Fabrics mixed from synthetic material and cellulose have a wicking effect as the cellulose acts as a wick onto which the synthetic polymer fibres melt.
- Wool and silk readily char and do not spread the flame.
- Raised pile fabrics are more of a fire hazard as they have a greater surface area in contact with air.
- Cellulosic fabrics readily burn and also produce flammable gases.

finish may need some ironing but resist wrinkling when being worn. The anti-wrinkling treatment is most often applied to cotton/polyester mixes. Drip-dry clothing undergoes anti-wrinkle treatment before it is tailored so that after washing, when it is hung up to dry, it regains its shape, needing little, if any, ironing. Permanent pleats and creases can be made in wool with a durable press treatment consisting of resins or chemicals. Another anti-wrinkle treatment is called 'liquid ammonia durable press' and is used on cloth made of 100 per cent cellulosic fibre.

Beetling This process makes linen yarns smoother and provides them with lustre and increased flexibility. Linen is pounded with wooden mallets to permanently flatten the yarn and close the cloth weave.

Bleaching Initially, most coloured fabrics are bleached using chlorine bleaches, such as sodium hypochlorite and sodium chlorite, or non-chlorine bleaches, such as hydrogen peroxide and sodium perborate. Fabric can also be bleached in the sunlight – a process known as grass bleaching – which is gentler than bleaching by chemicals and does not weaken the fabric as much. Optical brighteners may also be added to fabrics to mask yellow hues and make cloth appear brighter.

Calendering During this treatment, fabric is subjected to great pressure and/or heat under big rollers, like a giant ironing process. Calendering makes fabric smooth and lustrous, but it has a temporary effect on cotton unless resins are also applied, as in materials with glazes, embossing, moire or other treatments like Schreinering (a milling method which enhances the natural lustre of the fabric).

Decorative effects Heat, pressure and chemicals such as acids are used to create decorative effects on fabrics. For example, a number of finishes – such as creeping, embossing and moire – are made by passing fabric through engraved rollers.

Flame-resistant treatments These act in a number of ways: inhibiting the rate of ignition, slowing the spread of flame and encouraging a fabric to 'self-extinguish' if it catches fire. Flame-retardant finishes may require special care when washing: do not bleach or soak them in any washing product, and do not wash them with soap or a non-automatic powder as soap can mask the properties of the finish.

■ Glazing This creates a shiny, stiff fabric such as chintz. Old-fashioned treatments include starch and wax, which gradually wash out. Modern, more durable glazes are baked on to the fabric, or resins are calendered on (see 'Calendering', page 141).

■ Mercerizing A chemical treatment for cotton, mercerizing strengthens it, making it easier to dye and handle at the same time.

■ Mothproofing It is claimed that mothproofing protects cloth from moth damage either by killing the moth larvae when they try to eat the fabric fibre, or by making the fabric indigestible to the larvae.

■ Napping There are various ways of giving fabric a nap – that is, a raised surface such as on flannels – which gives extra warmth and stain resistance. The simplest napping method is brushing.

■ Permanent press Fabrics treated with a permanent press finish are less prone to wrinkling; however, they are more prone to taking up soil in the washing water and coming out grey.

■ Preshrinking Methods of preshrinking fabric include washing, mechanical means, and chemical and resin treatments. This treatment reduces the chance of more shrinkage occurring during home washing.

■ Resin treatments Resin-treated fabrics are prone to stains by oils. Some resin treatments involve formaldehyde, which is why it is often a good idea to wash a new item of clothing before wearing it. Resins such as urea, glyoxal, carbonate and melamine formaldehyde can be applied to cotton, linen and rayon for a number of effects: permanent creases, wrinkle resistance, shrinkage resistance, permanent stiffness, shine or lustre, water repellency and decorative effects.

■ Soil-release treatments Fabrics finished with soil-release treatments come cleaner on laundering. These treatments are applied to synthetic fabrics or blends and durable press fabrics. One treatment type uses fluorocarbons, which form a film on the fabric surface, preventing oil coming in direct contact with fabric fibres and making it easier for detergents to wash it away.

■ Soil-resistant treatments Used on natural and synthetic fabrics, soil repellents cause water and/or oil to bead on the surface rather than penetrate the fabric. They reduce a fabric's absorbency but not its ability to breathe.

- ▣ Stiffening **Starches and other sizings (sizing is any substance used to stiffen fabric) stiffen cotton and linen temporarily. They wash out and must be reapplied if you want the fabric to return to its original stiffness.**

- ▣ UV protection **These fabric qualities offer more protection from sunlight's ultraviolet content: thicker rather than thinner; darker colour rather than a lighter one; and tighter weave rather than a looser, more open one. In addition, chemicals can be added to a fabric to render it more opaque to UV. In some countries fabrics may be awarded sun protection factors.**

- ▣ Water-resistant treatments **Waterproof fabrics are impermeable to water because of a layer of, for example, plastic, rubber or vinyl resin. They are also impermeable to air. Water-repellent treatments add a coating that causes water to bead up on the fabric surface rather than soak through immediately.**

If you are in doubt about how to wash a particular fabric, consult the table on 'Fabrics and their washing requirements' on pages 144–51 in conjunction with the table on 'Fabric names' on page 152. Always follow the care label if there is one; otherwise, hand wash in tepid water or dry-clean.

PEGGING OUT THE COTTON *To bleach in the sun the material must be thoroughly washed and boiled in an alkaline solution of soap and washing soda, then bleached for two days and two nights. The material is stretched on the grass, fastened by…a loop of tape attached to each corner to pegs already placed on the ground. The process of boiling and bleaching must be repeated every alternate day until the fabric is quite white.*

Margaret Cuthbert Rankin, *The Science of Laundry Work* (1910)

FABRICS AND THEIR WASHING REQUIREMENTS

FABRIC	DESCRIPTION	SPECIAL REQUIREMENTS
Acetate	Widely used cellulose derived fabric	Wash gently in lukewarm water. Handle gently when wet. Take care with stain solvents
Acrylic	Synthetic fibre that does not shrink	Treat heavy knitted articles with care to avoid stretching. Gentle machine or hand wash, inside out to prevent pilling. Use fabric softener regularly to reduce static electricity. Use a low tumble dryer setting; dry knits flat
Angora	Fluffy fibre from the Angora rabbit	Hand wash with care. To dry, lay flat away from direct sun or heat. Brush with teasel brush (a spiky brush) when dry to raise the surface
Cashmere	Natural fibre from the downy undercoat of the Tibetan cashmere goat	Hand wash with care. Will quickly felt if washed too vigorously. To dry, roll in a dry towel, press to remove excess water, then repeat with a second towel. Finally, lay flat to dry on a fresh towel
Clydella	Mixture fabric of natural fibres, wool and cotton	Do not rub
Corduroy	Cut weft pile fabric with corded effect, usually cotton	Wash deep and bright colours separately
Cotton	Strong natural fibre which can withstand vigorous washing	Machine wash if you wish but be more cautious with loose weaves, trims and linings. Bleach when desired but rinse well afterwards. Dry in the sunlight for a lightening effect. Don't leave out in the sun for more than a few hours or it will yellow
Cotton (drip-dry)	Cotton with special finish for crease resistance and minimum iron	Machine wash
Denim	Twill weave, usually cotton or cotton blend	Allow for shrinkage. Not all denim is colourfast
Dylan	Shrink-resistant wool	Sometimes machine washable. Normal rinse. Normal spin, do not wring

MAX. WASH TEMP.	AGITATION	RINSE	SPIN	IRONING NOTES
40°C (104°F)	Gentle	Cold	Short	Damp iron on wrong side with cool iron
40°C (104°F)	Minimum	Cold	Short	Cool iron if required
40°C (104°F)	Minimum	Warm	Short	If desired, warm iron over damp cloth, or use steam iron
40°C (104°F)	Gentle; do not wring or twist	40°C (104°F)	Do not spin	Press on wrong side with warm iron under damp cloth, or use steam iron
40°C (104°F)	Minimum	Normal	Normal; do not hand wring	If required, warm iron on wrong side when damp
50°C (122°F)	Medium	Cold	Drip-dry	Do not iron. Remove creases by steaming
95°C (203°F) whites 60°C (140°F) colours	Maximum	Normal	Normal	If required, warm to hot iron when dry
50°C (122°F)	Medium	Cold	Drip-dry	Warm to hot iron when dry if required
95°C (203°F) whites 40°C (104°F) coloureds	Maximum	Normal	Normal	Hot iron when damp
40°C (104°F)	Minimum; do not rub	Normal	Normal; do not wring	Warm iron over damp cloth, or steam iron

FABRICS AND THEIR WASHING REQUIREMENTS

FABRIC	DESCRIPTION	SPECIAL REQUIREMENTS
Egyptian cotton	Fine quality natural cotton fibre in closely woven cloth	Machine wash
Elastane fibres	Synthetic stretch fibres	Wash according to other fibres in fabric and not above 50°C (122°F)
Fibreglass fabric	Woven from fine glass filaments. Flameproof and resistant to bacteria	Handle gently; liable to fray if machine washed. Abrasion can cause damage to the surface and loss of colour
Flame-retardant fabrics	Various fabrics designed to increase flammability	Do not soak, bleach or boil
Flame-retardant finishes	Various fabric finishes designed to decrease flammability	Do not use soaps or soap products. Medium agitation. Rinse carefully with cold water. Do not soak or bleach. Short spin or drip-dry
Foam backs	Fabrics to which a layer of polyurethane or polyester foam has been bonded to the back of the face fabric to give warmth without weight and to preserve shape	Not all foam backs are suitable for home washing. If in doubt dry-clean. Otherwise proceed as for face fabric
Glazed cotton	Cotton with special finish. Only permanently glazed cotton will retain sheen on washing	No special requirements
Helenca	Process which gives high stretch to yarns such as nylon and polyester	No special requirements
Lamb's wool	Natural fibre, fine-graded, high quality wool	Hand wash with care
Laminates	Two or more layers of fabrics bonded together	Not all are suitable for home washing. If in doubt dry-clean. Washable laminates should be laundered according to face fabrics
Lastex	Natural stretch yarn made from extruded rubber (latex)	If no advice on label, proceed at your own risk
Linen	Natural fibre made from flax	Wash at high temperatures. Can bleach and boil if white

(CONT.)

MAX. WASH TEMP.	AGITATION	RINSE	SPIN	IRONING NOTES
95°C (203°F) whites 60°C (140°F) coloureds	Maximum	Normal	Normal	Hot iron on wrong side when damp
50°C (122°F)	Medium	Cold	Short spin or drip-dry	Do not iron
40°C (104°F)	Gentle	Cold	Drip-dry	Do not iron
40°C (104°F)	Minimum	Cold	Short spin	Press lightly with a cool iron on wrong side while slightly damp
50°C (122°F)	Medium	Cold	Short spin or drip-dry	Cool iron
As for face fabric	As for face fabric	As for face fabric	As for face fabric	Iron according to face fabric
50°C (122°F)	Medium	Cold	Short spin or drip-dry	Hot iron on wrong side when damp. Finish by polishing on right side
60°C (140°F) white nylon 50°C (122°F) other	Medium	Cold	Short spin or drip-dry	Warm iron when dry if necessary
40°C (104°F)	Gentle	Cold	Roll in towel, then dry flat	Press lightly with warm iron under damp cloth or use steam iron. Brush up pile when dry
As face fabric	As face fabric	As face fabric	As face fabric	Iron if necessary according to face fabric
30°C (86°F)	Gentle	Cold	Short	Do not iron
95°C (203°F) whites 60°C (140°F) coloureds	Maximum	Normal	Normal	Hot iron when damp

FABRICS AND THEIR WASHING REQUIREMENTS

FABRIC	DESCRIPTION	SPECIAL REQUIREMENTS
Linen (delicate)	Lace or fine linen blouses	Hand wash or place item in old pillowcase before washing on gentle setting. Use mild detergent; avoid one with optical brighteners which can cause white spotting
Linen (sturdy)	Tablecloths, sheets, woven towels	Presoak overnight to remove stubborn stains. If tumble drying, remove while still damp to prevent overdrying which can make linen brittle
Lurex	Specially processed metallic thread incorporated into other fabric	Wash according to fabric type
Minimum iron	Easy-care finish	Wash according to fabric type
Modal	Viscose in modified form with improved wet strength	No special requirements
Mohair	Natural fibre from the Angora goat	Hand wash only
Nylon	Strong versatile synthetic fibre	No special requirements
Permanent press	Technique for giving permanent shape and creases to garments	Wash according to fabric type
Polyester	Very strong synthetic fibre	Wash regularly as attracts greasy soiling. Pretreat greasy stains. Wash inside out to prevent pilling
Polyester cotton	Blend	Do not allow to become heavily soiled before washing
Proban	Flame-retardant finish	Do not use soap

(CONT.)

MAX. WASH TEMP.	AGITATION	RINSE	SPIN	IRONING NOTES
40°C (104°F)	Do not wring	Normal	Roll in a towel to remove excess moisture then dry flat away from direct source of heat	Iron when still damp
50°C (122°F)	Minimum	Extra rinse	Fast; don't wring	Iron when still damp
As fabric type	As fabric type	As fabric type	As fabric type	Warm iron
40–50°C (104–122°F)	Minimum	Cold	Drip-dry	Warm iron if necessary when dry
40–60°C (104–140°F)	Maximum	Normal	Normal	Hot iron when damp. If necessary warm iron for polyester blends
40°C (104°F)	Gentle	Cold	Roll in towel, then dry flat	Press on wrong side under damp cloth with warm iron or use a steam iron. Brush up pile when dry
60°C (140°F) whites 50°C (122°F) coloureds	Medium	Cold	Short spin or drip-dry	If necessary, cool iron when dry
As fabric type	As fabric type	As fabric type	Do not wring	Not necessary
50°C (122°F)	Medium	Cold	Short spin or drip-dry	If necessary, cool iron when dry
60°C (140°F) whites 50°C (122°F) coloureds	Medium	Cold	Short spin or drip-dry	If necessary, warm iron when dry
50°C (122°F)	Medium	Cold	Short spin or drip-dry	Cool iron

FABRICS AND THEIR WASHING REQUIREMENTS

FABRIC	DESCRIPTION	SPECIAL REQUIREMENTS
PVC	Synthetic thermo plastic fibre	Shrinks over 70°C (158°F). Coats and raincoats: sponge c
Rayon	Read care label carefully as finishes and manufacturing processes are so varied. Specific care labels may recommend more vigorous handling	Either hand wash or use machine's gentle cycle if care label recommends machine washing. Use a mild, non-alkaline detergent. Dry knits flat; hang woven items
Rigmel	Shrink-resistant finish for cotton	No special requirements
Sanforized	Shrink-resistant finish	Wash according to fabric type
Sarille	Modified viscose with wool-like qualities	No special requirements
Scotchguard	Water- and oil-repellant finish	Wash according to fabric type. Rinse thoroughly
Silk and wild silk	Natural protein fibre made by silkworms	Use mild soap or detergent. Regular laundry detergent is alkaline and could damage silk fibres. Don't use chlorine bleach; use hydrogen peroxide or sodium perborate bleaches. Rinse thoroughly, dry gently. Don't soak for long periods.
Triacetate	Synthetic cellulose-derived fibre	More robust in wash and wear than acetate
Viloft	Tubular viscose fibre with high bulk and extra absorbency	Washes well often
Viscose	Widely used cellulose fibre used on its own and in blends	No special requirements
Viyella	55% lamb's wool, 45% cotton	Treat gently
Wool	Natural sheep fibre available in many qualities	Hand wash unless specifically advised to machine wash
Wool (machine washable)	Process which makes wool shrink resistant	Do not wring

(CONT.)

MAX. WASH TEMP.	AGITATION	RINSE	SPIN	IRONING NOTES
40°C (104°F)	Minimum	Cold	Short spin	Do not iron
30–40°C (86–104°F)	Gentle	Cold	Squeeze rather than wring	If in doubt, cool iron
95°C (203°F) whites 60°C (140°F) coloureds	Maximum	Normal	Normal	Hot iron when damp
As fabric type	As fabric type	As fabric type	As fabric type	Iron according to fabric type
40°C (104°F)	Normal	Normal	Normal	Hot iron when slightly and evenly damp
As fabric type	As fabric type	As fabric type	Drip-dry	Warm iron if necessary
30–40°C (86–104°F)	Minimum	Cold	Short spin, do not hand wring	Warm iron when slightly and evenly damp. Cool iron wild silk
40°C (104°F)	Minimum	Cold	Short spin	Cool iron when damp
50°C (122°F)	Medium	Cold	Short spin or dry	Not usually necessary
60°C (140°F)	Maximum	Normal	Normal	Hot iron on wrong side when damp
40°C (104°F)	Min., do not rub	Normal	Normal spin; do not hand wring	Warm iron on wrong side while slightly damp
40°C (104°F)	Min., do not rub	Normal	Normal spin; do not hand wring	Warm iron under damp cloth, or steam iron
40°C (104°F)	Min., do not rub	Normal	Normal spin; do not hand wring	Warm iron over a damp cloth, or use a steam iron

Many fabrics have several different names. Use the following table as a guide to using the main table on fabric care on pages 144–51.

FABRIC NAMES

FABRIC	OTHER NAMES
Acetate	Dicel
Acrylic	Acrilan®, Courtelle®, Dralon®
Nylon	Perlon®, Ultron
Silk	Shantung, Tussore (a wild silk with a slub)
Triacetate	Tricel
Polyester	Crimplene®, Dacron®, Diolene, Tergal, Terital, Terylene, Teteron, Trevira®
Flame-retardant finishes	Teklan, Timinox
Polyvinyl chloride fibres (PVC)	Rhovyl
Elastane	Lycra®

KEEP YOUR MACHINE CLEAN Many manufacturers recommend running a washing machine through a complete cycle with neither powder nor clothes every month or so. This keeps the machine clean and free from deposits.

WASHING DAY *Many a young housekeeper has felt at her wit's end when left without a servant. The young wife, perhaps, looks ruefully at the clothes to be washed, and wonders 'how on earth' Mary Anne ever got through them, and how she is going to.*

Mrs Lance Rawson, *The Australian Enquiry Book* (1894)

Washing guidelines

A whiter wash

Are your whites grey? Do some of your clothes have persistent grease spots you can't remove? You could try some old-fashioned whitening methods, such as these. Check the table on pages 144–51 for special instructions for individual fabric types.

- **Blue** Washing blue, made from the pigment indigo, counteracts the yellow tint that results from perspiration and the use of soap and soda.

- **Methylated spirits and cloudy ammonia** Adding 1 cup of each to the washing water every so often helps to keep whites actually looking white.

- **Borax** Add 1/2 cup borax to a machine wash. This is particularly effective if you dry the items in the sun after washing.

- **Sunlight** If you leave cloth in strong sunlight for a day, the sun plus oxygen and moisture from the air create a slow bleaching effect.

- **Frost** Bleaching also occurs when damp clothes become iced over. However, frost also weakens fabric, so handle items with care. To prevent tears, wipe the clothesline with boiling water and salt before you peg the clothes out in the first place. Ideally, wait until the washing has thawed before bringing it in.

Hand washing

Hand washing is still desirable for many items, such as woolly jumpers or delicate lingerie. It's sometimes the only option for travellers, or for students and others on tight budgets. For the best results, follow these steps.

1   Fully dissolve the granules of powder in the water.

2   Soak to loosen dirt but take care never to soak wool.

3   Agitate by picking up and dropping clothes in the water, or by kneading them gently.

4   Rinse clothes thoroughly.

5   Rinse your hands carefully after doing the washing.

6   Drip-dry clothes if you have the space, or roll them in a towel to remove moisture, then hang them up to dry.

Soaking success

Heavily soiled or stained articles may need soaking before washing. When soaking coloured items, follow this check list.

- Check that the dye can withstand soaking (if in doubt, do not soak).
- Fully dissolve the washing powder (there may be spotting if concentrated powder is left in contact with the fabric).
- Select a water temperature that is not too hot for the fabric type.
- Make sure the article is not bunched up.
- Soak white and coloured articles separately.

Stain removal

When dealing with stains on fabric, the golden rule is this: act fast. A speedy response may prevent a stain from setting and allow you to use a milder remedy. Some delicate fabrics may withstand methods that are appropriate for removing a fresh stain, but the same fabrics may be damaged by the harsher methods necessary for attacking set stains. If you leave the wrong stain to set on the wrong fabric, you could end up with woefully permanent stains; synthetic and drip-dry fabrics are more prone to this than natural fibres. For example, if you leave rust stains on cotton and linen, the cellulosic fibres may weaken and holes may also result.

Here are some general guidelines for stain removal.

- Remove the spill first Mop liquid spills on washable fabrics with a cloth and remove solids with the back of a knife.

TESTING FOR COLOURFASTNESS

To test how fast a dye is – that is, how strongly it retains its colour – take these steps.

1   Dampen a piece of the hem or seam allowance or any part of the article that is not conspicuous.
2   Iron a piece of dry white fabric onto it.
3   If any colour transfers to the white piece, the dye is not colourfast. Wash the article separately in cool suds and rinse at once in cold water. Dry immediately.

■ Never rub a stain **Rubbing only pushes the stain further into the fabric. Instead, use a pinching action with a clean cloth or a paper tissue to remove as much of the staining substance as possible.**

■ Outside in **When working with solvents on a stain, always work from the outer rim of the stain to minimize its spread.**

■ Test first **If possible, first test a stain remover, especially a solvent, on a hidden or less conspicuous area of a garment – for instance, the hem or seam allowance. (See 'Testing for colourfastness', opposite.)**

Washable stains

The following stains are washable. Check the table below ('Removal of washable stains') for specific instructions on how to remove them, depending on whether the stains are liquid or solid, fresh or dried.

■ Beetroot	■ Egg	■ Milk	■ Soup, stew
■ Blood	■ Fruit juices	■ Mud	■ Syrup
■ Chocolate	■ Gravy	■ Nappy stains	■ Tea
■ Cocoa	■ Ice blocks	■ Pickles	■ Tomato sauce
■ Coffee	■ Jam	■ Sauces	■ Washable ink
■ Cream	■ Meat juice	■ Soft drinks	■ Wine, spirits

REMOVAL OF WASHABLE STAINS

TYPE OF STAIN	REMOVAL METHOD
Excess liquid	Blot excess liquid with a dry cloth or paper towel before soaking
Food solids	Scrape off solids such as cooked egg before soaking
Fresh stains	Soak in cold suds for 30 minutes to prevent the stain from setting in the fabric, then wash normally
Dried stains	Lubricate with glycerine by applying a mixture of 1 part glycerine to 2 parts water to the stain. Leave for 10 minutes then treat as a fresh stain
Residual marks on white fabric	Bleach with a solution of hydrogen peroxide (1 part '20 volume' hydrogen peroxide to 9 parts water). Leave to soak for 1 hour, then wash as usual

How to remove stains

Use your stain removal kit, the description of the absorbent pad method below and the table on 'Stain removal' opposite to tackle stains.

THE ESSENTIAL STAIN REMOVAL KIT

Keeping a household stain removal kit in your laundry gives you a head start on stains. A basic kit should contain the following items, but take care with solvents and only use them if they are really necessary.

- Acetone or amyl acetate, solvents found in nail polish remover
- Bicarbonate of soda
- Blotting paper
- Borax
- Clothes brush
- Cotton wool, paper tissues, clean dry rags
- Cream of tartar
- Droppers
- Dry-cleaning fluid
- Eucalyptus oil
- Glycerine for lubrication
- Household ammonia
- Hydrogen peroxide
- Kerosene
- Lemon juice
- Methylated spirits
- Potassium permanganate
- Precipitated chalk
- Proprietary grease
- Salt
- Scraper
- Turpentine
- White vinegar

ABSORBENT PAD METHOD OF STAIN REMOVAL

For treating and washing stains, use the absorbent pad method. This requires two pads of cotton wool or something similar.

1 Soak one pad in the appropriate solvent.
2 With the solvent pad under the stain and the other pad on top, dab the stain.
3 When some of the stain has transferred to the top pad, turn it over so its clean side is in contact with the fabric and repeat.
4 Change the top pad and continue working until no stain comes through.
5 Wash as usual.

STAIN REMOVAL

TYPE OF STAIN	SOLVENT	METHOD
Ballpoint ink	Methylated spirits	Absorbent pad method (see opposite)
Bicycle oil	Proprietary grease solvent	Absorbent pad method
Black lead	Proprietary grease solvent	Absorbent pad method
Chalks and crayons	Detergent Use methylated spirits for stubborn marks	Brush off as much as possible while dry. Brush stained area with suds (1 dessertspoon to 570 mL/1 pt water). Wash as normal
Chewing gum	Methylated spirits Ice cube	Absorbent pad Rub the gum with an ice cube to harden it. You may be able to pick it off by hand, then wash as usual to remove any traces
Cod liver oil, cooking fat and heavy grease stains	Proprietary grease solvent	Absorbent pad method
Contact adhesives	Amyl acetate	Absorbent pad method
Dried fruit stain (for all but very delicate fabrics)	Boiling water	Stretch the fabric over a basin. Pour over almost boiling water
Dried fruit stain (very delicate fabric)	Lemon juice	Spread the fabric over blotting paper and sponge on the wrong side with hot water. If the mark remains, moisten with a little lemon juice and rinse with hot water
Felt pen ink	Soap Methylated spirits	Use hard soap to lubricate the stain. Wash as normal. For obstinate stains use methylated spirits and the absorbent pad method. Wash again to remove final traces
Fresh fruit stain	Salt	Before it has had time to dry, cover the stain in salt and wash without a soap (the alkali in the soap fixes rather than fades the stain)
Glue, tar, chewing gum on fabric and other surfaces; adhesive tape on vinyl	Eucalyptus oil	Place a few drops on the stain, leave for 2 minutes and wash. Repeat a few times if necessary. Finish with a wipe of methylated spirits and eucalyptus oil

STAIN REMOVAL (CONT.)

TYPE OF STAIN	SOLVENT	METHOD
Grass stain	Methylated spirits, cream of tartar	If the fabric is too delicate to wash, daub with methylated spirits on a clean cloth. If it can be laundered, soak in cold water then cover with a little cream of tartar and leave it in the sun
Hair lacquer	Amyl acetate	Absorbent pad method
Ink stain on coloured fabric	Milk, tomato	Soak the stained part immediately in slightly warm milk. Rinse. Or rub the stain with half a ripe tomato, then soak the fabric in cold water. The stain should disappear in the next laundering
Ink stain on white fabric	Salt, lemon	Sprinkle with salt immediately then rub with a cut lemon. Rinse and wash off
Iron mould on white cotton and linen only	Oxalic acid solution	Dissolve 1/2 teaspoon oxalic acid crystals in 285 mL (1/2 pt) hot water. Tie a piece of cotton tightly around the edges of the stained area to prevent the solution spreading and immerse the stained part. Leave for 2–3 minutes. Rinse thoroughly and wash in rich suds
Iron mould (rust marks) on wool, synthetic fabrics and all delicate fibres	Lemon juice	Flood the stain with lemon juice and leave for 10–15 minutes. Place a damp cloth over the stain and iron. Repeat several times as necessary. Rinse and wash as usual
Lipstick and blusher	Proprietary grease solvent	Soak light stains then wash in the usual way. For heavier stains, use the absorbent pad method
Lipstick alternative on washable fabrics	Kerosene	Sponge
Lipstick on non-washable fabric	Methylated spirits or eucalyptus oil	Absorbent pad method
Marking ink	Marking ink eradicator	Follow manufacturer's instructions

TYPE OF STAIN	SOLVENT	METHOD
Metal polish	Proprietary grease solvent	Absorbent pad method
Mildew on coloured articles	Detergent	Regular soaking followed by washing in rich suds. If the stain is not entirely removed, it may gradually fade with subsequent washes
Mildew on linen or cotton	Precipitated chalk	Wet the mildewed parts, rub with ordinary laundry soap, cover with precipitated chalk and rub it in. Leave for at least 1 hour then rinse. Repeat if necessary
Mildew on white cottons and linens without special finishes	Household bleach and vinegar	Soak in 1 part bleach to 100 parts water with 1 tablespoon vinegar. Rinse thoroughly then wash
Mildew on white drip-dry fabrics	Hydrogen peroxide solution	Soak in 1 part hydrogen peroxide ('20 volume') and 9 parts water until stain has gone. Rinse thoroughly and wash as normal
Mildew (old and persistent stain)	Potassium permanganate	Try soaking item in solution of 1 teaspoon potassium permanganate in 570 mL (1 pt) water
Mildew (set in)	Salt	Rub the stain with damp salt and expose to warm sunshine if possible
Mildew (slight stain)	Lemon juice	Sponge with lemon juice and place in the sun until the spores have disappeared (about 1 day)
Nail varnish	Amyl acetate	Absorbent pad method
Nicotine	Methylated spirits	Absorbent pad method
Paint (oil-based)	Turpentine or amyl acetate	Absorbent pad method
Paint (water-based)	Water	Sponge paint splashes immediately with cold water. Dried paint is permanent

STAIN REMOVAL (CONT.)

TYPE OF STAIN	SOLVENT	METHOD
Permanent ink	Oxalic acid solution (suitable for linens and white cottons only)	Dissolve ½ teaspoon oxalic acid crystals in 285 mL (½ pt) hot water. Tie a piece of cotton tightly round the stained area to prevent the solution spreading and immerse the stained part. Leave for 2–3 minutes. Rinse thoroughly and wash in rich suds
Perspiration (fresh)	Ammonia	Dampen with water then hold over an open bottle of household ammonia
Perspiration (old stains)	White vinegar	Sponge with white vinegar, rinse thoroughly then wash as usual
Perspiration (on wool)	Lemon juice	Sponge with a 1:1 solution of lemon juice and water then hang up to air
Plasticine	Proprietary grease solvent or white spirit, also called lighter fuel	Scrape or brush off as much as possible. Apply solvent using the absorbent pad method then wash to remove final traces
Scorch marks (light)	Glycerine	First try soaking in cold water and soap or detergent suds, then wash. If stain persists, moisten with water and rub glycerine into the stain. Wash. Try removing residual marks by soaking in a hydrogen peroxide solution. Heavy scorch marks that have damaged the fabric fibre normally cannot be removed. Alternative method: dampen the affected area and leave in the sunlight for a few hours. Soak a piece of linen in a solution of 3% hydrogen peroxide, place it over the scorch then press with a hot iron. (Test for colourfastness first)
Shoe polish	Glycerine and proprietary grease solvent	Lubricate stain with glycerine then use solvent and absorbent pad method. Wash to remove final traces

TYPE OF STAIN	SOLVENT	METHOD
Sour milk	Laundry detergent and cloudy ammonia	Rinse in cold water, then soak for 30 minutes in laundry detergent and lukewarm water with 1 teaspoon cloudy ammonia. Rinse and wash in lukewarm water
Stains on clothing (perspiration marks, oil and soluble grease)	Eucalyptus oil	Add 2 teaspoons eucalyptus oil to a wash load. Place an absorbent cloth under the stain. Moisten a clean rag with with eucalyptus oil and gently but firmly brush the stain from its edge into the middle
Sunscreen	Proprietary grease solvent	Absorbent pad method
Tar	Eucalyptus oil, proprietary grease solvent, benzine or lighter fuel	Scrape off surplus. Apply solvent using the absorbent pad method. Rinse and wash off as soon as possible
Verdigris (green stains from copper pipes) on wool, synthetic fabrics and all delicate fibres	Lemon juice	Flood the stain with lemon juice and leave for 10–15 minutes. Place a damp cloth over the stain and iron. Repeat several times if required. Rinse and wash as usual
Verdigris on white cotton and linen only	Oxalic acid solution	Dissolve 1/2 teaspoon oxalic acid crystals in 285 mL (1/2 pt) hot water. Tie a piece of cotton tightly round the stained area to prevent the solution spreading and immerse the stained part. Leave for 2–3 minutes. Rinse thoroughly and wash in rich suds

Iron away stains

Irons are handy for two types of stains.

- **Grease** **Some greasy stains can be removed with blotting paper and an iron. Place the stained part between two layers of blotting paper and press with the iron until all the grease is absorbed.**

- **Wax** **Let the wax harden, then scrape off all you can with a spatula. Place the item between two pieces of blotting paper and press with a warm iron. Use ammonia to remove any residual stain.**

Can I wash it?

Here is a special guide for tackling some of those difficult washing tasks around the home.

Doonas and eiderdowns

Dry-cleaning is usually the recommended option for doonas and eiderdowns, but if you have the space to tackle them at home, use warm soapy water and knead to aid cleaning. Rinse well in several changes of water. Do not wring or spin dry the doona, just squeeze out as much water as possible, then place it flat on grass, if you can, on an old sheet. Turn it over and shake it from time to time. When it is absolutely dry, shake it thoroughly and hang it on the line, then beat it gently to separate the filling.

Blankets

Don't wash a woollen blanket in hot water as it will felt (that is, become matted). Use warm water instead with a mild detergent and a gentle washing action. Do not leave a woollen blanket to soak for more than five minutes. A cup of ammonia will help to soften the fabric. Spin dry, shake vigorously and reshape it before hanging it on the line to dry.

Non-woollen blankets are invariably machine washable. If yours is heavily soiled, soak it for about 20 minutes first. Then wash it on a gentle cycle in warm water, followed by a cold rinse and a fast spin dry. Hang it out to dry on a line and, if possible, spread the weight of the blanket over two lines. Alternatively, lay it flat on an old sheet on the grass.

WASHING WITH BRAN

If you are game, wash dark cretonne (heavy printed cotton) and chintz (glazed cotton) curtains by hand in a bran bath. A bran bath is suitable for washing bright colours as it does not fade them. It also has stiffening and cleansing properties. However, do not use a bran bath for white or light colours as the bran water is tinted.

To make a bran bath, you'll need 300 g ($10^1/_2$ oz) bran for every 228 L (5 pt) of water. Then follow these steps.

1   Sew the bran into a bag of muslin, leaving plenty of room for it to swell once it is wet.

2   Put the bag of bran into the water in an enamel-lined or aluminium saucepan. Bring to the boil and stew for 45 minutes.

3   Pour off the water into a bowl, fill the saucepan again with cold water and stew the bran once more.

4   Unless they are very dirty, items can be washed in the bran water without soap. Squeeze the water through the articles and when they are clean, place them in a second lot of water from the second stewing.

5   Rinse in tepid water.

Curtains

Many curtains are washable, especially if you wash them by hand. Take them outside and shake them first to get rid of as much dust as possible. If you are washing new curtains for the first time, soak them overnight in salty water to remove fabric dressings (finishing treatments).

Pillows

It is possible to wash feather-filled pillows, but take care not to strip the feathers of their natural oils. Follow these steps.

1   Use a mild detergent or soap and wash them either by hand or in a front-loading machine. (A top loader may be too rough.)

2   Rinse the pillows thoroughly and, if washing by hand, squeeze out any excess water.

3   Otherwise spin dry in any type of washing machine.

4   Do not hang up pillows to dry as the filling will fall to one end. If you
     don't have a dryer, lay them flat. If you're drying them in a tumble dryer,
     use a low temperature. A couple of towels in the dryer will speed up the
     drying time, and two or three tennis balls will help to break up clumps
     of feathers. Make sure the pillows are completely dry before putting
     them away.

Gloves

How you clean gloves depends on the material.

Leather

As a rule, you should not wash suede and lined leather gloves, but some leather
gloves are washable. If you want to try washing leather gloves, follow these steps.

1   Empty the fingers of dust and lint.
2   Wash the gloves in warm water and mild soap suds.
3   Squeeze gently.
4   Rub extra soap on any stained patches.
5   Turn the gloves inside out and repeat the gentle squeezing.
6   Rinse the inside, then the outside.
7   Dry the gloves flat, working them several times with your hands as
     they dry to prevent them from stiffening. When they are half dry, put
     the gloves on to shape them. When they are completely dry, rub them
     with a little leather conditioner. If they do dry stiff, wet them a little and
     work them with your hands to soften them.

Wool

Wash woolly gloves by hand as they may pull apart in a machine wash.

1   Remove lint and dirt from the inside.
2   Wash them by hand with a mild detergent.
3   Rinse.
4   Roll them in a towel to dry.

Lace

If your lace gloves are machine washable, place them in a mesh bag. Use a gentle cycle, mild detergent and warm water only. If they are too delicate for the washing machine, use the method described in 'Washing delicate items', below. Dry them by first rolling them in a towel, then laying them flat.

Washing delicate items

Small lace handkerchiefs and other delicate items that could be damaged by rubbing can be placed in a screw top jar filled with warm, soapy water. Soap flakes are fine. Shake vigorously. Rinse in clean warm water in the same manner.

To wash delicate net or chiffon, place the item inside a clean muslin bag first. Wash it in warm, soapy water (again, use soap flakes) and knead it gently. Rinse in the same fashion.

Starching

Stiffening fabrics with starch serves two purposes: it gives them body and crispness, and also creates an extra barrier to dirt. Starches are available in dry, liquid and spray forms, but you can also make them yourself. Some starches are applied during ironing; others can be put in the final rinse of the wash. Sprays are convenient when ironing or for a quick touch up job on cuffs and collars.

To starch using liquids, dip clothes in the starching fluid after rinsing. Squeeze out excess water, hang the articles until nearly dry or roll in a dry cloth ready for damp ironing. Iron the garment on alternate sides until it is dry.

KITCHEN CUPBOARD STARCH RECIPES

- **Potato starch** Grate three or four potatoes and cover them with water. Agitate and let them stand for two hours. Agitate again and mix the pulp and water with your hands. Remove the pulp with a strainer, let the solids settle at the bottom of the container, then very carefully pour off the water.
- **Rice starch** Boil 1 cup rice in 1 L (1 3/4 pt) water until the rice is soft. Mash it by hand and strain it while the mixture is still cloudy. Refrigerate the liquid in a sealed container, shaking it from time to time.

To stiffen synthetic fabrics, use sizings. These usually contain a cotton derivative, sodium carboxymethylcellulose, which stiffens when exposed to heat.

Drying

If you can, dry your washing outside in the fresh air: a clothes dryer consumes energy and costs you money while wet clothes over a clothes horse disperse a lot of extra moisture into the home, encouraging moulds and dust mites.

If you live in a flat or apartment, you don't have a clothes dryer and drying inside is the only option, use only one room if you can and keep a window open for ventilation. Shut the door of the room, sealing it off from the rest of the house. Of course, after several days of wet weather, especially if you live in a cold climate, you'll have no option but to hang damp clothes up to dry all over your home.

TO CLEAN A CLOTHESLINE Cut a slit in a wine cork and run it along the line.

Pegging out

Hanging clothes out to dry in the sun and fresh air is a pretty straightforward task; however, if you follow these handy tips your clothes will last longer and ironing will be easier.

- Hang clothes straight away. If you leave wet clothes in the laundry basket, you risk colour runs and mould.
- Hang drip-dry clothes while they are dripping wet: they are designed to relax their wrinkles while drying.
- Lay knitted items flat in the shade.
- Place pleated garments in a stocking before hanging them up to dry. Roll them up if necessary.
- Dry white household linen and white clothing in the sun but coloured items and woollens out of the sun. The sun's bleaching effect is welcome on whites, but it can fade coloureds as well as shrink wool and cause white silk to yellow.
- Use plenty of pegs to support garments so they are less likely to be pulled out of shape.

SINGLE SOCK SOLUTIONS

Do you have bags of lonely socks waiting to be reunited with their partners? You could try these tricks.

- Count them in and out. Place a special receptacle for socks only next to the family washing basket. A wicker wastepaper bin is ideal. Make sure the socks go into and out of the washing machine in pairs.
- Peg the socks in pairs and fold them in pairs as you take them off the line.
- If you do end up with odd socks, put them away in the drawer or cupboard where they belong. When their partners 'come home', you can pair them.

- As a rule, peg the strongest part of the item – waistband, shoulders and toes, and the hems of t-shirts, dresses and shirts.
- Don't fold sheets before pegging them out as they will dry faster if allowed to billow between two lines. If you must fold them because you don't have enough line space, fold each sheet in four then refold and turn them from time to time to hasten drying.

DRYING KNITS If you have nowhere to dry a knitted top flat, run the legs of an old pair of pantyhose through both sleeves and peg the waist and toes of the pantyhose to the line. This technique helps support the weight of the garment and prevents peg marks.

Using a tumble dryer

When you do need to use your tumble dryer to dry your washing, here are some tips for using it efficiently.

- Make sure your tumble dryer is vented to the outside so that the moist air is extracted.
- Use the washing machine's fastest spin option to squeeze as much water out of the load as possible. This will cut down the drying time.
- Sort the clothes first, grouping together items that need a similar drying time, otherwise you'll end up with some damp clothes and some that are over-dried and possibly damaged.

- Use the correct temperature for the fabric.

- Don't overload the dryer: the load should tumble freely. However, remember that drying full loads is more efficient.

- Reload the dryer while it's still warm from a previous load.

- Clean the dryer's lint screen after each load. Lint build-up limits air flow and so increases drying time.

- Do not tumble dry items that contain elastic or rubber.

Ironing

With so many easy-care, drip-dry clothes available these days, it's possible to avoid using an iron altogether, but there are still many people who regard a newly ironed, crisp cotton shirt as being worth the extra effort. And there are also some people who insist on ironing every item of washing, including towels and socks.

WHICH SETTING?

FABRIC	IRON SETTING	DAMP OR DRY	WHICH SIDE?
Acrylic	Cool	Dry	Wrong
Cotton (dark)	Warm–hot	Either	Wrong
Cotton (pale)	Warm–hot	Either	Either
Linen (dark)	Warm	Damp	Wrong
Linen (pale)	Hot	Either	Either
Nylon	Cool	Damp	Either
Polyester	Cool	Damp	Either
Polyester mixes	Warm	Either	Either
Rayon	Warm	Damp	Wrong
Silk	Warm	Either	Wrong
Wool	Warm	Dry	Wrong

What happens to articles once they are washed also affects their ironing needs. If you pull an item into shape when you hang it out and then fold it smoothly when it is dry, you may not need to iron it at all. But even the smoothest of ironed fabrics will become wrinkled in a wardrobe that is packed with clothes.

STEAM IRON Hang jackets, trousers and tailored dresses in a steamy bathroom to relax wrinkles.

Ironing tips

What you choose to iron is your choice, but when you do, here are some tips on how to go about it.

- First, dampen the clothes. Steam irons automatically dampen fabric as they iron, but some items will still benefit from dampening before ironing. The most effective way of doing this is to sprinkle the item with warm water, then roll it up tightly and put it aside. If you are really organized, you could sprinkle them and leave them in a plastic bag overnight. Alternatively, sprinkle the clothes an hour before ironing. Failing that, spray or sprinkle while you iron.

SWEETLY PRESSED Add a couple of drops of your favourite essential oil to a spray bottle of water, and use it to dampen clothing and linen when ironing.

- Ironing brings out the best in a fabric, but it's important to follow a few basic rules. The iron must be hot enough to smooth a fabric's wrinkles, but not so hot that it damages it. Some fabrics should be ironed on the wrong side to avoid making them shiny, and others (such as wool) should not be ironed directly as this makes the fibres brittle.

- Unless the manufacturer specifically states that tap water is suitable for your iron, use either distilled water or demineralized tap water, both of which are available at supermarkets.

- Natural fabrics will simply burn if you iron them on too hot a temperature, but synthetic fibres may melt.

- Don't iron over plastic buttons and zips.

- Don't iron over metal objects that may scratch the plate.
- Use a pressing cloth over metal objects, especially when using an iron with a non-stick plate.

Cleaning the iron

It's a good idea to keep the plate of your iron clean with this old-fashioned method: from time to time rub it with a cloth soaked in strong cold tea, then wipe it with a soft clean cloth. If you exercise some care when using your iron, you will avoid damaging the plate with melted fibres or rust. If something does go wrong, look at the table opposite for some cleaning and repair solutions.

How to iron clothes

1   First, iron thicker areas — such as collars, cuffs and waistbands —as these will wrinkle less while you complete the garment.

2   Next, iron structured areas that are not flat — for example, sleeves.

3   Finally, iron the flat areas such as shirt backs.

IRONING LINEN If you have hung linen to dry or laid it flat, once it is the correct dampness for ironing, roll it up tightly and place it in a plastic bag. Put it in the fridge or freezer if you do not intend to iron it within a couple of hours.

How to iron table linen

- For a round tablecloth, start in the middle and work outwards.
- Iron napkins flat. Do not iron in creases.
- Iron damask, which is designed to be shiny, on the wrong side first, then on the right side.

Pressing needs

Knitted woollens and tailored items, such as suits, need pressing rather than ironing. This is best done professionally, but when that is not possible, or you want to touch up a garment, you can press at home.

HOW TO CLEAN A DIRTY IRON

PROBLEM	SOLUTION
Accumulated brown stains	Rub the cold plate with a cut lemon
Clogged steam vents	Use a cotton bud and warm soapy water. If this doesn't work, pour white vinegar into the water tank and turn on the iron for a few minutes. Iron a clean rag to remove deposits. Cool and rinse with cold water
Dirty non-stick plates	Clean with a cloth dampened in warm water and detergent
Dirty ordinary plate	Rub with bicarbonate of soda and a damp cloth
Melted synthetic fibre	Heat the iron and gently scrape away large pieces with a wooden spoon or paddlepop stick. Wearing an oven glove, remove smaller traces with cotton wool dipped in acetone (nail polish remover) and/or rubbing alcohol. If necessary, rub a regular plate with very fine steel wool, and a non-stick plate with a nylon mesh scrubber dipped in mild sudsy water
Plastic	Sprinkle some aluminium foil with salt and then iron it
Rust	Scour with salt and beeswax
Scratched surface	Rub with dampened salt and crumpled newspaper
Sticky plate (e.g. with starch)	1 Use a clean toothbrush. Heat the iron to warm and iron over a piece of waxed paper. 2 Clean with metal polish. 3 While the iron is hot, run it back and forth over a sheet of clean paper that has been generously sprinkled with salt.

To press, take a hot iron and a damp cloth made of calico or linen. Place the damp cloth on the garment and press heavily on the iron to remove creases. Continue pressing until the cloth is dry, but don't let it become singed. If the garment to be pressed is damp, do not dampen the cloth. Take care that the iron does not touch the garment itself or it may cause shiny patches.

STERILIZE AS YOU IRON A hot iron sterilizes tea towels and handkerchiefs.

Dry-cleaning

Despite its name, dry-cleaning is usually a wet process, but one that does not involve water. Professional dry-cleaning uses the solvent, perchloroethylene. Although 'perc', as it is known, is considered much safer than the earlier generation of solvents it replaced (including kerosene at first, then carbon tetrachloride and trichlorethylene), in high doses perc is a highly toxic carcinogen. A new process called 'wet cleaning', which avoids 'perc', is beginning to be used in some countries and is worth trying. Wet cleaning uses a combination of spot cleaning, steaming and hand washing.

Dry-cleaning at home

You can cut down on your dry-cleaning bills and avoid exposure to dry-cleaning fumes if you look after your clothes properly. Try the following.

- Brush clothes to remove lint and surface dirt.
- Hang jackets and other tailored items of clothing in the bathroom while you shower. Water particles penetrate the fabric, helping remove dirt and odours.
- Air clothes by hanging them outside.
- If you long for that professional pressed look, investigate the cost of aids such as trouser presses that are used by hotels.
- Even though some items are labelled 'dry-clean only', it's often fine to hand wash them, although you are taking a risk. Silk and rayon often respond well to hand washing if they are treated with care: use cool or lukewarm water, keep colours separate, squeeze out excess water by rolling the garment in a towel, then dry it flat. Woollen items labelled 'dry-clean only' are less successfully washed at home.

FEWER FUMES To reduce exposure to dry-cleaning fumes, remove the plastic from a dry-cleaned garment as soon as you come home, then hang it outside or in a well ventilated room before wearing it or putting it away in your wardrobe.

Home dry-cleaning kits

Instead of sending clothes to the dry-cleaner, you can try freshening them in the tumble dryer by using a kit comprising stain removers, a dry-cleaning sheet and a dryer-safe plastic bag. These kits are good at removing odours such as stale cigarette smoke and cooking smells but they don't clean as well as the professionals. They do, however, help minimize the number of visits to the dry-cleaners. They also use chemicals that, while not considered 100 per cent environmentally friendly, are less harmful to the environment than 'perc'.

THE IMPORTANCE OF CLOTHES CARE *First impressions are important...and the family with a well-cared-for look compares very favourably with a more expensively dressed family whose clothes have an air of slovenliness.*

The Book of Good Housekeeping (1947)

Old-fashioned dry-cleaning remedies

Salt, bran and clay are just three cleaning agents used in the past to care for garments that could not be laundered. Some of the methods require a little space and could prove quite messy. Choose an outdoors location or an easy to clean room such as a tiled bathroom, and protect your hair with a scarf.

Materials

To use the environmentally friendly dry-cleaning methods described on pages 174 and 175, you'll need these materials.

- Bran
- Flour
- French chalk
- Fuller's earth
- Ground rice
- Pipe clay
- Salt

- **General purpose dry-cleaner** Water and fuller's earth (an absorbent clay with a gentle cleaning action) remove grease and oil from materials such as felt. Mix the fuller's earth with water to form a paste. Spread it on the article. Let it dry, then remove it with a stiff brush.

- **Light and delicate items** Place the item on a clean towel, rub all over it with French chalk, giving extra attention to marked areas. Roll it up in the towel, leave it for 3–4 days, then brush lightly to remove the chalk.

- **Woollen coats and jackets** Mix together 2 cups each of flour and bran (the flaky outer husks of the wheat grain), then heat them in the oven, turning the mixture frequently to prevent it from browning. When it is as hot as possible without burning, spread it over the fabric. Fold the hot garment in a towel and put it aside. Two or three days later unwrap the garment, shake it energetically and brush.

- **Furs** Regularly wiping furs with a damp towel is sufficient to keep them looking good most of the time. When they are really dirty, the old-fashioned method calls for hot bran that has been heated in the oven. Gently rub the heated bran into the fur. Leave it on for half an hour, up to two hours, depending on how dirty it is. Remove the bran with a soft brush and hang it out to air. Another method, suitable for light-coloured fur, is to scatter cornflour thickly over the fur with your fingers. Brush out the cornflour with a soft, white-bristled brush.

LAUNDRY BAG *Outside hung a blue board on which was painted in large white letters, 'The Ideal Laundry. Careful Hand Work', and underneath, in smaller letters, the mysterious words 'Bag Wash'.*

Eve Garnett, *The Family from One End Street* (1937)

■ Leather jacket **Give a leather jacket a facelift by covering it with a paste made from pipe clay (fine white pure clay) and water. Use just enough water to make the clay spreadable. Rub it in one way only, from the bottom to the top. Allow the paste to dry, then shake the garment until all the clay has dropped off.**

■ Woollens **Salt applied with a linen pad is suitable for cleaning woollen coats, dresses and skirts. Lay the garment on a table and sprinkle a thin layer of salt over it. Spread it evenly with your fingers then, with a linen pad (a piece of linen folded several times), rub the salt into the cloth in long sweeping movements towards the hem. (A circular motion may roughen the surface.) Place the garment on a coat hanger and brush it vigorously with a stiff clothes brush. Cuffs, collars and hems may need a repeat treatment.**

■ White/light-coloured wool **Here's an alternative treatment for white or light-coloured wool garments: apply ground rice, as for salt on general woollens above, but leave the powder on for several hours.**

The linen press

Whether your linen press is a roomy cupboard at the top of the stairs, or a pine chest in your bedroom, make sure you regularly turn it out and clean it thoroughly. When returning freshly laundered bed linen to the linen press, place them at the bottom of the pile. That way you'll avoid always using the same few sets and wearing them out first.

Storing linen

The same rules apply to storing sheets, towels and other household linen.

■ Before you store any item of household linen – whether it is a sheet, towel or tablecloth – make sure that it is clean and absolutely dry. Dirt attracts insects, while dampness encourages moulds. The two together create unpleasant odours.

■ Don't store any starched items, as silverfish eat the starch and damage the fabric fibres in the process.

■ Store linen items unironed and loosely folded or rolled to prevent them cracking at the creases. Even when an item is new, it can be difficult to iron these creases out.

■ For long-term storage of delicate items, including antiques, wrap them in acid-free paper and store them in acid- and lignin-free boxes to prevent acid damaging the cellulosic fibres. (Lignin is a constituent of plants.)

■ Do not store antique, heirloom or delicate linens in cedar chests as the cedar gives off fumes that can yellow and damage cellulosic fibres.

■ Place a bar of scented soap among your stored linen and replace it every few months. Not only does this make your linen smell sweeter, but it also gives added life to your soap: it will dry out and last longer.

■ Place sachets in drawers. Make simple drawer sachets by spooning a mixture of oatmeal and a few drops of essential oil or perfume into muslin bags.

■ Dried lemon and orange peel in a muslin bag is a moth deterrent.

For more natural moth deterrents, see 'The bedroom', page 287.

Pomander

A pomander can be hung in a wardrobe for several months.

INGREDIENTS

1 firm-skinned orange

Fresh cloves

1 teaspoon orris root powder

1 teaspoon ground cinnamon

METHOD

1 Wash and dry a firm-skinned orange and stud it evenly all over with some fresh cloves.

2 Place the orris root powder and the cinnamon in a brown paper bag with the orange and shake the bag to coat the orange.

3 Store the bag in a dark place for a month, then remove the orange and brush it free of powder.

4 Tie a ribbon around the orange and finish with a loop at the top.

Lavender bag

The essential oil of lavender kills germs and is fragrant. Put lavender sachets or bags in a drawer to prevent their contents from becoming musty. This lavender bag will retain its scent longer if you keep the stalks on.

INGREDIENTS

Lavender in full bloom

Newspaper

Muslin or fine cotton

Ribbon

METHOD

1 Cut the lavender and spread the stems out to dry on newspaper, either in the sun or in another warm place.

2 Cut fabric, such as muslin or fine cotton, to the size and shape required and stitch into a simple bag shape.

3 When the lavender is dry, insert a bunch into the bag so that the stems stick out of the opening.

4 Close the opening with hand stitching or a length of ribbon.

5 Trim the stalks to a length of 4 cm (2 in).

Folding napery

▨ Bed linen **Sheets are best folded by two people.**

▨ Tablecloth **Roll a tablecloth around a cardboard tube or fold it loosely to avoid creases as much as possible. If it is not too wide, try hanging a tablecloth on a clothes hanger with a thick crossbar.**

▨ Circular tablecloth **To fold a circular tablecloth, follow these steps.**

1 Fold it into a semicircle.
2 Fold the rounded edge down to the folded edge to form a lozenge shape.
3 Fold the lozenge shape in two to form a rectangular type shape.
4 Fold it in half and then in half again until it is of a manageable size.

▨ Napkins **For daily use, simply folding napkins into squares or rectangles is sufficient. Napkin rings allocated to each family member are handy if you use table napkins every day: you don't have to wash them after every use. For entertaining, more complicated folds include the bread roll holder and the bishop style.**

LINEN COLLECTION *Afternoon tea cloths, tea napkins, bridge cloths, breakfast tray sets, cocktail sets and tray cloths are seen in an almost endless variety.*

The Home Lover's Encyclopedia

RICHES FROM RAGS

Making your own rags saves money and is a good way to reuse old clothes. Rags can be made from any soft absorbent, colourfast material that will not leave little tufts of lint everywhere. Once they are at the end of their first lives, sheets, towels, t-shirts, shirts, sweatshirts and brushed cotton pyjamas are excellent candidates for rag making. If you cut them with pinking shears they will fray less. Also cut off any zips, buttons and thick seams to avoid scratching vulnerable surfaces.

Recycling worn house linen

Once items of household linen start to show some wear and tear, consider how they could be recycled.

- Cut up a tablecloth into smaller cloths, napkins and tea towels. Housewives used to be advised to make 'tea, breakfast, carving trolley and tray cloths' (*The Book of Good Housekeeping*, 1947).

- To prolong the life of a sheet, cut and sew it 'sides to middle'; remake it as pillow and bolster cases and aprons; or use it as an ironing board cover or a drop sheet when decorating.

- Cut down an old woollen blanket to make cot and pram covers and warm sleeping bags for babies and toddlers. You'll need to bind the cut edges in some way – sew them either using wool and blanket stitch or ribbon.

- An old pillowcase can be put to good use in the laundry. Place delicate linen items, hosiery and lace in one before washing them in the washing machine.

- Curtains can find new life in dress-up boxes, as garment bags to protect coats and evening wear, or cut and sown to make cushion covers.

the bathroom

Bathrooms are both utilitarian spaces — where children splash in the bath and reluctantly clean their teeth — and places where we find time for a moment's indulgence: freshening up in the shower after a long day or enjoying a few minutes of privacy while shaving. Looking after the bathroom involves keeping it well ventilated, clean and hygienic. It is also one of the critical rooms in the house: here how much water you use, how much energy you use to heat it and how much pollution you cause when cleaning it, all have an impact on the environment.

BATH TWICE A DAY *to be really clean,*
once a day to be passably clean,
once a week to avoid being a public menace.

Anthony Burgess, *Inside Mr Enderby* (1963)

the bathroom

The clever bathroom

The clever bathroom is easy to keep fresh and clean with low-toxic products and makes use of several water- and energy-saving devices.

- **A dual flush system** is used to minimize water usage in the toilet.
- **Flushing water** for the toilet comes from your household's recycled water tank.
- **Water for the shower, bath and basin** is supplied from the household's rainwater tank.
- **A reduced water flow shower rose** is fitted to the shower, reducing water flow while still giving a satisfying hard shower.
- **Hot water** is supplied by a solar hot water system.
- **An extractor fan** keeps the moisture down, reducing the potential for mould growth.
- **Cleaning products** are non-toxic, which means the water going down the drain can be recycled to water the garden.
- **Non-absorbent, washable surfaces on walls and floors** are easy to care for. They also reduce the growth of bacteria and potential allergens such as moulds.
- **Toiletries** include a range of non-perfumed and low-allergy products.
- **Soap scraps** are saved to make soap gel.

Water wise in the bathroom

The bathroom is the scene of many a water wastage crime: taps left on after someone has brushed their teeth, long showers, deep baths, litres or gallons of water on its way to the sewage treatment plant every time the toilet is flushed. Whether you think this matters or not may depend on the source of your water: when it just keeps on coming out of the tap, you probably don't give it a second thought, but when you rely on a rainwater tank, for instance, the inconvenience of running out is often motivation enough to be more careful.

HOW MUCH WATER DO YOU USE?

- To measure what your average shower uses, hold a bucket under the shower for ten seconds. Measure this volume and multiply it by 6 to give you the number of litres (gallons) per minute.
- Collect and measure the water you use for hand washing or teeth cleaning.

JAPANESE BATH The Japanese wash themselves down before entering the bath, which is considered a place for relaxing and soaking rather than cleaning.

Shower

- Fit a low-flow shower rose. These use 7–12 L (1 1/2–2 1/2 gal) a minute of water, compared with up to 20 L (4 1/2 gal) a minute with a standard shower rose.
- Alternatively, fit a flow restriction disc (a plastic insert) to your current shower rose.
- Have shorter showers. If you cut down from a five minute daily shower to a three minute one, you could save as much as 40 L (8 3/4 gal) of water per shower.

TURN IT OFF Don't leave the tap running while you brush your teeth – turn it on and off as needed.

Toilet

- Flushing the toilet accounts for about one-third of an entire household's water use. Cisterns commonly contain 3–11 L (1/2–2 1/2 gal) of water.
- Fit a dual flush system. New models use 6 L (1 1/3 gal) for a full flush and 3 L (1/2 gal) for a half flush.
- For a single flush toilet, reduce the flushing volume by placing an old juice container full of water, or even a brick, in the cistern.

Grey water for flushing

One load of washing can produce enough water to flush the toilet for a day. Here are some other methods of reusing water for the toilet, depending on your motivation.

- **Bucket from bath to toilet** **Where your shower is fitted over a bath, leave the plug in the bath while you shower. Then use a bucket to scoop water out of the bath and flush the toilet.**

- **Holding tank** **Laundry water or bath water can be pumped or fed by gravity into a holding tank fitted above a toilet, which leads to the toilet cistern. It also needs an overflow pipe (water can be directed for reuse somewhere else if the holding tank is full) and may need a low-pressure valve fitted to the cistern to allow it to accept water being fed by gravity rather than by mains pressure.**

- **Hand basin toilet** **Water from the hand basin is fed directly into the cistern. In theory this could be a very neat, direct system, with the top of the cistern shaped like a hand basin, but such cisterns are not generally commercially available. Alternatively, a separate hand basin could be plumbed so that it fills the cistern.**

See 'The outdoors', page 315, for more information on using grey water.

Composting toilets

A sure way to reduce water usage in the toilet is to fit a composting toilet which uses no water at all: waste is turned into compost by aerobic decomposition (aerobic refers to chemical reactions taking place in the presence of oxygen rather than anaerobic, without oxygen). The pan is placed directly over the composting chamber. A fan can be fitted to extract odours from the room. Heating — either electrical or solar — can reduce the amount of liquid in the compost as well as aid the micro-organisms' decomposition process.

Depending on which system you use, you can add other organic matter such as leaves or chopped paper to assist decomposition, which is finished in the garden, where the compost is usually buried in an area used for shrubs and flowers rather than vegetables, for at least six months.

Although most composting toilets take up a fair amount of space and are therefore difficult to fit in an existing house, smaller models are available.

Biogas digesters

In China and India, biogas digesters are used to deal with used household water. Organic matter gives off biogas — a mixture of gases such as methane, carbon dioxide, ammonia gas and nitrous sulphide — when kept in anaerobic (that is, without oxygen) conditions. This gas can be used to fuel engines and stoves. However, in most countries these systems are still in the experimental stage as far as domestic use is concerned.

General bathroom care and cleaning

When giving the bathroom a good going-over, it makes hygienic sense to start with surfaces less likely to be contaminated with bacteria. Start by placing disinfectant in the toilet bowl and let it soak while you clean the walls and floor, basin, bath and shower. Move on to the bidet if you have one, then the outer surfaces of the toilet, finishing with the inside of the toilet bowl.

Bacteria and other disease-causing organisms are often spread from hand to mouth after touching a contaminated surface. Therefore it is sensible to clean and disinfect door handles, the flushing handle and other places that are frequently touched after someone has been to the toilet.

All-round cleaners

There are several choices for cleaning the basin, bath and outside of the toilet.

- Commercial bathroom cleaner **A thick liquid, paste or powder containing bleach, abrasives and detergents with an overall acidic composition.**

- Mild detergent **A solution of washing up liquid is a good all-purpose cleaner and can be used on floors and walls as well as fittings.**

- Bicarbonate of soda **A mild abrasive which can be used as a general cleaner, or to remove tough spots. Can be used as a solution, a paste or powder.**

- Borax and lemon juice or vinegar **An all-purpose cleaner which keeps moulds at bay on shower curtains and other surfaces. A paste of borax and lemon juice left for half an hour will remove stubborn stains.**

- A solution of washing soda and water **A tough, all-purpose cleaner.**

■ White vinegar **Use with a brisk scrub.**

■ Tea-tree **Diluted tea-tree oil keeps the brush and bowl germ-free.**

If you don't want to use commercial products, it's easy enough to make your own. See 'The kitchen', page 84, for a number of low-toxic, basic cleaner recipes that will keep all the surfaces of your bathroom sparkling.

MOULD ATTACK Improving ventilation is the long-term solution, either by opening windows immediately after a steamy bath or shower, installing extractor fans, or fitting the room with wall vents so that steam and moisture can escape. Wiping away condensation will also help. Paint and grout is sometimes impregnated with fungicide.

FRESH AS A DAISY

To freshen the air in the bathroom and remove odours, make sure it has adequate ventilation. If necessary, open the window and try one of the following non-toxic air fresheners.

■ Position 1/4 cup white vinegar in an open bowl on a high shelf.

■ Do the same with a bowl of clay-type cat litter.

■ Make a simple spray air freshener by combining 1 teaspoon bicarbonate of soda and 1 teaspoon lemon juice in 2 cups hot water.

■ Scented candles can help to banish bathroom smells, even if they're lit for only a short while.

■ Lemon essential oil kills germs and is fragrant. Add a couple of drops to the final rinsing water when cleaning the bathroom.

■ For an antiseptic air freshener, dissolve 1.5–2 mL (1/4–1/2 teaspoon) of any antiseptic essential oil (thyme, bergamot, juniper, clove, lavender, peppermint, rosemary or eucalyptus) in 5 mL (1 teaspoon) methylated spirits, and then blend this with 500 mL (2 cups) distilled water in a pump spray. Use your customized air freshener on the fine mist setting.

Walls and floors

Ceramic tiles are traditionally used for the floor and walls in the bathroom and have certain advantages for both surfaces. They are non-absorbent and do not deteriorate upon contact with water. While mould can grow on tiles, it is easily removed. Tiles are cold on the feet, but washable cotton mats remedy this.

Cleaning ceramic tiles

Frequent sweeping helps protect ceramic tile floors as well as keep them clean. Sand and grit, for instance, being harder than many glazes, can abrade glazed tile surfaces, causing them to become dull prematurely. Washing removes dirt build-up. Use any non-acidic cleaner, with a gentle, or non-abrasive action. Detergent solution is fine. Use a toothbrush for hard to reach spots, including the grout between tiles. If you suspect the glaze is particularly delicate, closely observe whether a particular cleaner has dulled the surface. If it has, polish with a soft towel and avoid it in future.

OUT DAMNED SPOT

- **Mould and mildew** Mix 1/4 cup chlorine bleach in 2.5 L (about 5 pt) of water. Scrub with a brush or toothbrush.
- **Limestone deposits** Scrub with a little white vinegar and water, and rinse.
- **Blood** Use hydrogen peroxide or household bleach.
- **Coffee, tea, food, fruit juice and lipstick** Wash with detergent in hot water then hydrogen peroxide or household bleach. Rinse and dry.
- **Nail polish** Wipe off with acetone, then, if necessary, use bleach.
- **Grease and oil** Use an all-purpose cleaner.
- **Inks and dyes** Steep the stain in household bleach until it disappears. Rinse and dry.
- **Chewing gum, wax and tar** Chill with an ice cube then scrape away with a wooden spatula. Use paint stripper to remove any remaining trace.
- **Rust** Use lemon juice in conjunction with mild detergent to remove stains such as rust on ceramic floor tiles. Squeeze lemon juice into a glass and add a few drops of dishwashing detergent. Cut an absorbent cloth into pieces the size of the stain and saturate them with the mixture. Place the cloth pieces onto the stain, wiping off any excess solution. Leave for a few hours. Repeat if necessary, then rinse with water.

NO SOAP Do not use soap to clean ceramic tiles as it may leave a thin film of scum, which will gradually build up over time and can be difficult to remove.

Soap gel

Recycle your soap scraps into liquid soap gel that you can use in a recycled pump pack. It's great for washing your hands and is useful whenever you want to use pure soap.

INGREDIENTS

Handful of soap scraps

Water

Essential oil (optional)

METHOD

1   Place the soap scraps in a saucepan, cover them with water and leave for 24 hours, stirring occasionally.

2   Bring to the boil over a moderate heat, stirring continuously, then lower the heat to a simmer.

3   To completely dissolve the soap, whisk or mash it.

4   Remove from the heat and allow it to cool.

5   Add a few drops of essential oil, if desired. Pour into a pump dispenser for hand washing.

ALLERGY TIP If you suspect you may be allergic to chemical cleaners used in the bath, there are gentler alternatives that you can try.

■ Bicarbonate of soda.
■ Any shampoo that you know you can tolerate (shampoo contains detergents that help shift scum and oil).

The hand basin

A regular wipe over with or without a cleaner, plus a weekly thorough going-over keeps the basin clean. Be sure to rinse the plug hole well to avoid leaving bathroom cleaner on it which could damage the coating. Scrub around taps and the plug hole with bicarbonate of soda to remove mould.

To clean taps

Wipe taps with chrome, plastic, gold and brass finishes regularly to remove traces of toothpaste and other toiletries. Clean with a solution of washing up liquid or bicarbonate of soda, using a toothbrush for crevices. To remove lime scale, wrap a cloth soaked in lime scale remover or vinegar around the tap and leave according to the manufacturer's instructions, or for up to half an hour.

The bath

Train the family to rinse the bath after they have used it. Leave a cloth and light spray cleaner within easy reach so they can also wipe it over regularly to keep soap and scum deposits at bay. An all-purpose bathroom cleaner will do the trick: use a commercial one or your own, made up into a solution and poured into a spray bottle.

WARNING

1   Do not use abrasive cleaners on acrylic baths as they may scratch.
2   Products designed to remove lime scale may cause enamel to dull. Try using a
     plastic scourer, neat washing up liquid and elbow grease.

Once a week or so, you'll need to do a more thorough clean, scrubbing around the taps and plug hole and tackling any lime scale build-up. Bicarbonate of soda is ideal for scrubbing around taps and plug holes, while vinegar removes lime scale.

TOYING ABOUT Don't leave bath toys, sponges and loofahs in the bath where they will remain almost constantly wet. To keep bacterial counts down and prevent moulds from growing, let them dry out between uses. Some people disinfect them between uses. Choose toys that you can drain easily after a bath, wash regularly and dry. Soak every now and then in a bleach solution.

The spa bath

It is important to follow the manufacturer's instructions on maintaining and cleaning your spa bath. You will probably need to clean out scum left in the pipe work, perhaps once a week. You can do this by filling the bath with warm water and a disinfecting agent, such as sterilizing tablets. Leave for five minutes. Empty the bath, then refill it. Turn on the spa and leave the water to circulate and rinse for another five minutes before emptying it.

HOT AND STEAMY To reduce the amount of steam produced when you run a bath or a spa, run the cold tap first, then the hot one. Less steam means reduced moisture and less chance of creating the warm humid conditions in which fungi and moulds thrive.

The shower

Wipe over the floor of the shower recess with an all-purpose cleaner and use a lime scale remover as needed, perhaps once a week. Shower screens can be cleaned with a solution of washing up liquid.

Dealing with a mould-ridden plastic shower curtain

If you have a problem with mould on your shower curtain, dry the curtain soon after showering. This will at least cut down on the amount of mould.

To clean mould from the curtain, you can use commercial mould removers but these often contain thickened chlorine bleach. Scrubbing with baking soda is a less toxic alternative. Another method is to rub the curtain with a paste made with vinegar or lemon juice mixed with borax. Rinse well. Black stains are difficult to remove, but leaving the curtain to soak overnight in a weak bleach solution may help.

Some shower curtains, especially nylon ones, are machine washable, but the plastic curtains are vulnerable to cracking so you should proceed with caution. Some shower curtains are impregnated with fungicides.

To clean dirty grout

You can buy products that whiten and kill moulds with fungicides. Alternatively, scrub with a solution of household bleach (1 part bleach to 4 parts water).

To clean sealant

To remove mould from sealant, wipe it with neat vinegar or rub over a paste of bicarbonate of soda. As a last resort, spray on a bleach solution (1 part bleach to 4 parts water) and leave it for 30 minutes. Scrub, then rinse clean with warm water.

The toilet

Toilet cleaners are at the harsh end of the cleaning scale in both environmental and health terms. Most are based on strong acids, such as sodium hydrogen sulphate. Other ingredients may include paradichlorobenzene (PDB), fragrance, detergent and bleach. These chemicals should be used with caution as they can damage the skin and eyes; in addition, they do not readily break down.

DON'T MIX TOILET CLEANERS Never use more than one toilet cleaner at a time, including bleach, as toxic gases may be produced.

All the outer surfaces of the toilet — rim of the bowl, seat, outside of the bowl — can be cleaned by wiping over with a solution of detergent or a cleaner of your choice. Clean the bowl with a toilet brush and disinfectant, either a commercial toilet cleaner or the gentler alternative below. To clean a toilet brush, hold it under the flushing water and rinse it in bleach.

Natural toilet cleaner

Try this gentler alternative to commercial toilet products.

INGREDIENTS

1 cup borax
1/4 cup white vinegar or lemon juice

METHOD

Mix the ingredients together and pour into the toilet bowl. Leave at least a few hours —overnight if possible — then scrub the bowl with a toilet brush. Add a few drops of pine oil to this recipe for extra disinfectant power.

NATURAL DISINFECTANT To make a disinfectant from essential oils, dissolve 20–30 drops of any oil with disinfectant properties — cinnamon, clove, pine, niaouli, tea-tree, thyme, bergamot, juniper, peppermint, rosemary or sandalwood — in 5 mL (1 teaspoon) methylated spirits. Mix with 1 L (2 pt) distilled water and store in an airtight plastic or glass bottle.

Drains

When drains are operating smoothly, you probably don't give them a second thought. But when plumbing blocks up or smells, you begin to appreciate the convenience of modern sanitation.

How to unblock a toilet

If the pan is clogged and water is overflowing, turn off the water supply to the toilet. The tap is usually just behind the toilet. First, wait a while to allow the water to subside — sometimes a blockage will clear of its own accord given enough time. If it doesn't, turn to the plumber's friend, the plunger. When using a plunger to unblock a toilet, some experts recommend a plunger with a metal disc above the rubber cup to prevent the cup turning inside out. Plunging requires more vigour for a toilet than a sink as there are no flat surfaces with which to make a good seal.

Wash the plunger by flushing the cistern while the plunger is still in the pan, then adding a little detergent and bleach to the pan water.

Depending on your confidence, or your skills, plumber's eels (jointed flexible tubing which can be pushed into drains to remove blockages) are a possibility, but it may just be time to call the plumber.

For more information on looking after drains, see 'The kitchen', on page 77.

Caring for towels

As bacteria love a moist environment, towels and face washers or flannels should be allowed to dry thoroughly between uses; on a sunny or windy day, dry them outside. Making sure each household member has his or her own towel will cut down the transfer of bacteria from one person to another.

As some toiletries contain substances that can damage towels and face washers or flannels, rinse them in cold water if they come into contact with, for instance, skin creams. Skin creams containing benzoyl peroxide can cause colour loss. Hair perming and neutralising solutions are also particularly damaging.

Snip pulled threads on towels before they spread.

Caring for combs and hair brushes

Your hair will only be as clean as the implements you use on it, so keep them scrupulously clean.

Combs

Tortoiseshell or bone combs are best not washed, as water may split and roughen them. They should be cleaned with small brushes instead.

Hair brushes

To clean brushes the old-fashioned way, dissolve a walnut-sized piece of washing soda in hot water in a basin. Comb out the hair from the brushes then dip them, bristles downward, into the water, keeping the backs and handles out of the water as much as possible. Repeat until the bristles seem clean. Rinse in a little cold water, shake well and wipe the handles and backs, but not the bristles, with a towel. Place in the sun or near a heater to dry. Do not use soap on bristles as this will soften them, as does wiping them.

NITPICKING: THE PROBLEM OF HEAD LICE

Commercial head lice treatments can contain a range of chemicals (see 'What's in a name?', page 349), all of which are toxic in varying degrees, and not necessarily effective, as head lice have built up a resistance to certain products.

There is a time-consuming but non-chemical treatment for head lice which does work. Comb hair conditioner through the hair every other day with a nit comb over a two week period. In this way you remove the lice after they have hatched but before they can lay new eggs (also known as nits). If you prefer to use a chemical, choose a pyrethrin-based one if possible; carbaryl and malathion are the next best. To avoid cross-contamination, check each member of the family and take action if anyone has an infestation.

Home-made toiletries

Ready-made shampoos and bath lotions are welcome conveniences of modern life, but home-made toiletries are luxurious and making them can be fun. If you are sensitive to cosmetic ingredients, making your own toiletries also ensures you know exactly what's in them.

The earliest cosmetics were made at home and housekeeping manuals have traditionally included several recipes for head-to-toe care. Some of them contain ingredients we'd be hard-pressed to find these days. Cleopatra is supposed to have bathed in asses' milk — a 'luxury' it would be rather difficult to arrange today, and possibly distasteful too. But many home-grown indulgences are more attuned to our senses and circumstances, and use simple ingredients that are still appealing. Here is a selection of old and new tips and recipes to try at home.

Life's little luxuries

- **Essential oils** Add a few drops of essential oil to a hot bath. Sage, lovage and orange are said to stimulate. Lavender, mint, rosemary and marigold are relaxing.

- **Scented candles** For an evening bath with a difference, light some candles in the bathroom and turn off the lights.

- **Bicarbonate of soda** To soothe irritated and sunburnt skin, add bicarbonate of soda to your bath.

- **Epsom salts** Add epsom salts to a warm bath or foot bath to ease swollen ankles and feet, and to relieve the early symptoms of a cold.

WARNING:

AROMATHERAPY OILS IN THE BATH

Essential oils and aromatherapy oils are sold in an extremely concentrated form. They are ideal bath mates when added drop by drop to running water. But their soothing qualities can turn toxic if too much is used. Never use more than 10 drops of oil in a bath.

Bath bags

For an alternative to bubble bath, gather a square of muslin into a little bag shape, fill it with flower petals or herbs, tie the bag and hang it over the taps as you fill the bath. Here are some simple ideas for the filling.

- **Oatmeal and petals** Fill with oatmeal and petals of rose, lavender and chamomile.
- **Fresh herbs** Fill the muslin with your favourite aromatic herbs, such as mint, lavender, rosemary and lemon grass. Either mix them together or use each one individually.

Children's bubble bath

The children can help make this as long as a supervising adult deals with the boiling water.

INGREDIENTS

4 tablespoons flower petals or heads (e.g. rose or lavender)

300 mL (10 oz) bottle of baby shampoo

300 mL (10 oz) boiling water

12 drops essential oil (such as lavender)

METHOD

1   Place the petals in a bowl, cover them with boiling water and leave for 15 minutes.

2   Strain the flower water into the other bowl.

3   Add shampoo and essential oil.

4   Pour the mixture into plastic bottles.

5   Shake each bottle for several minutes. Store any extra bottles that are not in use in a dark, cool place.

CIRCULATION AID Alternating hot baths and cold showers is said to improve the circulation.

MRS BEETON ON TREATMENT OF THE HAIR

Under 'Recipes for the lady's maid', Mrs Beeton writes: 'Twice a month wash the head with a quart of soft water, in which a handful of bran has been boiled, and in which a little white soap has been dissolved. Next rub the yolk of an egg, slightly beaten, into the roots of the hair, let it remain a few minutes, and wash it off thoroughly with pure water, rinsing the head well.' Reaching for a bottle of shampoo has never seemed more convenient!

Egg shampoo

INGREDIENTS

1 egg

Hot water

Few drops liquid ammonia

METHOD

1   Separate the yolk from the white of a fresh egg.

2   Beat the yolk with a little hot water. Add a few drops of liquid ammonia for greasy hair.

3   Wet the hair thoroughly with hot water and rub the beaten yolk into the scalp.

4   Massage in for two or three minutes.

5   Rinse with soft hot water, gradually using cooler water.

RAINWATER FOR HAIR Soft water is said to be best for hair as it contains fewer minerals. Rainwater fits the bill perfectly as it is a natural source of soft water.

ON SHAMPOO *The best and safest shampoo for any head is the egg shampoo. It gives lustre and softness to the hair. The scalp gets ammonia and sulphur in its simplest forms, and the hair obtains just the gentle emollient it needs.*

News Chronicle Housewife's Handy Book (c. 1930)

Once they have been opened, the following skin creams must be kept refrigerated as they do not contain preservative.

Skin cream

An excellent cleaner or massage cream may be made as follows –
1 oz oil of almonds
2 oz lanolin
1 oz extract of roses
2 oz glycerine

...And if you like to be extravagant...
1 drip of attar of roses

Melt lanolin over heat. Add almond oil, remove from fire, beat well, gradually adding glycerine and the extract of roses.

News Chronicle Housewife's Handy Book (c. 1930)

Scented cream

INGREDIENTS

50 mL (1 1/2 fl oz) unscented base cream (available from chemists)

8 drops essential oil (e.g. lavender, chamomile, or a combination)

METHOD

1   Add the essential oil to the base cream.

2   Stir well.

Flower-infused cream

INGREDIENTS

175 g (6 oz) emulsifying wax
25 g (3/4 oz) dried flowers (such as marigold
and rose petals)
75 g (2¹/2 oz) glycerine
75 mL (2¹/2 fl oz) water

METHOD

1   Melt emulsifying wax in a bowl over a
    saucepan of boiling water.
2   Remove the bowl from the heat and stir
    in dried flowers, glycerine and water.
3   Place the bowl back on the pan and
    simmer for three hours.
4   Strain the cream through muslin placed
    over a sieve and squeeze out the
    excess liquid.
5   Allow to cool a little.
6   Pour into sterilized dark glass jars.
7   Leave to set, tighten the lids and label.

Pawpaw mask for oily skin

INGREDIENTS

Half a ripe pawpaw
1 tablespoon fuller's earth
1 tablespoon natural yoghurt
1 tablespoon orange blossom water

METHOD

1   Rub the pawpaw flesh through a sieve
    with a wooden spoon, then add the
    fuller's earth and yoghurt.
2   Mix thoroughly, then add the orange
    blossom water.
3   To use the mask, smooth it over your
    face and leave it for 15 minutes until it
    is almost dry. Break the mask up by
    rubbing your hands over your face then
    rinse with warm water. Finish with a
    cold splash.

MOUTHWASH For a safe and effective mouthwash, mix bicarbonate of soda with
water and gargle it.

Eau de cologne

INGREDIENTS

150 mL (5 fl oz) vodka

50 mL (1 1/2 fl oz) distilled or boiled water

60 drops orange essential oil

30 drops bergamot essential oil

30 drops lemon essential oil

6 drops neroli essential oil

6 drops rosemary essential oil

METHOD

1   Combine the vodka and oils in a bottle
    and leave for a week. Shake daily.
2   Add water, shake and set aside for
    4–6 weeks.
3   Strain through a filter and funnel into a
    second sterilized bottle.

Rose water and glycerine hand lotion

INGREDIENTS

150 mL (5 fl oz) rose water

100 mL (3 fl oz) glycerine

1 drop pink or yellow food colouring

METHOD

1   Add the rose water and colouring to
    the glycerine little by little.
2   Mix together with a hand whisk.

TO REFRESH SORE FEET Add 5 drops of peppermint oil to a bowl of cold water. Bathe the feet for 10 minutes.

STERILIZING GLASS JARS To sterilize a glass jar, place it in a saucepan with enough water to cover. Bring it to the boil, then boil for five minutes. Use tongs to remove the jar. Dry it in a warm oven.

Bathroom safety

The combination of slippery surfaces and hot water can result in accidents, especially when young children or the elderly and frail are involved. To make your bathroom a safer place, take the following precautions.

- Never leave a young child alone in the bath. If the phone rings or someone knocks on the front door, either ignore the summons or take the child with you.

- If you have small children, never leave the bathroom door open when running the bath, or when there's water in the bath.

- Use shower curtains or screens to keep the floor as dry as possible.

- Avoid scalds by reducing your hot water temperature at the source (see page 63) or installing thermostatically-controlled mixer taps or fitting childproof hot taps.

- Use non-slip mats in the bath and shower.

- Install side grips and rails for extra stability near the toilet, bath and shower if a member of your household is elderly or infirm.

- Keep medicines out of reach of young children.

HOW HOT?

Children are more sensitive to hot water and usually prefer it at a maximum of 35°C (95°F), while babies are better off with bath water at 30°C (86°F).

- Hot water is 37–42°C (98.6–107.6°F).
- Warm water is 33–36°C (91.4-96.8°F).
- Cold water is 15–20°C (59–68°F).

Bathroom recycling

- Cut hand towels and face washers from old towels and spruce them up with cheerful borders.

- Use old toothbrushes for cleaning and for hobbies such as ceramics.

- Recycle chipped attractive mugs into tooth mugs but wash them regularly to avoid bacterial growth.

- Wash out a plastic bottle that has been used for soft drink or washing up liquid and give it to the children to use as a bath toy: they'll have fun filling it up and pouring it out.

- Yoghurt pots and margarine tubs make excellent sorters for the medicine cabinet.

ON CHOOSING TOWELS *A good towel is downy, spongy and resilient when crushed in your hand...A loosely twisted yarn is more absorbent than the tightly twisted yarns used in towels designed for friction rub-downs...Hold a towel to the light to see if the weave is close and firm — if it is, you should be able to see only pinholes of light.*

The Book of Good Housekeeping (1947)

the living room

Today's living room is central to family life. You use it for relaxing, reading, listening to music or watching television, and for receiving friends. These days, it is also just as likely to be known as the family room and to incorporate an informal dining area adjacent to the kitchen or a home office in one corner. As it is both a public and a private room, you no doubt want the living room to be comfortable yet durable, and casual yet smart, showcasing your most valuable possessions.

A SOFA IS A PIECE OF FURNITURE *which affords a great sense of comfort to its possessor.*

John Claudius Loudon

the living room

The clever living room

The clever living room is multifunctional and comfortable for the whole household. It is easy to care for and, with adequate storage, clutter-free.

- **Quarry tiles on a thick concrete base act as a solar heat store, remaining cool in the summer and warm in the winter. This minimizes dust and dust mites, and is easy to clean.**

- **The walls are painted with washable satin-finish, water-based paint.**

- **Woollen rugs add extra warmth underfoot.**

- **Double-glazed windows reduce outside noise and help regulate the temperature, while window vents provide ventilation.**

- **Thick curtains reduce heat loss in the winter and can be drawn on extremely hot summer days to prevent overheating.**

- **Shutters fitted outside provide extra heat control.**

- **A high-performance combustion stove warms the room in winter and makes it cosy and comfortable. Conducted heat vents have a greater heat output than conventional open fires, while complete combustion and filters minimize the emission of pollutants. The chimney is checked for cracks and swept every year to keep it working efficiently and safely.**

- **The television and sound system are switched off to conserve energy when they are not in use.**

Flooring

It is important to take time to consider all the options when choosing the best type of floor for your living area, as it is a decision you will probably need to live with for a considerable period of time. Obviously, floors need to be tough and easy to clean, but the ideal choice depends on your circumstances. A single person may find that taking out the vacuum cleaner once a week is enough to keep a carpet clean and looking good, while a mother of three young children may curse a carpet and find a timber floor, which can be wiped or swept clean so quickly, a blessing. The question of comfort is also subjective, depending on climate and personal preference. Carpets are often favoured in colder climates for being cosier, while stone or tile floors are blissfully cool in warm places.

WIPE YOUR FEET When you come indoors, it takes a minimum of eight steps to remove dirt from the soles of your shoes.

ALLERGY ALERT

The main consideration for people with hay fever-like allergies, or an allergy to dust mites, is to what extent the flooring collects dust and how easy it is to clean and clear of dust. Dust mites favour humid conditions, so whether a type of flooring remains dry or absorbs moisture is also a consideration.

- Hard surfaces such as vinyl, linoleum or wood are less hospitable to dust mites and easier to keep clean than fitted carpets or carpet tiles.
- Tightly woven short-pile carpet is also less inviting for dust mites.
- The static charge of nylon carpet attracts dust and helps prevent allergens from becoming airborne.
- Unsealed cork and unglazed ceramic tiles may harbour mites.
- Linoleum, made from linseed oil, gives off a strong odour that can cause respiratory irritation. (Open the windows after the first few days of installation.)
- When it is new, vinyl flooring out-gases high levels of many chemicals, particularly plasticizers.
- Anti-allergy carpet fibres contain antibacterial and anti-fungal agents that inhibit the growth of house dust mites, as they cannot digest skin scales unless they have been first broken down by bacteria and fungi. The carpet should be vacuumed routinely with an HEPA filter vacuum cleaner. (High efficiency particulate air filters can remove the tiniest particles, such as mould spots and tobacco smoke particles.)

Choosing the floor that's right for you

If you are choosing flooring, here are some of the points you need to consider.

- How easy is it to lay? Can you lay it on any type of sub-floor? Tiles and mosaic, for instance, usually need an absolutely flat floor while slate needs a very strong floor.
- Is it noisy? Stone and marble floors are noisy compared to soft flooring such as carpet and vinyl.

■ How do you clean it? Does it stain easily? Spills are easily wiped from hard surfaces while carpet often involves more of a drama. Wood flooring is easy to clean, but slate tends to stain.

■ How slippery is it? Ceramic tiles and seagrass can be slippery when wet, but sisal is not.

■ Is it hard or soft on feet and dropped items? Coir is rough on bare feet, linoleum is springy underfoot and tiled floors are unforgiving on dropped dishes and glassware.

■ Is it cold or warm to the touch? Many people like carpet for its warmth underfoot; timber is also warm, while tiles and stone floors are cold.

■ Is it the best type of flooring for anyone prone to allergies? See 'Allergy alert', page 217.

■ Is there an environmental cost? The sustainability of a material's source, how far and how easily it is transported, and the processes it undergoes before being laid in a home are just a few of the issues that determine how environmentally friendly a particular type of flooring is.

Timber

Timber floors are warm and durable, and good quality ones tend to improve with age. There is a vast range of timber flooring from which to choose and there are various forms, including boards and blocks and battens that can be laid in herringbone and other parquet patterns. It might surprise you to learn that timber products also include linoleum, which is made from powdered cork, linseed oil, wood resin and wood flour combined with chalk and pressed on to a backing of hessian or jute canvas.

■ Cork is another sustainable timber product. The cork oak tree regenerates itself after stripping and all the bark is used without waste.

■ Using wood produced locally, if possible, makes sense on economic grounds (shorter distances to transport), and also on climatic grounds (it withstands local conditions and weathers best).

■ Softwood such as pine may be from a sustainable resource if it originated in a properly managed forest plantation.

SUSTAINABLE TIMBER

The Forest Stewardship Council, an international non-profit organisation that promotes forest conservation and certifies forests worldwide, has an international system of certification to help consumers pick sustainable timbers. These timbers include those listed in the table below.

Hardwoods

- Alder
- American ash
- American whitewood
- Apple
- Aspen
- Australian blue gum
- Beech
- Birch
- Elm
- European ash
- Hickory
- Lime
- Maple
- Oak
- Pear
- Poplar
- Sycamore
- Walnut (American, European and Australian)

Softwoods

- Douglas fir
- Larch
- Pine
- Spruce
- Western hemlock
- Western red cedar
- Yew

- Recycled timber planking is a visually appealing choice as well as an economical and environmentally sound one. Old planks are often wider and of a higher quality wood than is readily available now. Avoid endangered tropical hardwood species.

TO CLEAN FLOORCLOTHS The once ubiquitous painted and varnished floorcloth is now consigned to craft books. Should you need to clean one, Mrs Beeton recommends washing it with a damp cloth, followed by a wipe with milk and a final rub over with a dry cloth.

Varnishes and finishes for timber floors

In its natural state, timber is not waterproof so you must take care to avoid overwetting it. You can stain timber flooring with an oil-, water- or spirit-based stain and seal it — with wax varnish, polyurethane varnish or oil — for extra protection. You also need to protect your flooring from dents caused by heels and castors.

SYNTHETIC VARNISHES

Many synthetic varnishes, including urethane varnish, contain volatile organic compounds (VOCs) — see 'The clever house', page 23. Urethane also contains synthetic rubber, acrylics and additives such as insecticides and fungicides. Epoxy varnishes too contain synthetic resins and phenols, some of which are carcinogenic and are banned in some countries.

Many wood preservatives are solvent based and those designed for the exterior may contain arsenics and creosote. They can cause irritation of the skin and mucous membranes as well as headaches, dizziness and nausea.

Most wood sealants are based on polyurethane.

NATURAL VARNISHES

Traditional natural varnishes are based on plant resins combined with linseed oil and thinners. Although they are less durable than synthetic ones, natural varnishes offer subtle colours and scents as well as being kinder to the environment.

- **Plants are exploited for their pigments, resins, oils, starches and waxes. For example, linseed oil, used since the 15th century in varnishes, is a versatile oil used to make wood water resistant both inside and out.**

- **Beeswax is suitable for all interior wood, giving it lustre and golden tones. Pure beeswax 'feeds' and protects wooden surfaces while enhancing its natural beauty and grain. Mixtures of plant extracts and beeswax are also available and are particularly suited to flooring. They give a durable, water-resistant finish and are pleasantly scented. Liquid beeswax can be used on stone, wood, cork and clay, producing an anti-static surface.**

- **Water-based preservatives contain much lower levels of VOCs, smell less strongly and may be less irritating for people with respiratory conditions. A translucent wood protection called lazur contains tree and plant oils, herb extracts and a lead-free drying agent. It allows the wood** to breathe while preventing water penetration. It does not emit fumes, has a pleasant scent and is biodegradable.

- An alternative to a synthetic wood sealant is natural resin-oil primer, which can be used on interior and exterior wood as well as cork and clay. Resin and oil finishes are another natural alternative for flooring. These water-resistant finishes have a soft sheen and can be tinted with natural stains and pigments.

- Wood stains made from plant extracts are also available.

Cork

Cork, from the cork oak tree (*Quercus suber*), is hard wearing yet has some cushioning effect. Its mottled surface disguises dirt, but as it is absorbent, it is often sold sealed with a 'wear layer' made of vinyl.

Vinyl

Made from plastic, vinyl flooring comes in a vast array of styles and colours, including other material look-alikes, including tile, timber and slate. A vinyl floor is easy to lay, comfortable underfoot and very easy to clean, basically only requiring sweeping and a damp mop.

Linoleum

Like vinyl, linoleum is a good choice for an easy-care floor, as it only really needs sweeping and damp mopping. It can also be polished for greater protection and shine. It is made from wood flour, cork, linseed oils and various resins which have been baked together, rolled under pressure and pressed on to jute backing.

Stone

Stone is healthy and non-polluting when it is placed in plain cement mortar and on a damp-proof foundation.

Radon, a naturally occurring radioactive gas (see 'The clever house', page 27), can be a problem in some areas of granite, limestone and slate, but stone can be tested. Quarry workers and stone masons may contract silicosis from inhaled stone dust. Quarries can disfigure the landscape and upset local ecology, although increasingly companies must provide environmental impact reports and restore industrial sites

KNOW YOUR STONE

■ The calcareous stones consist primarily of calcium and include marble, limestone and travertine. They are relatively porous and soft, and can be damaged by even weak acids. Marble, for instance, stains easily and is etched by vinegar, lemon juice and other acids.

■ Travertine is a type of limestone with a marble-like appearance.

■ Siliceous stones contain silica – the main constituent of sand – and include granite, slate, quartz, sandstone, bluestone and brownstone. These are less porous, harder, but vulnerable to strong alkalis and strong acids. Granite, for instance, is highly stain resistant.

after working on them. Transporting, quarrying and handling stone are all high-energy activities.

Stone is a popular choice for the energy conscious as it provides thermal mass – a heat conserving and shielding effect – as well as a certain grandeur. Stones traditionally used in the home include marble, granite, limestone, slate and travertine. Stone may be protected with a sealant, polished or honed. A polished floor is shiny and may even be reflective (and slippery) whereas a honed floor has a satin, smooth finish.

Quarry tiles

Quarry tiles are hard wearing and very easy to keep clean. They are an ideal choice for allergy sufferers and families with pets, but they can be cold and hard – and very unforgiving when breakables are dropped.

Glazed quarry tiles need only mopping with a cleaning solution. Unglazed quarry tiles can be polished with a liquid or solid wax polish. They are fairly stain resistant because their surface is relatively non-porous. They are not stain-proof, however.

Terrazzo

Terrazzo is a mixture of cement and marble chips. An expensive flooring option, it can be cleaned with a mop and a mild detergent solution.

Natural fibres

Fibres such as jute, sisal and coir are used to make matting. While natural fibres are harvested from abundant renewable sources, pesticides and other chemicals are frequently used in their production.

Carpets

Carpets tend to be popular in colder countries as they are warm and lend a cosy feel. Good quality carpets are often hard wearing too. The downside is that they require extra care to keep them free of dust and other allergens. Some carpet finishes and extras, such as underlay, especially in new carpets may also emit volatile organic compounds. Foam backings usually contain formaldehyde. Alternatives are hessian or felt. Air foam-backed carpets when installing them and keep the windows open until the 'new' smell dissipates.

ESCHEW FLOOR DAMAGE

High heels are hard on floors, whether they are wooden or carpet. *The Hoover Book of Home Management*, published in 1963, has the following advice about minimizing damage wrought by the then fashionable stiletto-heeled shoe: 'A tactful way with visitors is to have a supply of tiny plastic heel guards at the ready for those sharp high heels...' Consider this: a 57 kg (125 lb) woman in high heels exerts 900 kg per 6.5 cm^2 (2000 lb per 1 in^2) at each step.

THE DANGERS OF CARPET *Like many other household products and furnishings, new carpet can be a source of chemical emissions. Carpet emits volatile organic compounds, as do products that accompany carpet installation such as adhesives and padding. Some people report symptoms such as eye, nose and throat irritation; headaches; skin irritations; shortness of breath or cough; and fatigue which they may associate with new carpet installation. Carpet can also act as a 'sink' for chemical and biological pollutants including pesticides, dust mites and fungi.*

US Environment Protection Agency,
Indoor Air Pollution: Introduction for Health Professionals (1994)

A glossary of carpet terms

When you're considering carpet as a flooring option, it will make matters easier if you know what the sales people are talking about.

Fibre

A range of fibres with differing advantages and disadvantages is available. Natural fibres include wool, silk, jute, coir and flax, while some synthetic options are nylon, polyster, polypropylene, acrylic and viscose. In broad terms, wool is the most hard wearing but also, apart from silk which is rarely used, the most expensive. Blends offer a compromise between the two extremes.

- **Wool** Combines hard wear with good looks. Low combustibility. Produces no static electricity.

- **Jute** Mainly used in backing materials but sometimes in surface fibres for flat woven rugs.

- **Coir** Yarn spun from coconut husk fibre. Coir can be woven or made into cut-pile carpeting and rugs.

- **Flax** Occasionally used in loop pile and flat weave rugs and carpets.

- **Nylon** Also called polyamide. With modern stain-resistant treatments, this tough fibre is less prone to soiling than early nylon carpets. More flammable and prone to static than wool but often added to wool to increase wearability in lower pile weights and densities.

- **Acrylic** Not as hard wearing as nylon and less fire resistant than wool, but it does have bulk and resistance.

- **Polyester** Less resistant to flattening than some fibres but wears well.

- **Polypropylene** Hard wearing and easy to clean but scars if exposed to flame.

- **Viscose** Prone to flattening but relatively inexpensive.

Weight

Carpets come in three different weights. Some countries have specific labelling schemes that manufacturers may adhere to. Manufacturers may also have their own guidelines.

- **Lightweight** Suitable for light use such as bedrooms.

- **Medium weight** For medium use such as in dining rooms.

- **Heavy weight** For halls, living rooms and stairs.

Pile

Pile refers to the way the carpet is constructed. Piles come in different types and also different densities. The higher the density, the more hard wearing the carpet.

- **Loop pile** A series of small loops.
- **Cut pile** Loops cut to form a flat, level surface.
- **Velvet pile** A short dense pile which feels luxurious but is prone to shading and marking from furniture and tread.
- **Shag pile** Longest cut pile. A lightweight rake can be used to fluff up the pile.
- **Cut and loop pile** A combination forming a textured, sculpted effect.
- **Berber** Has flecks of contrasting colour throughout; can be cut or loop.
- **Twist pile** Tightly twisted cut pile that resists flattening and is therefore hard wearing.
- **Cord** Woven carpet made from a mixture of yarns and very low loops like corduroy. Very hard wearing but not necessarily comfortable to the touch.

Woven

A woven carpet is made on a loom. The two main types are Wilton and Axminster, named after the looms used to make them. There are various rules for manufacturing both of these, specifying, for example, the numbers of colours used and the type of pile.

Tufted

Tufts are inserted into a pre-woven backing, held in place by latex or a polyvinyl compound and another backing, usually hessian. Tufted carpets may have a secondary foam backing which acts as an underlay.

Underlay

Underlay is available in rubber, rubber crumb or felt. It prolongs the life of a carpet and makes it more comfortable to walk on.

Cleaning your floor

Whichever material you choose for your floor, it will last longer if you clean it regularly and give vulnerable spots some protection. Consider these measures.

- Place door mats at all entrances, inside and out.
- Position rugs where spills are likely, such as by the sink or fridge.
- Place other protectors such as glides and covers under furniture.
- Avoid walking on the floors with high heels.
- Lift rather than slide furniture across floors.

ON HANDS AND KNEES

Whether you use stringy-topped mops or the squeegee-fitted ones, mops save your back. But there is a school of thought that says they just don't get floors clean like an elbow grease-powered hand holding a towelling cloth or a scrubbing brush. If you go for the low down approach, wear gloves to protect your hands, and kneel on something soft to save your knees.

For the definitive floor wash, change the washing water as soon as it is dirty (otherwise all you are achieving is spreading dirty water over the floor), and rinse with fresh water and a well cleaned (or a second) mop. Change the rinsing water if it becomes dirty.

How to clean timber floors

The more protection you provide for a timber floor, the longer its sheen will last. It's a question of finding the balance between convenience and wear. Sweep regularly, mop spills with a dry cloth or paper towels, and remove sticky patches with a damp cloth. The basic rule of thumb is sweep first, mop second. Water alone will remove light soiling and is fine for frequent cleaning.

For a tougher clean, you will need to consider the type of finish or sealer on your timber floor, as each benefits from slightly different treatments.

Oil-finished timber

Sweep, then clean an oil-finished timber floor with a damp mop. Wash with 1 part methylated spirits to 10 parts hot water. Mop spills with a dry clean cloth and remove sticky foods with a warm damp cloth. To remove sticky food from an oil-finished timber floor, sprinkle an absorbent powder (talcum powder or flour) over it, then wipe with a warm damp cloth.

If you wish to polish an oil-finished floor, use a liquid acrylic and spirit-based wax polish rather than an oil-impregnated mop.

Polyurethane finish

Mop sparingly with hot water alone or a mild soap or detergent solution. Avoid letting the wood become too wet. About once a month, mop with a mixture of 1 part methylated spirits to 10 parts water. Rinse with a clean damp mop. Buff with a dry cloth tied to the end of a broom. A timber floor finished with polyurethane needs sanding and resurfacing every few years.

Wax polish finish

Brush off dust and debris regularly and wipe over with a damp mop or cloth to remove sticky and oily stains. Polish and clean with liquid acrylic and spirit-based wax polish. To avoid a build-up of polish (which will eventually have to be removed — see the recipe on page 228), apply it sparingly only where it is needed, such as heavy traffic areas, and don't apply too much.

NO-NO'S FOR TIMBER FLOORS

- Ammonia and other strong alkalis may dull the surface.
- Abrasive cleaners can scratch the surface and make it dull.
- Oil products may cause slipperiness and leave a sticky residue.
- Wax on top of a sealed wood floor will make it very slippery.
- Varnish applied over a waxed wooden floor will not dry and you'll end up with a sticky goo.

Varnished, shellacked or lacquered finish

Floors with these finishes are sometimes protected with a couple of coats of solvent-based floor wax. Once they have been waxed, clean them using mineral spirits. Do not damp mop them.

Removing stains and scratches from timber floors

When it comes to removing stains from timber floors, they fall into two main categories: floors with hard finishes and those without. In the group with hard finishes are polyurethane and other varnishes; in the second group are natural finish, wax finish and penetrating stains. If you're not sure which finish you're dealing with, take a closer look at the stain you are trying to remove. If it appears to be in the finish, the wood probably does have a hard finish. If it's in the wood, it very likely does not have a hard finish.

Alternatively, drop a little water on the flooring. If it makes a white mark, it is without a hard finish. The mark will disappear when the water dries.

To strip old polish from a timber floor

For an alternative to proprietary stripper, try this recipe.

INGREDIENTS

135 mL (4½ fl oz) floor cleaner (your own strong cleaner such as 'Strong all-purpose cleaner 1' — see 'The kitchen', page 84 — or a commercial one)
500 mL (1 pt) household ammonia
4 L (8½ pt) cold water

METHOD

1   Apply with a mop, tackling the job bit by bit, and allowing it to soak in to dissolve the old wax.
2   Use a sponge mop or newspapers to clean off the old wax.
3   Reapply where necessary.
4   Wipe over with a damp soft cloth then dry with a clean one.

RESTORING TIMBER FLOORS

DAMAGE	WITHOUT HARD FINISH	WITH HARD FINISH
Scratch	Wax	Touch up kit (available from a flooring retailer)
Food	Clean up with a damp cloth, rub dry, then wax	Use a specialized cleaner
Chewing gum, crayon, candle wax	Apply ice, or iron over an ink blotter. Use a solvent-based wax to loosen	Ice or specialized cleaner
Oil and greasy stains	Rub with kitchen soap, or saturate cotton with hydrogen peroxide and cover stain with cotton, then saturate second piece of cotton with ammonia and place over the first. Repeat. Dry and buff	Specialized cleaner
Cigarette burn	Shallow burn: rub with fine sandpaper or steel wool moistened with wax. Deep burn: remove charred parts, rub with fine sandpaper, stain, wax and buff	Shallow burn: touch up kit comprising stain and refinish. Deep burn: replace individual planks
Water mark (and white spots)	Fine steel wool and wax, then fine sandpaper. Clean with fine wool and mineral spirits. Dry, stain, wax and buff	Not usually a problem
Water mark/dark spots	Try above. Household bleach or vinegar. Soak for 1 hour. Rinse with damp cloth, dry. Fine sandpaper, stain, wax and buff	Specialized cleaner with scrub pad
Mould on timber	Wood cleaner	Specialized cleaner and a scrub pad if stubborn
Heel marks	Rub wax in with fine steel wool and hand buff to return shine	Rub wax in with fine steel wool and hand buff to return shine

Basic wooden floor cleaner

Here's a good, safe cleaner for damp mopping your timber floor.

INGREDIENTS

1/4 cup liquid soap

1/2–1 cup white vinegar or lemon juice

9 L (9 1/2 qt) warm water

METHOD

Mix all the ingredients together in a bucket and apply with a mop or sponge mop. For best results, rinse with clean water.

How to clean cork floors

Unsealed cork should be vacuumed or swept frequently but never cleaned with water. Clean it with solvent-based cleaners and use only solvent-based waxes to polish it. It can be buffed with a power buffer.

Vinyl-sealed cork can be wiped with a damp mop and liquid washing up solution. For extra protection in the kitchen or bathroom, apply emulsion polish. Even cork finished with a layer of vinyl should not be overwetted.

How to clean vinyl and lino floors

Both vinyl and linoleum are easy floors to care for.

- For general cleaning, sweep with a soft brush or vacuum. Using a solution of detergent or floor cleaner, wipe with a damp cloth or mop, then rinse.

- To remove scuff marks from vinyl floors, dip a cloth in undiluted washing up liquid or white spirit. Rub and rinse. Despite the extra work, it is worth rinsing a vinyl floor after cleaning, otherwise a smeary and sticky build-up of detergent occurs.

- To remove marks from a lino floor, rub lightly with a fine nylon pad and neat detergent.

- If you wish to polish lino, use an emulsion, water-based polish. Apply a thin coat at a time and allow each coat to dry completely before applying the next. Do not use wax polish.

REMOVING STAINS FROM LINO AND VINYL FLOORS

Quick action is always best: wipe, mop and scoop spills as soon as possible. Avoid using undiluted bleach (it may cause yellowing) and abrasive cleaners (they can scratch or dull the surface). If you are left with stains, try the following.

- Wipe the stain with an all-purpose cleaner.
- Try a pencil eraser.
- Use lemon and salt for rust stains: cut a lemon in half, sprinkle with plenty of salt and rub in the stain. Using a rag or sponge, rinse with water.
- For thick grease or tar, try mineral spirits, but use it with caution, testing on a tiny portion first as mineral spirits can take the shine off. Another way to remove tar is to cool it with an ice cube and pry it off with a spatula when it is brittle.
- A bleach solution made of 2 cups water and 1/4 cup chlorine bleach will remove many stains including beer, wine and other alcoholic drinks, coffee, tomato sauce and mustard. Organic stains such as blood, grass stains and pet accidents can be treated with this solution or lemon juice, or lemon and salt.

Spit and polish

- Floor polishes come in two main types: water based and solvent based. It is important to use the right sort for your floor. Generally, vinyl and lino should be polished with water-based floor polishes containing synthetic polymers; solvent-based ones — which contain wax — may make the colours run and soften the floor material.

- Thoroughly clean floors before polishing them by both sweeping or vacuuming then washing. Although it's not necessary to remove old polish every time you polish the floor, it is a good idea to start from scratch every three or four coats, otherwise you may end up with a thick build-up of polish which is both difficult to remove and dull because of inbuilt dirt.

- Remove old polish with 1/4 cup ammonia and 1/4 cup heavy duty detergent in 2.5 L (51/2 pt) water and rinse carefully afterwards to ensure all ammonia is removed. Ammonia left on the floor will prevent polish being applied evenly.

- Two thin coats are better than one. Apply floor polish in thin coats. It looks better, does not hold the dirt as a thick layer does, and is easier to remove when it's time for a new coat. Apply with a sponge mop or applicator. Pour polish into a shallow container rather than directly on the floor for ease of application.

- Many polishing products do not need rubbing but if you like extra shine, buff with a soft cloth or lamb's wool pad. Quick and light rubbing is the most effective technique.

- Some products are sold as all-in-one wash and polishes. Whether they are an asset is debatable: some say the dirt is only trapped in the glossy layer and builds up over time.

How to clean a stone floor

Prolong the finish of a stone floor by using rugs and mats in heavy traffic areas, such as entrances to the house. Cleaning protects by removing sand and other dirt that can scratch and dull a stone surface. Vacuum or sweep at least once a week. When necessary, wash with a mop, cloth or scrubbing brush (not a hard one) using a mild detergent. Rinse thoroughly with plenty of clean water and dry with a soft cloth.

NO SOAP Do not use soap to clean stone as it may leave a thin film of scum that will gradually build up over time and can be difficult to remove satisfactorily.

How to clean quarry tiles and terrazzo

Glazed quarry tiles and terrazzo only need sweeping and damp mopping. For a more thorough clean, mop them occasionally with a cleaning solution or detergent.

If unglazed tiles are left unglazed, they will absorb stains, particularly oil-based ones, which can then be very difficult to remove. In areas where spillages are likely to occur, such as kitchens and family rooms, or simply to add protection, unglazed quarry tiles can be polished with a liquid or solid wax polish.

Before polishing, treat marks with very fine steel wool dipped in white spirit. Wash, rinse, dry, apply polish and buff.

To restore a dulled surface, apply a pigmented wax dressing or polish. To restore faded colour, remove old polish with steel wool and white spirit. Wash and rinse. When dry, apply a pigmented wax polish sparingly and then buff.

How to clean your carpet

To protect your carpets, use doormats, preferably one inside and one outside each entrance point. This removes a great deal of dirt that would otherwise get walked on to the carpet. Always wipe your feet and train others to do so too. Some families habitually remove their shoes on entering the home and this keeps floors cleaner as well as looking good for longer. Place castors and protectors under furniture legs to help prevent the pile from being crushed.

THREE GOLDEN RULES OF CARPET CARE

Manufacturers recommend regular care to keep your carpet looking its best.

1   **Vacuum at least once a week, more often in heavy traffic areas.**
2   **Get working on spills and stains immediately.**
3   **Wet clean every one to two years or as needed.**

In a dirty carpet, the soil embedded at the base of the tufts grinds away at the fibre, gradually wearing it down. So vacuuming regularly is not just about keeping up with the Jones's clean appearance. Keeping the carpet clean also prolongs its life. Carpet sweepers remove crumbs and other surface dirt, while vacuum cleaners pull out the dirt from deeper down. When tougher action is called for, there are several options to choose from: spot treatments, carpet shampoos and cleaners, and carpet-cleaning machines.

WOOL AND ALKALIS Alkalis must never be used on wool as they damage the fibre and can also cause dyes to fade.

Stain protectors

There are two main types of stain protectors used on carpets. Stain protectors act as a shield to hinder the penetration of dirt and liquids, while a stain-resistant finish reacts as stains occur and prevents stains from being absorbed. In a way they give you a head start in mopping up spills as they delay absorption. Both types can be used in combination and can be applied during manufacture or once they are laid, although they work better if applied during the carpet's production.

Carpet shampoos

Carpet shampoos come as liquids, powders and foams — and are packaged in trigger sprays and aerosols.

- **Liquid shampoo wets the carpet pile, takes up oily and greasy dirt, traps it in suspension then dries to a brittle foam which can be vacuumed away, taking the stain with it. The ingredients usually include a polymer that helps the foam to dry brittle, colour brighteners and deodorizers.**

- **Powder shampoo contains solvents and surfactants to emulsify the soil before it is absorbed by the powder. Cleaning powders are saturated with solvents or detergents so they can battle stains. To use, first vacuum the carpet, sprinkle the powder liberally, brush it into the pile and repeat the vacuuming. Powders do not work as well as wet cleaning with a liquid shampoo but they are a convenient refresher and distort the pile less.**

- **Aerosol foam shampoo is suitable for lightly cleaning small areas. Usually the foam is sprayed onto the carpet sparingly, worked into the pile with a moistened sponge or brush and left to dry before vacuuming again.**

HOW STICKY IS YOUR CARPET SHAMPOO?

Pour a little carpet shampoo into a saucer and leave it overnight. Pour off the excess and allow the remainder to dry. If it leaves a sticky residue, that stickiness can attract household dust on your carpet as well as on the saucer.

The same test can be carried out with foam cleansers.

CRUSHED ICE To reinstate the pile on a synthetic carpet where, for instance, furniture legs have stood, place an ice cube over the spot.

Hot water extraction

Often incorrectly referred to as steam cleaners, hot water extraction machines can be rented to use at home but care must be taken not to overwet the carpet. (Overwetting can distort the pile and the backing.) The carpet pile is injected with hot water and shampoo solution under pressure so that the soil is suspended in the water, which is extracted almost at once by a high suction wet vacuum system. It works extremely well with very dirty carpets because it removes deep-seated dirt but it's not as effective on surface dirt. It also removes excessive detergent from successive wet cleanings. For a really dirty carpet, try successive wet cleanings combined with hot water extraction or get the carpet professionally cleaned. The most effective solution for a rug is for it to be factory cleaned.

What type of vacuum cleaner?

There are several different types of vacuum cleaner available.

- Traditional vacuum cleaners **suck dust into a bag. Their efficiency is reduced when tiny holes in the bag become clogged with dust.**

- Bagless cleaners **eliminate this problem by using technology that does not require a bag. They tend to be at the top end of the market, but they do not always perform very much better in tests.**

- Upright vacuum cleaners **are good for pushing around open spaces and are kinder on your back as they force you to adopt a better posture.**

- Cylinder cleaners **are harder on your back but better for getting round corners, under furniture, on the stairs and so on. Some tests suggest cylinders are better 'dust busters', while uprights make swifter work of animal hairs as some models also include brushes which pick them up.**

- Three-in-one cleaners **vacuum, shampoo and pick up water spills. Water and a cleaning solution are sprayed onto the carpet and immediately sucked back, along with the dirt.**

How dirty is your carpet really?

Your carpet might look clean enough, but consider what the vacuum cleaner is going to pick up. Perhaps we should all adopt the the Japanese custom of leaving our shoes at the door.

- **Sand and oil** Street dirt is usually a mixture of sand and oil, brought into the house on the soles of your shoes. While sand and grit can damage flooring, oil causes stains and traps further dirt.

- **Skin flakes** These make up the majority of household dust. Much of it ends up on the floor where it provides food for dust mites and moulds.

- **Pollens** From flowers and trees, pollen can accumulate indoors when floors are not regularly cleaned.

- **Hair of the dog** Pet hairs from dogs and cats can be very difficult to remove. Some vacuum cleaners come with extras such as special filtration to remove odour, and special nozzles to pick up animal hairs.

- **Mites** Dust mites live in carpets and bedding, producing faeces. Some people are allergic to them.

- **Hypoallergenic vacuum cleaners** These feature extra fine filters (HEPA filters) which trap fine particles and prevent them from re-entering the air as many other vacuum cleaners do.

- **Moulds** These thrive in house dust and where it is found, such as in carpets and upholstery.

What's eating your carpet?

Carpets can be attacked by moth and carpet beetle, which if left unchecked, can do irreparable damage to your valuable investment.

- Regular and thorough vacuuming, particularly under furniture and along the skirting boards, will keep carpets free of moths and beetles.

- If carpets are infested, the first sign is often a loosened pile and the second — when you look closer — is insect droppings, cocoons and cast skins.

Basic stain-removing foam for carpets and upholstery

INGREDIENTS

50 g pure soap

1/2 cup washing soda crystals

1/2 cup white vinegar

1 1/2 teaspoons eucalyptus oil or tea-tree oil

Few drops lemon or lavender pure essential oil for fragrance

5 L (10 1/2 pt) cold water

4.5 L (9 1/2 pt) hot water

METHOD

1   Grate the soap into a large saucepan and cover with 1 L (2 pt) of the cold water. Bring to the boil, add washing soda and stir until completely dissolved.

2   Stir in eucalyptus oil, vinegar and essential oil.

3   Pour into a bucket, add the hot water then stir in the remaining cold water.

4   When cool, beat to a light foam and spoon over the stain.

5   Leave it for ten minutes, then wipe with a sponge dipped in white vinegar to remove the alkalinity left by the cleaning solution.

6   Rinse with plain warm water (by either spraying the liquid onto the carpet or by patting it on with a clean white cloth or paper towel) and blot thoroughly.

◼ To treat, spray or dust an insecticide such as a permethrin onto the contaminated areas. Spraying with wettable powder gives protection for more than 12 months and is less likely to cause enhanced soiling than liquid sprays.

◼ Avoid organophosphates, such as dichlorvos, and organochlorines, such as dieldrin (see 'What's in a name?' on page 349).

The thrills of spills

Speed is your ally when removing spills from carpets. Fast action can make the difference between removing all trace of an accident, leaving a carpet spotless and living with a mark that spoils the effect of the whole carpet.

- The first line of action is simple enough: blot liquids and scoop solids. To blot spills use kitchen paper, tissues or an absorbent cloth or rag, and make sure these are white or colourfast. Use a blunt knife blade or a spoon to scoop.

- The next step is to use a cleaning solution. If in doubt, try the gentlest treatment first. Many spills can be removed with clean warm water. Many more can be salvaged using the foam only from a solution of frothed-up detergent and water (see the recipe on page 237).

- A mild bleach, sodium hydrosulphite, can be used safely on most light-coloured carpets.

- As with all stain removal, work from the outside of the stain towards the centre to avoid spreading it. Use small amounts of cleaning solution at a time so as not to overwet the carpet, and blot between applications with a cloth or tissue.

- Do not rub hard as this can spread the stain and distort the pile. Rinse with clear tepid water, especially if bleach has been used.

- Place a thick wad of white tissues or cloth on the treated area and weigh it down with a heavy object until dry.

- For rugs, start on the reverse side first, using a soft brush and a circular motion. Rinse with a cloth that has been wrung well in plain water, then proceed to the front of the rug. To dry, wipe the rug with a clean towel and air it by opening windows, using fans if necessary to speed drying. When the rug is dry, brush it with a soft dry brush to raise the pile. If you have the room, clean it outside in the fresh air.

BUBBLE AID Liquid spills can be treated by sparingly pouring on soda water or mineral water. The bubbles cause the spillage to rise to the surface where it can be quickly blotted.

On the spot: A to Z of carpet stains

Most stains can be treated in one of three ways, or a combination. Familiarize yourself with each of the three methods, then use the list below to find and treat your particular problem.

- **Treatment A** Mild detergent (1 teaspoon neutral detergent – that is, no alkalis or bleaches – in 1 cup lukewarm water).
- **Treatment B** Vinegar solution ($1/3$ cup white vinegar in $2/3$ cup water).
- **Treatment C** Ammonia solution (1 tablespoon household ammonia in $1/2$ cup water).

STAIN REMOVAL

STAIN	REMOVAL METHOD
Ball point pen	Sponge with a dry cloth and methylated spirits, or a small amount of dry-cleaning solvent, before sponging with Treatment A. Finally sponge with clean water
Beer	Sponge with Treatment A, followed by Treatment B, before sponging with clean water
Blood	Blot with cloth or paper towels. Use cold water, working it into the pile. Blot again and repeat as necessary. Small amounts of blood should come out fairly easily. If this does not work, try the following steps: sponge with Treatment A, then Treatment C, then sponge rinse with cold water
Butter	Sponge with a small amount of dry-cleaning solvent, then sponge with Treatment A
Chewing gum	As for butter
Chocolate	Sponge with Treatment A, followed by Treatment C. Repeat with Treatment A before sponging with clean water
Coffee	As for beer
Cola drinks	As for beer
Crayons	Sponge sparingly with dry-cleaning solvent, followed by Treatment A. Finally, sponge with clean water

STAIN REMOVAL (CONT.)

STAIN	REMOVAL METHOD
Dirt	As for chocolate
Egg (raw)	As for beer
Food	Remove excess then wipe with cloth wrung out with Treatment A
Food colouring	Professional carpet cleaner
Fruit juice and fruit	As for beer
Furniture polish	As for crayons
Glue (white craft)	Sponge with Treatment A, followed by Treatment B, then Treatment A again. Finally, sponge with clean water
Gravy	As for crayons
Ice cream	As for chocolate
Ink	Blot excess. Natural inks such as Indian ink are very difficult to remove
Iodine	Sponge with Treatment A, followed by Treatment C, then Treatment B and finally Treatment A again. Finish with clean water
Lily pollen	If dry, vacuum excess. If wet, soak up with dry cloths
Milk	As for chocolate
Mud	Let it dry completely first, then brush with a stiff brush to break it up. Finally, vacuum
Nail polish	Use non-oily polish remover on a cloth for small stains, then sponge with Treatment A. Finally, sponge with clean water
Paint	While still wet, emulsion can be rinsed off with water. If dry, break up the paint with the edge of a blunt knife and then vacuum. To remove gloss, use sparing amounts of white spirit but be warned, it can remove colour from carpet. When dry, for a superficial stain, try shaving off the paint with a sharp knife — only try it if you are confident of a steady hand, otherwise you may risk holes
Pen (marker)	As for crayons
Red wine	Blot with paper towels or a dry cloth. Sprinkle with white wine, which is acidic, to neutralize the stain, or water, and blot again. Remove the remaining stain with a clean cloth and methylated spirits

STAIN	REMOVAL METHOD
Rust	Put lemon juice on the mark, leave for 1 minute and rinse with water. Repeat if necessary
Shoe polish	As for crayons
Skin cream	As for crayons
Soft drinks	As for glue (white craft)
Soot	As soot is oily, do not attempt to remove with water and detergents. Vacuum as much away as possible and tackle small stains with a solvent cleaner
Soy sauce	Sponge with Treatment A, followed by Treatment C, before sponging with clean water
Tar or oil	Remove with a spirit-based cleaner
Tea	Using a paper towel or dry absorbent cloth, blot as much as possible. Add a little water and soak up again until the colour is gone. You can also safely try Treatment A or methylated spirits dabbed on the residue. Alternatively, try sponging with Treatment A, followed by Treatment B, before sponging with clean water
Urine (dried stain)	Sponge with Treatment A, followed by Treatment B, then Treatment C, then Treatment A again. To finish, sponge with clean water
Urine (wet stain)	Blot, then sponge with clean water. Sponge with Treatment C, followed by Treatment A. Finally sponge with clean water
Vaseline	As for crayons
Vomit	Scoop and blot as much as possible
Water stains	Professional help only
Wax	As for crayons
White wine	As for glue (white craft)

REMOVING INK STAINS FROM CARPET *When ink is spilt on a carpet, take up the moisture immediately with blotting paper, then rub the place with a rag dipped in milk, preferably boiled, and dry with a dry cloth, rubbing hard. Or salt may be sprinkled on the stain, and then rubbed with a cloth moistened in warm water.*

Home Lovers Encyclopedia

THROW SALT OVER YOUR SHOULDER BUT NOT ON RED WINE

Tradition has it that salt heaped liberally over a spill of red wine will soak it up and save the stain. But professional carpet cleaners do not recommend it on carpets. Instead they suggest a combination of white wine and methylated spirits (see the 'Red wine' entry in the table on page 240).

Caring for valuable or delicate rugs and carpets

Delicate rugs and carpets, such as antique ones, need special treatment.

- Vacuum with reduced suction, using the gentlest power on your cleaner.
- If you don't have a vacuum cleaner with adjustable power, adjust it yourself by placing a screen of plastic on the nozzle or even on the carpet itself.
- Vacuum slowly in the direction of the pile.
- Avoid wet cleaning.
- Do not use old valuable carpets in areas of high traffic or in places such as doorways where they are likely to receive harsher, dirtier treatment.
- For serious spillages, blot and gently scrape as much as you can, then wrap the carpet tightly in plastic to avoid drying the stain. This helps prevent it setting. Whisk it off to a professional cleaner.
- When storing carpets and rugs, roll rather than fold, and roll pile side out to prevent wearing.
- If storing delicate or antique rugs, line them with acid-free paper before rolling and place in acid-free boxes.

Walls

Walls take a battering at various spots around the house – consider points of entry or tight areas when items are carried through the house – but inevitably, the rooms where the family spends most time are the most likely to show signs of wear. In a living/family room, walls are especially prone to smears and scuffs and grubby finger marks.

Choosing a wall covering

Your choice of wall covering will depend partly on the size and nature of your family. For example, if you have children who are still at the food-smearing, wall-drawing stage of their development, designer wallpaper or moire silk may not be the most sensible options!

Paint

Of the two most commonly used finishes, paint is the most popular as it's relatively inexpensive, easy to keep clean, and once a wall is finished well, you can slap a coat of paint on quite quickly and transform a room.

Wallpaper

As well as being decorative, wallpaper is also useful for disguising irregularities in the smoothness of the wall surface. It comes in a wide range of types.

- **Plastic wall 'papers' will withstand scrubbing and scuffing.**
- **White lining paper is a pure white paper designed to provide a smooth surface for painting.**
- **Off-white lining paper is used under wallpaper as a base.**
- **Reinforced papers smooth down very uneven surfaces, such as old plaster walls, ready for papering.**
- **Standard wallpapers are inexpensive but not hard wearing.**
- **Other types of wallpaper include embossed, wood chip (designed to be painted to disguise surface imperfections), high relief, flock, vinyl, foamed polyethylene and foamed vinyl.**

Other wall finishes

For alternatives to paint and wallpaper you can choose from fabric, cork or ceramic tiles, and wood panelling. Of the fabric coverings (perhaps more popular in the past than nowadays), the most common are hessian (paper-backed or not), grasscloth (a fragile fabric made by weaving grasses onto a fine cotton warp, then bonding it to a paper backing) and silk (usually adhered to a paper backing). As a general rule, the fabric coverings are the most difficult to clean.

- Cork **for wall covering is manufactured from pressed layers of tree bark. It is warm to the touch and a good insulator of both heat and sound. It should be sealed for ease of cleaning and maintenance.**

- Ceramic wall tiles, **slabs of fired clay decorated on one side with glaze, are hard, durable, water resistant and stain resistant.**

- Wood panelling, **which comes in a variety of sizes and styles, can be used to line a room completely, or as a decorative feature. Like timber flooring, it needs to be painted or sealed in some way to make it a practical choice for wall covering.**

Alternative paint products

Many commercial paints emit volatile organic compounds (VOCs) — see 'The clever house', page 23. A growing number of paint manufacturers offer paints with natural products as their base.

- Protein-based paints **use proteins such as casein, milk products, bone and glue. They do not emit VOCs, have little, if any, odour and are non-allergenic. However, they are moisture sensitive and only suitable for interior use. Available in matte finish only, these paints are not washable.**

- Resin-based paints **use wood resin and vegetable oil. They have a pleasant smell, are available in a range of finishes and varnishes, and are both durable and washable. However, being solvent based, they contain potentially irritating turpentine and white spirit, and require good ventilation.**

- Synthetic resin-based paints **are available in a wide variety of finishes and varnishes. They are washable, durable, do not emit VOCs and are non-allergenic.**

LEAD ALERT

The best indicator of the presence of lead in the paint in your home is your home's age. Before 1950 lead was routinely added to paint, and you can safely bet that paintwork dating before and up to this time will contain lead. New paint over the top seals in lead, but cracks, peeling and flaking can allow lead dust into the air. Disturbing the paint in other ways — pets scratching, children knocking or home renovation — can also release paint dust. The easiest way of dealing with lead paintwork in good condition is simply to paint over it with modern paint. If the paintwork is in bad condition and needs to be removed before you can redecorate, where at all possible, use methods that do not create dust or fumes.

The dos and don'ts of lead paint removal

■ Don't use solvent- or caustic-based liquid strippers.

■ Do use solvent-free, water-based paint stripper.

■ Don't use a hot air gun unless absolutely necessary.

■ Do keep the hot air gun below 45°C (113°F) — this will soften paint without burning it (burning the paint releases dangerous fumes).

■ Do wear protective clothes, gloves and a good quality face mask with an appropriate filter.

■ Do shut off the work area and keep others out, especially young children and pregnant women.

■ Do cover furniture and carpets, or better still remove them.

■ Don't use sandpaper — use waterproof abrasive paper instead.

■ Do wash your hands and any exposed skin straight away after working, and wash your work clothes separately from others.

■ Do put any paint peelings in a sealed bag and put it out with the rubbish.

■ Do clean the room afterwards with water and detergent.

■ Lime-based paints use limewash or lime plus animal or vegetable fats. They are non-allergenic but form a dusty film when dry. Available in matte only, they are only marginally washable.

■ Stone-paint is based on silicate. Highly durable, washable, anti-fungal by nature and non-allergenic, it comes in matte only and is usually used on exteriors. It can rub off against clothing, and is alkaline (therefore requiring protection when being applied). From an environmental point of view, its manufacture requires a great deal of energy.

■ Oil-bound emulsions are latex paints based on vegetable oils. They are washable and fairly durable inside. Although they are generally non-allergenic, oil-bound emulsions can produce allergy symptoms in some people. Certain versions contain VOCs. Best used for interiors, they are available in matte only.

TIPS FOR WASHING WALLS

■ To stop water running down your arms, wear towelling wrist bands to absorb drips.
■ Working in pairs is much easier – one person washes and the other rinses and towel dries.

General care of painted walls and ceilings

■ Dust occasionally with either a soft attachment on the vacuum cleaner, a broom with a soft cloth tied onto the brush or a dry cloth. Start at the ceiling and work down.

■ Spot clean regularly to keep walls looking good. Scuffs at door entrances, finger marks near light fittings and door handles, and sticky finger marks at child height on the wall are the hot spots. A railing on both sides of the stairs is one way to prevent finger marks appearing by the walls up stairwells. To spot clean, try (in order of most gentle method first) a damp, clean, colourfast cloth; a clean cloth dipped in a mild detergent solution; any of the strong all-purpose household cleaner recipes (see 'Laundry', page 126); or a cream cleanser.

■ Regularly remove cobwebs from the ceiling and give corners a brush with a long-handled broom covered in a soft cloth, or a long-handled duster. Washing the ceiling is a messy job, involving drips and buckets of water. It may be something you feel you only really need to do before painting but, on the other hand, a good clean can be almost as revitalising as painting, especially if the ceiling has been discoloured by mould.

THE WHOLE WALL AND NOTHING BUT...

In the past, walls needed washing at least seasonally because heating tended to be dirtier and walls showed up particles of soot from the fire or oven. Cleaner types of heating mean it is hardly necessary now but should you feel the urge, this is how to go about it.

To wash painted walls, doors and ceilings, use a mild detergent solution. If you need something stronger use, for instance, a solution made with 100 g (3½ oz) washing soda to 4 L (8½ pt) water.

1   Prepare the room first by laying drop sheets on the floor and over any furniture that may receive an unwelcome shower. Some paints take to a wash better than others. Gloss, for instance, is usually fine but an old-fashioned paint such as whitewash may get washed off itself if it is too harshly treated. If you are in doubt about the washability of your paint surface, test wash an area that is not on public display.
2   Dry clean the wall with a duster or vacuum cleaner before wetting it.
3   When washing, start from the bottom and work up, rubbing the surface briskly with your cleaning solution, rinsing off and drying with a soft towel. Catch drips fastidiously as you go as dirty drips can be even harder to clean up than the original dirt source, but they don't stain a damp wall that's already been cleaned.
4   To rinse, wipe drips with a clean damp sponge. You need two buckets — one for your cleaning solution and one for rinsing water. Depending on the area of the wall, you may need to change the water frequently.

General care of wallpaper

Washable wallpapers are coated with a thin transparent vinyl layer, which makes them easier to clean and more difficult to stain. Dust regularly with a soft brush and wipe over with a damp cloth dipped in mild detergent and warm water. Rinse with a damp cloth and a bucket of clean warm water.

Non-washable wallpaper requires gentler treatment. Dust regularly with a soft brush or cloth. Spot clean by dabbing with powdered borax and brushing out. Another home-made remedy is to rub gently with a piece of bread rolled into a ball, or a soft rubber eraser.

General care of other wall coverings

■ Fabric **Gently dust with a soft brush or damp cloth. Spot clean with a sponge or soft bristle brush soaked in mild detergent or soap solution. For tough stains try a solution of mild bleach. Rinse well and dry with an absorbent towel to avoid streaking.**

■ Cork **Wipe with hot water, without detergent. When you need something stronger, wipe with a mixture of 1 part methylated spirits to 10 parts water, and rinse with a clean damp cloth. For extra shine, buff with a dry cloth tied to the end of a broom. If you have unsealed cork, consider waxing it for protection.**

■ Wood panelling **Dust or vacuum clean with the soft brush attachment. For grubby finger marks, use a cloth dampened in a mild detergent solution.**

■ Ceramic tiles **Keep clean using a damp cloth and a solution of washing up liquid. For stains, rub with neat washing up liquid. See 'The bathroom', page 193, for more on cleaning ceramic tiles.**

The young artist: The toddler years

Budding artists are prone to exhibiting their talents on floors and walls. Swift action may save the day. In addition, when using a cloth to attempt to remove a stain, make sure that you switch spots on the cloth as soon as one area becomes discoloured.

First test your removal method in an inconspicuous area, if possible, because cleaners that are strong enough to tackle the stain may also tackle the paint. If practical, remove excess material with a spatula, then rub gently with a sponge or cloth with a little paste made of baking soda and water. This should remove crayon, pencil, ink and marker pen as well as general scuffs, but see the specific tips below.

Wax crayon

■ **For hard non-porous surfaces such as glass, use white spirit or powder detergent on a soft cloth and rub gently using small circular strokes.**

■ **For wooden furniture, use a strong all-purpose cleaner and soft cloth.**

■ **For varnished and painted woodwork, brick and stone, brush with a nail brush dipped in dry-cleaning solution. Then mix dry-cleaning solution with powder detergent and rub again. Rinse with clean water and dry.**

- For carpet and soft furnishings, rub or press the mark with dry-cleaning solution, probably a few times, using a clean cloth or paper towel. If any colour remains, try a very mild bleach solution, but test a small area first.
- For wallpaper, use a pencil rubber then an all-purpose liquid cleaner.

Liquid paint

For varnished and painted woodwork and painted walls, try dabbing with a damp cloth. If this fails, try powder detergent and a damp cloth, but be careful of glossy surfaces as they may become scratched or dull. Finally, try nail polish remover.

Chalk

- On wallpaper, use a damp cloth and a liquid cleaning solution or household soap. If that doesn't work, try rubbing with an eraser.
- On brick or stone, brush with a stiff brush then scrub with a paste cleaner or powdered detergent and water.
- On vinyl flooring or desk surfaces, use a liquid cleaner.

Furniture

Your living room furniture is an investment that needs to be treated with care and respect to ensure it remains in optimum condition for as long as possible.

Wooden furniture

A little maintenance will keep wooden furniture looking its best.

What sort of finish?

There are three main ways of finishing wood for tables, chairs and other furniture.

1 French polish This is a beautiful satin finish, achieved by repeated applications of shellac dissolved in spirit.

2 Lacquer This hard-wearing finish can be applied directly onto wood or on top of a veneer of wood, paper foil or plastic.

3 Wax Repeated rubbings of wax polish and turpentine give a rich gloss.

Cleaning and caring for wooden furniture

Housework used to be tackled according to a routine of specific tasks every day, so dusting and polishing furniture would have been a major weekly job. There's certainly something very appealing about the smell of newly polished furniture.

Protection is better than a cure

All wooden furniture can be dusted with a soft cloth.

- Lacquered furniture can also be wiped with a damp duster using a fine water mist spray on the duster to avoid getting the wood too wet. Dry with a second cloth and buff with a soft cloth. While it is not necessary to polish lacquered furniture, an occasional application brings a shine to a dull surface.

- Regular waxing of waxed furniture helps protect it from heat and moisture. Once or twice a year should be sufficient. Solid wax produces better results even though it's harder to apply.

Be sure to protect tabletops and other wooden surfaces by sticking felt underneath ornaments and using coasters or mats to protect surfaces from the heat of cups or liquid from vases.

WAX WARNINGS

- Furniture polishes with added silicones or aerosol polishes give instant shine to wooden furniture but they do not fill scratches and other blemishes like wax. In addition, the solvents in these kinds of polishes can soften underlying wax and give the surfaces a milky look. The only remedy when that happens is to strip the finish entirely and start again.
- Furniture cream waxes contain a high percentage of solvents that can soften and remove lower layers of wax.
- Do not apply wax over a build-up of dirty wax. Remove the dirty wax first with a cloth dipped in white spirit. Wipe the wood, following the grain until all the dirt is removed. Allow to dry, then wipe with a clean dry cloth before reapplying the wax paste.
- Do not apply wax to a dusty surface as you will seal in the dirt, making it impossible to clean away. Always dust and clean first.
- Apply wax polish sparingly, otherwise it will be difficult to buff up.
- Let wax dry before buffing for a good shine.

Removing stains and marks

Inevitably, wooden furniture will suffer the occasional mishap. When attempting to remedy marks and stains, proceed with caution, starting with the mildest methods first. Try repeated gentle methods rather than one harsh treatment. While there are many commercial products available, it is worth trying home remedies first, but make sure you work in a well ventilated place.

- **Greasy finger marks** Wipe with a just damp cloth that has been wrung in a mild solution of soap flakes. Dry thoroughly.

- **Heat marks** White marks may indicate that the finish has been damaged. Try burnishing out the mark with a cream metal polish, rubbing it briskly in the same direction as the grain. Follow with a polish of wax. Do small sections at a time, wiping the polish away as you go.

- **Rough patch** Smooth with very fine steel wool dipped in liquid wax polish. Proceed with great caution on veneered surfaces.

- **Water marks** Try removing marks left by wet glasses as you would heat marks (see above).

- **Scratches** Mask light scratches with a similar coloured wax crayon or shoe polish. Leave it to absorb before buffing briskly.

- **Alcohol spots** Burnish with a cream metal finish, rubbing briskly in the direction of the grain. Follow with a light wax polish.

Home-made furniture polish

INGREDIENTS

55 g (2 oz) beeswax

140 mL (4³/4 fl oz) turpentine

2 tablespoons linseed oil

2 tablespoons cedar oil

METHOD

1   Grate the beeswax into a heatproof bowl.

2   Pour in the other ingredients. Stir.

3   Place the bowl over a saucepan of simmering water until the ingredients melt.

4   Allow to cool before using.

5   To use, rub sparingly over wooden furniture with a soft cloth.

Upholstered furniture

While timber is ideal for tables, dining chairs and storage units, the idea of trying to relax for very long in solid timber chairs is a little daunting. With inner springs, padding and various other methods of cushioning the body, upholstered furniture has a place in every comfortable living room. Furniture can be upholstered in a variety of materials but the two most common are fabric and leather.

Fabric has the advantage of being available in limitless colours and styles to suit all tastes and budgets, but will tend to wear and get dirty over time. Leather is an ideal covering for chairs and sofas that are going to take a beating from children or pets. Although it can be an expensive option in the first place, there are savings to be made on cleaning and replacement costs when compared with the life of traditional fabric upholstery. Leather might also prove less of a dust-haven for the allergy prone. However, whether fabric or leather, all upholstered furniture needs care and maintenance to remain looking its best.

Cleaning and caring for fabric upholstery

All upholstery benefits from a regular vacuum to remove dust and other debris that finds its way into crevices. Preventative measures, some more fashionable than others, include these.

- Soil repellents and stain repellents **work by making spills bead up rather than soak into the fabric.**

- Antimacassars **are coverings thrown over the back of sofas and chairs to protect them from grease in the hair. Typically, these take the form of small lacy circles or rectangles.**

- Throws **are particularly handy for protecting upholstery from the rigours of pets and young children.**

- Loose covers **may be laundered.**

- Arm guards and back guards **protect the most vulnerable spots on chairs and sofas.**

SHAMPOOING FABRIC UPHOLSTERY

Like carpet fibres, upholstery fabric is worn away by dirt. Regular shampooing — perhaps once a year or once every two years — helps keep sofas and the like clean. Loose covers are usually designed to be washed, but check the care labels. If in doubt about shrinkage, wash the covers in cold water and replace them on the furniture when they are still slightly damp.

Hand shampooing is good for delicate dirty upholstery. Follow the instructions on a commercial shampoo. In general, use a soft brush dipped in the foam made by a shampoo. Rinse by wiping the foam off with a well wrung cloth dipped in clean water. Dry thoroughly, then vacuum.

For furniture with fixed upholstery, you might consider a home steam extraction machine which pumps liquid into the fabric and sucks it out again, eliminating the problem of wet seats, arms and cushions, which take forever to dry. Even so, good ventilation helps speed up the drying time.

Cleaning and caring for leather upholstery

To spot clean minor stains, wipe leather upholstery with a little water, taking care not to get the leather too damp. To more thoroughly clean leather upholstery, dust, then use saddle soap or a similar product. Let it dry thoroughly before using the furniture again. If the leather is beginning to crack or seems dry, use a leather conditioner but test in an inconspicuous spot for its effect on colour.

Window treatments

Curtains, blinds and shutters not only enhance the decorative effect of your living area, they also make it more energy efficient, keeping excess heat and harsh light out during summer and helping to prevent heat loss during winter.

Blinds

- **Dust blinds regularly.**
- **To refresh the colour, wipe linen blinds with a cloth wrung out in methylated spirits and vinegar, then wipe with a dry cloth.**
- **To remove stains, rub with a piece of bread.**
- **To wash a really dirty roller blind, take down the blind, keeping it rolled up but leaving the roller. Wet the blind and leave it for a few minutes. Give it a bath in warm water and detergent by gradually unrolling the blind and sponging it as you draw it into the bath. Keep going until you reach the end but do not dip the spring part. Rinse in the same gradual**

fashion. Let it drip on the clothesline for a few minutes then place on a towel on a table and dry from one end to the other with a second towel.

TO REVIVE VELVET CURTAINS Dust makes velvet and plush curtains dull as well as enticing for dust mites. Go over with a brush of medium stiffness – against the pile for velvet and with the pile for plush – then hang in the bathroom over a hot bath to revive the pile.

Lighting

Choosing lighting is very much a personal decision, but do bear in mind that for a multifunction room, such as a living or family room, there will be lots of different lighting requirements that need to be addressed.

- Natural light is best, whether from windows, skylights and light tubes (small, highly efficient skylights). Keeping these clean allows more light to enter your home.

- Make the most of reflected light: pale-coloured ceilings, walls and furnishings bounce light around rooms, making the best use of daylight and artificial light. Use diffusers over lights, light-coloured shades, light tubes and skylights to spread light over large areas.

- Fluorescent lighting is the most efficient and is now available in a range of shapes and colours.

- A single high wattage bulb is more efficient than a cluster of lower ones.

- Locate lights where you need them and use spot lights for reading, sewing and so on.

Movement sensors, light sensors and timers automatically switch lights on and off, and dimmers allow you to lower light levels.

How to clean lampshades

Which cleaning method you use will depend on what material the lampshade is made of.

- Fabric **Clean with a vacuum cleaner using the dusting brush attachment, adjusted to low power suction if possible. Attempt to clean spots with a mild detergent solution but be careful: you risk making water marks and/or dissolving the glue which holds the shade together.**

- Glass or plastic **Dust regularly. If necessary, wash with a clean cloth and detergent solution.**

- Paper and parchment **Brush often with a feather duster.**

- Raffia and straw **Vacuum with the brush attachment.**

LIGHTS ON

Light quality varies subtly, depending on whether it's direct, diffused, reflected, natural or artificial. Even artificial lighting comes in many forms, with different uses.

- **General lighting** Usually a central ceiling light. Dimmers give you more control, and hence more variety and flexibility. Several lights — for instance, downlighters and uplighters — create a more pleasant effect.
- **Task lighting** To illuminate activities that require good light, such as reading, computer work, sewing or drawing, use spotlights, mini-spotlights and desk lights, or fluorescent lights close to the work area. These lights should be shaded to avoid glare.
- **Mood lighting** For atmosphere, use table, wall or floor lamps or concealed shelf lighting. Lower wattage and pearl bulbs help create a softer, more diffuse light.

A cosy fire

If you have an older style home, you may have open fireplaces in the living rooms and bedrooms. Open fires produce polluting combustion by-products (see 'The clever house', page 19) and are not efficient methods of space heating, but their warmth does more than heat a room. New, more efficient solid fuel fires — including sealed wood burners — display the leaping flames we enjoy so much but also conserve energy.

To clean fireplace surrounds

1 Vacuum all loose soot and ash.

2 Rub off as much remaining soot as you can with a dry brush or cloth.

3 Wash the surround with a strong all-purpose cleaner recommended for the surface, whether it is brick, stone or marble. Alternatively, apply a weak solution of ammonia in water with a stiff brush.

4 Wash glass doors as you would any glass, unless the manufacturer's instructions advise otherwise.

THE IMPORTANCE OF SWEEPING CHIMNEYS An annual clean sweep removes blockages, preventing poisonous gases from building up in the house. It also removes soot and creosote build-up, which if not cleared, can fuel serious fires.

To clean fireplace accessories

1 Brush with a dry brush or cloth.

2 Wash in an all-purpose cleaner of your choice.

3 Apply paste wax for shine and to help prevent rust.

Home entertainment equipment

Dust and dirt can damage televisions, sound systems, video cassette recorders (VCRs) and other home entertainment appliances, so dust them regularly by wiping them with a soft cloth or flicking them with a feather duster. To reduce static electricity, wipe over appliances with an antistatic cloth.

General care and cleaning of home entertainment equipment

Remember to switch off and unplug all appliances before cleaning them.

- To remove greasy marks and other spots, use a cloth dampened with methylated spirits.

- To clean disc and tape compartments, wipe them out with a cloth. To reach the corners, use a cloth dampened with methylated spirits over a cotton bud.

- Clean the stylus of a record player by brushing dust off with a paintbrush. Dip the brush in methylated spirits and brush gently again.

- To clean a television screen, remove dust with a soft cloth, then wipe with a cloth dampened in either a glass-cleaning solution or warm water. Never spray directly onto the screen as this can cause damage.

- Clean VCR heads with a cleaning cassette (available from your local video hire store). A bad case may need professional cleaning. Regularly clean the VCR as dirty equipment damages tapes.

- Store your VCR in a cool, dry place, and avoid any sudden changes of temperature.

- Play and rewind VCR tapes at least once a year to redistribute tension evenly along the tape.

- Store CDs in the cases provided, away from sunlight and direct heat.

- Hold each CD by the edge.

- Dust CDs with a soft clean cloth, always wiping from the centre outwards. Do not wipe in a circular motion following the lines.

- To remove finger marks from CDs, use a cloth dampened in mild detergent. If this does not restore the CD to full quality, try a little isopropyl alcohol (rubbing alcohol, available from chemists and some supermarkets).

ANTISTATIC CLOTH Soak a lint-free cloth in fabric softener and water. Squeeze out the excess and dry the cloth before using it.

Caring for books

The best way to keep books at their best is to read them, but there are also several other things you can do to ensure they remain in good condition.

■ **Regularly open books to help reduce dampness as well as prevent dust from setting too deep.**

■ **Store books in glass-fronted cabinets to protect them from dust and sunlight, ideally at a temperature of around 15°C (59°F), but make sure there is adequate ventilation.**

■ **Store heavy books flat to prevent the pages tearing away from the spine, and use book ends to stop books slumping against each other and becoming damaged.**

■ **Dust books once a year by brushing the page edges with a thick make-up brush while the book is closed.**

MUSTY BOOKS To rid a book of a musty smell, store it for a few days in a paper bag filled with crumpled newspaper. The newspaper will absorb the smell. For stubborn odours you may need to repeat this process several times, using fresh newspaper each time.

STORING VALUABLES

When storing valuable paintings or antiques, be aware of their natural enemies.

■ Light may trigger chemical changes, such as fading.

■ Humidity over 50 to 60 per cent encourages mould; too little humidity makes paper brittle, and wood shrink and crack.

■ Lack of ventilation also promotes mould. Ensure valuables are stored in a way that allows plenty of air to circulate.

■ Specialist materials are available for storing valuables – for instance, for wrapping paintings. If in doubt, use acid-free tissue paper.

Caring for photographs

Your photographs will last much longer if you look after them properly.

▓ Store treasured photographs in good quality paper albums interleaved with acid-free paper.

▓ Store photographs in a cool, dark, dry place — under the bed is ideal.

▓ Use photo corners rather than glue to secure photos in place.

▓ Store negatives and old prints out of sunlight, at an even temperature. Place them in polyester covers to prevent the surfaces sticking together and to avoid bleaching of colours.

Caring for pictures

Calculated neglect is the best treatment for paintings. They need a little of the right attention but nothing too harsh. Keep paintings away from humid places or rooms that may vary abruptly in temperature. Bathrooms and kitchens, attics and basements, then, are usually out of bounds. Also, don't hang pictures near windows, where rain or sun could damage them, or near smoky candles.

Seek specialist attention for very valuable artwork. For other less expensive or cherished pieces you can apply some home treatment.

▓ To clean unpainted wooden frames use a soft cloth dipped in linseed oil.

▓ Clean painted frames with a cloth dampened with mild soap solution.

▓ To remove discolouration from gilt frames, rub with a piece of lemon, sponge with a solution of 1 teaspoon bicarbonate of soda in 0.5 L (1 pt) warm water, then polish with chamois leather.

▓ Dust picture glass with a soft cloth. To remove marks, use a little methylated spirits or other glass cleaner — just enough to make the cloth damp — on a soft cloth. Never spray the glass with a liquid as some may seep behind the glass and come into contact with the painting.

▓ Never touch paintings that are not behind glass as skin oils can cause damage over time. Just gently dust these paintings with extreme care once a year. Use a fine soft brush and work from top to bottom.

Flowers in the house

Flowers add colour and grace to any room of your home, not just the living room. A few tricks can make their beauty last longer.

Cutting flowers

To prolong the life of cut flowers, follow these tips.

■ **If cutting flowers from the garden, cut on a cloudy day or early in the morning to minimize moisture loss. Make clean cuts with pruning shears or a sharp knife.**

■ **Plunge the stems into a bucket of tepid water as soon as you have cut them.**

■ **Encourage flowers to absorb water by cutting the stems every few days.**

■ **When recutting green stems, cut a 5 cm (2 in) slit up the stem from the base, then cut the bottom of the stem at a 45-degree angle.**

■ **Cut stems under water to prevent air bubbles entering the stems.**

■ **Let flowers stand in deep water for several hours before arranging them.**

■ **On woody plants, scrape away the bark on the lower 5 cm (2 in) of the stem, then slit it and recut.**

■ **Remove lower leaves on stems as when they are submerged, they rot, producing gas that can hasten wilting.**

■ **Trim buds that will not blossom to allow more water to go to flowers.**

■ **If you are arranging tulips, add a few drops of vodka to the water to keep the stems standing straight.**

Preserving flowers

Preserve flowers by adding 2 teaspoons medicinal mouthwash to every 4 L (8½ pt) water, although you could also try aspirin or a little sugar. Alternatively, the acid in a clear soft drink also works — add 1 can soft drink to every 4 L (8½ pt) water.

Plant life

Fungus on house plants is unhealthy for you as well as the plant. First, trim badly affected leaves and discard them. Make up a spray using 1 tablespoon bicarbonate of soda to every 4 L (8½ pt) water. Repeat every few days until there is no sign of the fungus.

TO REVIVE CUT FLOWERS Plunge the stems into boiling water. By the time the water is cool, the flowers will have revived. Cut off the ends of the stems and place the flowers in fresh cold water.

Home office

Whether it's a couple of pieces of furniture in the corner of the living room or a custom designed room, a home office has become a common feature of modern households. It may be a place of business, a place to do the household accounts, or just a computer games room for the kids.

For a healthy home office, take care to consider these factors.

- Make sure your desk chair is the correct height and gives adequate support to your lower back. Adjustable swivelling chairs with castors allow the most flexibility in movement and positioning.

- Ensure proper ventilation. A lot of office equipment emits gases such as ozone, which can worsen allergy symptoms.

- Turn off computers, photocopiers and printers when they are not in use as they produce ozone (see 'The clever house', page 27).

- If possible, put photocopiers in a separate room, as they are the worst ozone culprits.

- Ensure there is adequate lighting by placing the desk near a window, with the computer screen at right angles to the window. Set up a good desk lamp.

Caring for your computer

- Place your computer where air can circulate around it.

- Do not expose it to long bursts of sunlight or direct heat.

- Do not store a computer in dusty or damp environments.

- Make sure the cables are not laid next to a heater, nor are likely to be tripped over.

- Do not move the computer when it is running as the hard disc is vulnerable to damage by jarring.

Cleaning office equipment

Home office equipment is often valuable and needs to be cleaned carefully to keep it working at its best.

General equipment

When cleaning and servicing telephones, answering machines, keyboards, printers, photocopiers (body and flat bed glass) and typewriters, read the manufacturers' instructions first before proceeding.

- Dust regularly with a soft cloth and a synthetic paintbrush around buttons and keys.

- To keep items free of marks, wipe them occasionally with a cloth dampened with methylated spirits. (This is not recommended for computer keyboards.)

- Use dust covers on keyboards, printers and typewriters.

The computer

- Dust the screen and body with a damp, lint-free soft cloth. Do not allow moisture to seep into any openings.

- Do not use alcohol or other solvents, abrasives or sprays of any kind.

The keyboard

1   Turn the keyboard upside down to shift crumbs and dust. If you leave these particles to settle deeply, they may cause intermittent faults.

2   Turn the keyboard back the right way up and dust the keys with a small soft paintbrush.

3   If the keyboard is very dusty, use canned air to clear dust from around the keys.

The mouse

1   Remove the track ball cover.

2   Remove the track ball.

3   Clean inside the mouse with a cotton swab dampened with alcohol.

4   Replace the track ball and cover.

ON STUDIES *A great advantage of the separate study or den, from the housewife's point of view...is that it need not be cleaned or even tidied too often. Many men have a rooted dislike of having their highly-organised muddles moved so much as an inch.*

The Book of Good Housekeeping (1947)

the bedroom

The bedroom is the most private room of the house, a room that should promote rest. Make your bed a sanctuary of peace and comfort: buy the best quality bed you can afford and keep it dressed in crisp clean linen.

ONCE A WEEK, *when a bedroom is to be thoroughly cleaned, the housemaid should commence by brushing the mattresses of the bed before it is made; she should then make it, shake the curtains, lay them smoothly on the bed, and pin or tuck up the bottom valance, so that she may be able to sweep under the bed.*

Mrs Beeton's Book of Household Management (1861)

the bedroom

The clever bedroom

The clever bedroom is comfortable and airy. The bed is properly supportive, the bed linen is clean and fresh, the wardrobe is neatly stacked and well ventilated and, for allergy sufferers, the room is as free of dust as possible.

- **The ideal bedroom temperature** should be around 18°C (64.4°F). Children and the elderly are particularly sensitive to temperature.
- **The mattress** has been manufactured for maximum back support.
- **To protect against dust mites,** the mattress and pillow are encased in microporous covers (for allergy sufferers only).
- **Woollen or cotton bedding** is best. It is less flammable than many synthetic fabrics, and also breathes, letting water vapour pass through.
- **Clothes** are well cared for, and hung and stored in such a way as to prolong their life. Old favourites are mended and patched; clothing which has lost favour is recycled or passed on to charity.
- **Children's sleep wear** is made from approved fire-safe fabric. To reduce fire hazards, most countries have strict standards relating to children's sleep wear: choose a fabric that is designated less flammable than others and a snug style that reduces the chance of clothing catching fire.

AIR THE BED Each morning air the bed to allow moisture from the mattress to evaporate. Open the bedroom window first thing in the morning to refresh the air.

The bed

The bed has an interesting history. The first beds were pits dug into the earth and lined with springy vegetation such as grass and bracken. At night, tribespeople cloaked themselves with animal skins to keep warm.

The earliest type of elevated bed was made from a wooden frame latticed with thongs and supported by four forked branches stuck into the ground; a mattress of skins was laid over it. By the end of the Middle Ages wealthy people slept in wooden beds with canopies.

Your bed should be neither too soft nor too hard. A slatted timber base with a quality mattress, such as a pocket sprung mattress made from natural fibres, or a futon, is recommended. Slatted wooden or metal bases provide better air circulation than divans; it is also easier to clean under a raised bed.

A divan bed has a base with a solid-sided frame, sometimes incorporating drawers and storage. It may be fitted with springs and padding, and be covered with fabric. The mattress sits on top.

Bedding

Today's typical well dressed bed wears several layers of bed clothes. First, the mattress is protected by a mattress cover (which also provides some extra comfort) and a bottom sheet. Over the occupant lies a top sheet. For warmth, one or two blankets and/or a doona are placed over the sheet. Both sheets are washable, and they prevent the other bedclothes from getting soiled or irritating the sleeper. A bedspread or cover protects the whole arrangement during the day.

BLANKET STITCH When the edges of your blanket have frayed but the blanket itself still has life, trim any loose threads and use a thick woollen yarn to blanket stitch each side.

Allergy alert: dust mites

Beds are breeding grounds for household dust mites (see 'The clever house', page 33), which love the warmth, moisture and constant supply of skin flakes produced by a sleeping body. If you are sensitive to mites you may find that respiratory problems or even eczema rashes worsen at night. By trying some of the following steps, your symptoms may ease.

SPECIALIZED ANTI-MITE BEDDING

Barrier covers, designed to prevent you coming into contact with the mite allergen, are fitted over mattresses and pillows. The old-fashioned ones are made of plastic, which can make a night's sleep damp and uncomfortable as your body's sweat cannot pass through the cover. Modern covers are made from a soft, microporous material that allows water and air to permeate it. Covers that are impregnated with acaricide (a specialized pesticide which kills acarids such as mice and ticks) are also available.

Bedclothes

■ Clothes and bedding stored in divan drawers should be wrapped in breathable plastic bags to prevent dust mite droppings falling on them.

■ An electric blanket keeps the bed dry, making it less inviting for mites and moulds.

■ Avoid padded headboards, especially buttoned ones.

■ Launder bedding frequently to reduce dust and kill dust mites. Experts recommend washing sheets, pillowcases and doona covers weekly in hot water (56°C/132.8°F or above) to kill dust mites. If you prefer not to wash in hot water — perhaps for environmental reasons — or have bed linen which cannot be washed at 56°C (132.8°F), add a mite-killing chemical such as benzyl benzoate to the wash and give the linen an extra rinse.

PUTTING THE FREEZE ON MITES Place bedclothes, soft toys and favourite blankets in a chest freezer for a few hours, or overnight, to kill mites. You can then wash them out in warm, hot or cold water (or vacuum them if they're not washable).

■ In hot climates, hang bedding in the sun for a few hours.

■ Steam treatments kill mites near the surface but those deep inside mattresses and other soft furnishings remain unaffected. To be effective, the steam must be sufficiently hot for long enough not only to kill the dust mites but also to denature the allergen. Dead mites and allergen must be vacuumed afterwards. Carry out this treatment every three months or so.

■ Doonas are a better allergy option than blankets as you can put them in an anti-mite cover.

When you buy anti-mite bedding, follow these tips.

■ Buy a mattress with a guarantee.

■ Make sure the cover fully encases the mattress, pillow and doona.

■ Choose a water-permeable cover, to allow the fabric to 'breathe'.

■ Don't buy a non-breathable type such as polyvinyl as it is uncomfortable.

- Check that the seams are double stitched for durability and have a good quality zipper.
- Buy a washable cover.
- Buy laminated covers rather than ones coated with polyurethane and polytetrafluroethane.

Furniture

- To reduce the amount of dust on furniture, keep the number of pieces in the bedroom to a minimum.
- Regularly vacuum under the bed.
- Damp dust furniture and ornaments, and keep the tops of tall furniture free of dust.
- To make cleaning easier, choose easy-to-move pieces with a minimum of detailing.
- Keep the doors and drawers of wardrobes and chests closed.
- Remember that upholstered furniture encourages dust mites.
- Keep curtains dust-free by, for example, regularly vacuuming them or, if possible, washing them every three months at 56°C (132.8°F) or above.

The more specialized treatments listed below are sometimes recommended. In many cases a specialist should apply them. In some cases the effect is short-lived, so concentrating first on reducing the dust may be more rewarding. In addition, these treatments can be hard to find in some areas.

- Tannic acid can be used to 'denature' or change the structure of allergens such as pollens as well as the dust mite allergen so that they no longer cause an allergic reaction. It should be applied 3–4 times a year. Although it may discolour pale fabrics and carpets, it is generally considered harmless to people and animals.
- Heat treatment also kills mites and denatures the allergen. This method is suitable for furniture, mattresses, bedding, soft cushions and curtains, and should be done annually. Items are slightly dampened with tannic acid solution and heated to 100°C (212°F) in a tent-like envelope.

■ Liquid nitrogen freezes mites to death and loosens allergen-containing dirt, which can then be removed from bedding and carpets with a vacuum cleaner. This treatment must by applied by a specialist twice a year. It is safe and leaves no residues, but may not be sufficient on its own nor available in all countries or areas.

Flooring

■ Consider removing the carpets and instead fit wooden floors (or another hard surface) and a washable rug.

■ If you choose carpet, vacuum it thoroughly every week.

Ventilation

■ Open windows, air blankets and the doona, and air the bed by pulling down the covers and leaving it for an hour or so before making the bed again.

Vapours

■ Do not hang newly dry-cleaned clothes in your bedroom.

■ Do not smoke.

■ Avoid using hairspray or other strong-smelling toiletries.

■ Keep pets out of your bedroom.

■ Be wary of new curtains, upholstery and floor finishes, all of which can out-gas chemicals.

Babies' bedrooms and bedding

Paradoxically, in preparing a room for a new baby, parents may introduce new hazards: new surfaces may include paints and varnishes, and curtains and carpets can emit numerous gases. Ensure there is excellent ventilation in a newly decorated room and try to finish it well before it needs to be used.

■ When buying a cot, new or second-hand, make sure it meets the manufacturer's cot Standard for your country.

■ The mattress should be firm and clean and exactly the right size for the cot — a baby can become trapped in gaps.

■ The waterproof mattress protector must be a strong and tight fit.

NATURAL HEAT PACK *A bag lightly packed with bran and warmed in the oven for a few minutes retains its heat, and is a substitute for a hot water bottle.*

The Home Lovers Encyclopedia

Sleeping like a baby

Campaigns to reduce the risk of infants succumbing to SIDS (sudden infant death syndrome), or cot death, have focused on the following recommendations.

- **Put your baby to sleep on his back.**
- **Do not cover your baby's head or face while he is sleeping.**
- **Place baby to sleep with his feet at the bottom of the cot.**
- **Tuck in the bedclothes securely.**
- **Do not use quilts, doonas, lambskins, pillows or cot bumpers in the cot.**
- **Do not use electric blankets, hot water bottles or wheat bags.**
- **Avoid smoking during pregnancy.**
- **Do not expose your baby to cigarette smoke, especially in his first year of life.**

A good night's rest

To ensure the best possible night's sleep, consider these tips.

- **Temperature We sleep best between the relatively cool temperatures of 13°C and 19°C (55.4°F and 66.2°F). The elderly and the very young may need a slightly warmer room. If you are too hot, or too cold, you may sleep fitfully. Make sure you have the right weight covers: if you find you feel cold in the early hours of the morning, pulling up a second blanket from the bottom of the bed is probably all you need. While doonas are often too hot for summer, and even a sheet and blanket may be too hot, a sheet alone is not always enough. Try two sheets, or a sheet and a cotton blanket or cover.**
- **The right bedding Are you someone who feels cosier under a heavy pile of blankets? Or do you prefer the lightest of light quilts? The state of your sheets may not make the slightest bit of difference to you, but it's**

THE THOUGHTFUL HOST

Whether your guest accommodation is a sleeping bag on a stretcher bed in the dining room or a comfortable bed in a dedicated guest room, there are some simple details a guest will appreciate.

- Bedside lamp
- Wastepaper bin
- Extra blanket
- Clothes hanger on the back of the door
- Spare toothbrushes and towels

worth making yourself as comfortable as possible. Check out the sheet fabric; perhaps you'll sleep better with cotton sheets. Consider whether your laundry detergent could be causing you irritation.

- **Darkness** Most people sleep better in darkness. Fit heavy curtains to eliminate problems such as street lighting.

- **Relaxation** A warm bath before bedtime can help you to relax and prepare for sleep. Some people find that avoiding caffeine during the afternoon and evening helps.

Cleaning and care of clothes

Looking after the contents of your wardrobe means your clothes will always look their best and last longer.

To prolong the life of your clothes

- Hang your jacket as soon as you take it off rather than sling it on the nearest object.

- Don't launder more often than necessary: if you wear a shirt for just an hour or so, hang it up to air and fasten the top, middle and bottom buttons before putting it back in the wardrobe. If necessary, spot clean it rather than wash it.

- Dirt and sweat cause fabrics to deteriorate, so when clothes really need washing, do it sooner rather than later.

- When doing anything messy, protect clothes with an apron or overall.
- Use a scarf to protect the necks and collars of coats and jackets, especially leather ones, as hair and skin oils can stain.

Putting clothes away

Clothes need air to stay fresh. The cupboards, wardrobes and closets where you store your clothes should be dry and airy. Slatted shelves allow air to circulate: several shallow shelves are more effective than one or two deep ones and have the added benefit of making it easier to find items.

Don't be tempted to put even slightly damp clothes away. Wait until they are bone dry, as even the slightest touch of dampness will give clothes a musty smell that will be hard to remove.

For tailored jackets and skirts or trousers that you don't wash after each wear, air and brush them before putting them away.

Hanging and folding clothing

Many items — jackets, trousers, skirts and dresses — should be hung up rather than folded and placed on a shelf or in a drawer.

Before you hang up your clothes, fasten zips and do up the top, middle and bottom buttons: this will help them to hold their shape. Empty the pockets, especially in wool garments that easily distort.

Hang trousers by the cuffs (the leg bottoms) or fold them over a hanger that has either a thick dowel bar or a paper guard to prevent a horizontal crease forming.

PADDED HANGERS

Wide, shaped clothes hangers prolong the life of tailored clothing by spreading the weight and reducing the stress on the fabric at the point of hanging. They also help preserve shape. Padded hangers do these jobs even better.

Perfect folds

Clothing folded in the correct manner fits more easily into its storage space and stays neater for longer.

To fold a shirt

This basic method is also suitable for t-shirts, casual jackets, sweatshirts and pullovers/jumpers.

1   Fasten the top, middle and bottom buttons, and straighten the shoulders and sleeves.
2   Place the shirt on its front and fold back one shoulder so the shirt's side seam lies in the middle of the back.
3   Fold the sleeve flat.
4   Repeat with the other side.
5   Fold the tails up to make a straight line at the cuffs.
6   Fold in thirds, bring the bottom up towards the waist and the front of the shirt down.

To fold a dress

1   Lay the dress front down.
2   Fold the top as if it were a shirt.
3   Fold the bottom to the knees.
4   Fold at the waist.

To fold trousers with a front crease

1   Align the inside seams with the outer seams of the legs.
2   Give a tug to straighten and create a fold at the front of the legs.
3   Fold in half at the knees.

To fold trousers without a front crease

1   Flatten and smooth the legs.
2   Fold in half lengthways, with the back folding inwards.
3   Fold in half at the knees.

To fold a skirt

1   Lay the skirt front down with zips and fasteners closed.
2   Fold the sides towards the centre.
3   Fold in thirds or halves, depending on the length of the skirt.

To fold a pair of socks

1   Place one sock on top of the other.
2   Fold the top of one sock over the pair.

To fold a suit jacket

If possible, avoid folding a suit jacket. You should always hang it on a hanger and if you are travelling, place it in a garment bag. If you must fold it, follow these steps.

1   Undo the buttons.
2   Put your hands into the shoulders of the jacket.
3   Turn the shoulders inside out by holding on to the shoulder pads.
4   Pull the shoulders together, turning the jacket inside out.
5   Align the seams and sleeves, and smooth and open the lapels.

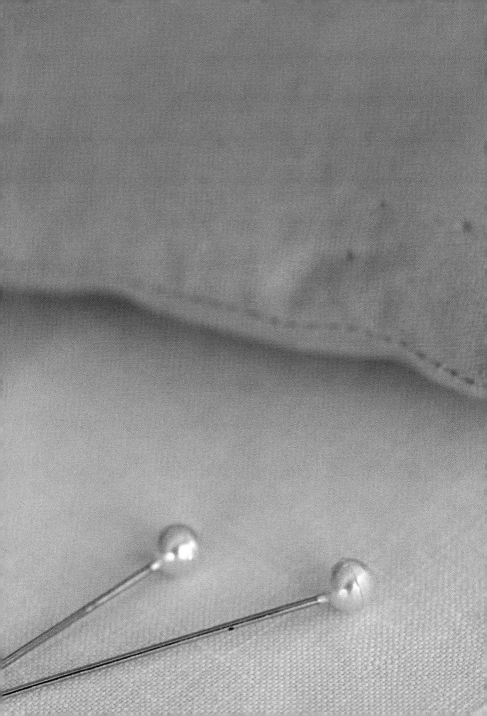

New life for old clothes

Patching, mending, cutting down and reusing clothes used to be a way of life. Nowadays we tend to throw out or give away a piece of clothing as soon as we're bored with it. But you can give clothing a new lease of life. Here are some ideas.

- **Dyeing** When the colours of a garment have faded but the fabric is not worn, dyeing – especially professional dyeing – revitalizes and smartens. This is also a good option for faded towels and bed linen.

- **Darning** Once darning socks was the norm, but these days cheap factory products have almost made it a redundant skill. Darning is still useful for repairing small holes that would otherwise make a woollen item unwearable.

  1 Take care to match the colour of the thread. If darning a patterned garment, using two colours may disguise the repair better.
  2 If possible, work on the wrong side.
  3 Take stitches well beyond the hole into the strong part of the fabric.

- **Patching** This repair method is ideal for children's play clothes and also useful for adults' clothes that can take a bit of character – for example, elbow patches on a comfortable tweed jacket or favourite woolly jumper. Circular or diamond patches wear better and show less than squares and rectangles. Choose soft supple leather for elbow patches and for strips along the end of a sleeve or along the front of a pocket. Cut a generous size that amply covers worn areas with plenty of margin. Use a blanket stitch or buttonhole stitch with a little slack to allow for movement. Use button thread.

- **Shortening** Trousers with holes at or below the knee can become gardening shorts.

- **New buttons** New trims and buttons dress up and contemporize.

- **Fancy dress** Eccentric hats, uncomfortable but glamorous shoes and other purchasing mistakes, especially ones made from unusual fabrics, make desirable items in a children's dress-up box.

- **The cover up** Big old shirts are ideal for dirty work like cleaning, hobbies and gardening.

- **Odd socks** Odd or old socks are useful for storing safety goggles, as ladder end pads and for various jobs around the house, including polishing.

- **Pyjama legs** If not too worn, these can be secured in place over ironing boards.

THE BASIC SEWING KIT

Even if all you do is sew on loose buttons, every house deserves a small repair kit.

- **Scissors** A small pair with sharp points for cutting thread; dressmaking shears if you plan to tackle fabric.

- **Needles** A range according to likely tasks: ordinary, embroidery, darners, upholstery.

- **Thimble** Protects the middle finger when pushing a needle through fabric.

- **Threads** White, black and beige are a good base.

- **Pins, tape measure and fastenings** Include a button collection.

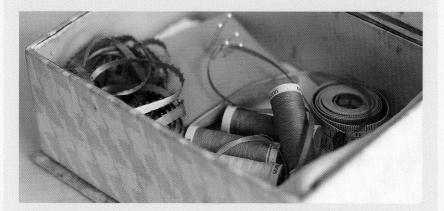

COMMON REPAIRS

- **To mend an L-shaped tear** When clothes catch and tear on a sharp object, pull the edges together and tack them to a piece of finely woven cloth on the wrong side of the fabric. Using threads from the garment, if possible, make a series of diagonal stitches across the tear in one direction, then in the opposite way so they form a trellis pattern.

- **Pockets** A worn pocket is a liability and an unnecessary one at that. For holes in trouser pockets, cut off the worn area and sew in a new piece in a tough fabric such as drill or calico. Alternatively you could fit an entirely new pocket – these are available ready-made if you don't want to start from scratch. To fix patch pockets that have ripped from the back, unpick the top corners, and place a strip of cotton behind the tear or weak area. Fix it with running stitches then lightly darn on the right side. Finally, reattach the pocket firmly.

FRESH AIR

■ To add a fresh smell to your wardrobe or chest of drawers, place a couple of teaspoons of pot pourri or dried lavender in a piece of lightweight fabric such as muslin or cheesecloth and tie with a ribbon.

■ To remove the smell of moth balls: scrub with equal parts white vinegar and lemon juice. Repeat if necessary.

Storing clothes

Before putting clothes away for long-term storage, or to store until next season, make sure you follow this check list.

■ **Do wash or dry-clean them. Dirt is more likely to attract pests such as insects, and encourage mildew.**

■ **Do air items, especially ones you've steam ironed or damped down before ironing.**

■ **Do use muslin or canvas storage bags, or clean white or undyed sheets.**

■ **Do place items on wire racks rather than shelves to allow air to circulate properly.**

■ **Don't starch items to be stored as starch attracts meal-seeking silverfish, which do not discriminate between the starch and the clothing fibre.**

■ **Don't store in dry-cleaning plastic or other garment bags that do not breathe as moisture may be trapped inside. In addition, dry-cleaning bag plastic may cause yellow streaks over time due to plasticizers.**

■ **Don't put clothes or shoes away while they are still damp.**

For advice on storing household linen, see 'The laundry', page 178.

WRINKLE LESS When packing a suitcase or putting away valuable clothes, placing tissue paper (acid-free for storage) between fabric layers with the garments themselves helps reduce creasing and wrinkling.

Moths

The webbing clothes moth (*Tineola bisselliella*) is the most common fabric moth. It is particularly attracted to wool and furs, and its larvae eat the fibres, leaving a rash of holes. Stored, unused clothing is most vulnerable as moths do not attack clothes that are in constant use. Regular airing and shaking does much to guard against moth attack. Pockets should be turned out and fluff brushed off.

Rid clothes of insects by washing in hot water, 50–60°C (122–140°F), or by dry-cleaning. It is important to do this before storing the clothes.

NATURAL MOTH TREATMENTS

- If you suspect moths have invaded an article, wrap it in a clean damp towel, and put it in a low oven to steam out the grubs, or place it underneath a damp towel and press it with a hot iron.
- If you can actually see moths, brush the article with a solution of 3 tablespoons turpentine and 2.8 L (3 qt) water.
- To defend drawers and cupboards from moth invasion, keep them free from dust and fluff by regularly airing and vacuuming them. Wipe over with a repellent such as eucalyptus oil.
- Cotton wool buds dipped in essential oils are said to keep moths away from clothing. Try lavender, lemon grass, camphor or rosemary and place a couple in each drawer between items of clothing. Or dot a few drops of essential oil on sheets of blotting paper, fix the scent with orris root powder and use them as drawer liners.
- Herbal deterrents include sachets of cedar chips, dried lavender flowers, dried rosemary or southernwood. Place these among your clothes, where they not only help to deter moths and silverfish, they also keep clothes smelling fresh.
- Line drawers with brown paper, butchers' paper or wallpaper off-cuts. Scatter herbal repellents underneath the paper.
- Make sachets from light fabrics such as muslin and fill them with a mixture of ground cloves, nutmeg, mace, caraway seeds, cinnamon (30 g or 1 oz each) and orris root powder (90 g/3 oz). This amount of mixture will fill several sachets.

If these treatments cause irritation you may need to store moth-vulnerable clothing in sealed plastic bags.

Commercial moth treatments are not only toxic to moths, but also to humans. They include naphthalene and PDB (paradichlorobenzene), which is an organochlorine. They kill moths, larvae and eggs in an airtight situation where they saturate the insects. If you must resort to these, they are best used only in spaces that are not living areas, such as attics or garages.

Cleaning and care of shoes

- Shoes will last longer if given one day's rest after wearing to allow moisture to evaporate, so have at least two pairs for each season.
- Keep your shoes on shoe trees when not in use to keep the shape and avoid cracking.
- Caring for the leather helps prevent cracks developing.
- Use a hard brush to remove mud; never scrape with a knife.
- Repair damaged shoes as soon as they need it. Delaying repair is a false economy.

SHOE CARE KIT

- Stiff brush for removing dried mud
- Soft woollen rags or old wool socks for applying polish
- Soft polishing brushes, separate ones for each polish colour

WATERPROOFING WITH TALLOW *A good way of making new shoes or boots waterproof is to rub the soles with tallow. Continue to rub it in until the leather will absorb no more; the grease will clog the leather and make it waterproof.*

The Book of Hints and Wrinkles

TO WATERPROOF FOOTWEAR, THE OLD-FASHIONED WAY Melt equal quantities of beeswax and mutton suet. Rub over the top and soles while still liquid and wipe off the excess.

TO REMOVE MILDEW ON LEATHER Rub vigorously with petroleum jelly.

To soften leather

- Rub with lemon juice or castor oil. Olive oil helps prevent the leather from cracking and drying.

- To help wear in new shoes, carefully pour a small amount of methylated spirits or rubbing alcohol into the shoes at the heels and let it soak in. Wear the shoes while still wet.

- Where a shoe pinches over a toe or joint, press a very hot damp cloth over the spot, and leave it for a few minutes so that it expands and softens the leather.

TO FRESHEN UP SUEDE SHOES *Brush gently with fine glass paper or with a fine wire brush. When too shabby to wear, smear well with metal paste (out of a box), or boot polish, and brush it in very hard. Do this several days in succession, and the shoes will then look like kid ones.*

Household Hints, *The Olio Cookery Book*

REPAIRING CUTS IN LEATHER *A pebble beach at the seaside is the greatest enemy for shoes, for walking among pebbles cuts up the leather. The best way to repair the damage is to rub them well with warm milk, to which a teaspoonful of soda has been added. Wait until they are dry, then polish in the usual way.*

The Book of Hints and Wrinkles

Removing stains on shoes

Always proceed with caution, especially for pale-coloured footwear.

- Grease stains on leather **Daub with petrol then egg white.**
- Grease stains on suede **Rub with rag dipped in glycerine.**
- Tar **Remove with petrol.**
- Other stains **Sponge with a solution of warm water and vinegar. Polish when dry with a soft cloth soaked in linseed oil. Remove all traces of the oil with a soft clean cloth.**

TO DEODORIZE SHOES Sprinkle bicarbonate of soda inside. Leave for a day or two, then shake out and air.

Drying shoes

Leather that remains wet can become irreversibly damaged; drying wet shoes too quickly can cause cracking.

- **Never dry shoes in front of a fire or heater.**
- **Stuff shoes with balls of newspaper or sand — the latter dries them quickly without altering their shape.**
- **Fine leather shoes can be revived after a dousing if you coat them in oil or petroleum jelly. Boots and tougher shoes can be rubbed down with saddle soap.**
- **To polish leather that is a little damp, first rub over with a cloth to which a few drops of kerosene have been added.**

Storing shoes

The best shoe treatment consists of using shoe trees to keep them straight. If you store shoes for a long period, put them in individual shoe bags or wrap them in tissue paper.

Cleaning and care of accessories

There's not much use keeping your clothes looking clean and in good order if you don't do the same for the bits and pieces that go with them.

Old-fashioned ways with hats

■ To clean a straw hat **Brush dirt off with a clean vegetable brush. Place on a light coloured surface. Starting at the top, apply a hydrogen peroxide solution diluted with an equal quantity of water: little by little wet it, scrub it, then dry with a clean towel. Dry in the shade. Reblock the hat — the milliner's term for reshaping — by moulding the crown over a pudding basin while still damp.**

■ To revitalize a panama hat **Beat together an egg white, the juice of half a lemon and a teaspoon of salt. Apply the mixture evenly to the hat with a brush. Wipe off the excess with a damp cloth, and dry away from direct sunlight.**

■ To stiffen straw **Brush on the wrong side with one of the following: egg white, white hard varnish or gum arabic.**

■ To clean a felt hat **Brush to remove dust, then clean according to colour.**
   1 **Dark felt** Rub with a cloth dipped in household ammonia.
   2 **Light felt** Rub with hot oatmeal or hot fuller's earth.
   3 **Grey felt** Brush with hot bran.
   4 **White felt** Brush with a thin paste of magnesia and water. Leave to dry, then brush off.

Storing hats

To keep dust at bay and prevent denting them, store hats with care.

■ **In hat boxes on a shelf**

■ **Wrapped in clean muslin**

■ **With their crowns stuffed with tissue**

HAT TRICKS After gently hand washing a beret in warm soapy water, rinse, roll in a towel to remove excess water, then slip it over a matching size plate to dry. This will help to keep its shape. Press with a slightly damp cloth.

Jewellery

A little bit of knowledge goes a long way when looking after jewels.

- **Do store precious jewels in padded boxes or bags to protect against sunlight, dust and humidity.**

- **Do avoid extremes of temperature.**

- **Do keep precious pieces separate from each other to protect against scratches and tangles.**

- **Do take extra care cleaning jewellery with loose stones as the dirt may be all that is holding them in place.**

- **Do take the gentler options first when cleaning, starting with a soft brush such as a paint or make-up brush on very dusty pieces.**

- **Do take valuable pieces to professionals for cleaning if you are in the slightest doubt about how to go about it yourself.**

- **Don't spray accidentally with hairspray or perfume as these can dull some surfaces.**

- **Don't use any substance on jewellery without being absolutely sure it is recommended for all the materials the jewel is made from. This includes water, detergent, ammonia, bicarbonate of soda and jewellery cleaning cloths and dips.**

How to wash jewellery

A lot of jewellery can be washed in a mild detergent and water solution, and gently brushed with soft bristles, but stones set with glue should not be washed. While transparent gems such as diamonds, sapphire and ruby are hard and do not absorb water, opaque gems such as opal, amber and so on should be wiped only with a damp cloth then patted dry. (See also 'Do not wash', opposite.)

Hard water can leave a chalky residue on precious stones. If you live in a hard water area, clean with distilled water.

Never clean jewellery in the sink as you risk losing pieces down the drain should they come apart. Use a bowl instead.

WHAT ABOUT AMMONIA?

Many experts recommend ammonia for cleaning jewels such as diamonds, and many proprietary jewellery cleaners contain ammonia. If you want to give it a go, be sure that it is safe for the particular piece you have in mind. Ammonia will damage many substances, including pearls. Generally, ammonia is usually thought to be safe for hard stones such as diamonds, rubies and sapphires. When using ammonia, add 1 part ammonia to 4 parts warm water in a jar or bowl. Let jewels soak for five minutes to loosen the dirt, brush gently and rinse. Use a soft lint-free cloth to dry.

Once you are sure a jewel can be washed, proceed as follows.

1   Put some water and some washing up liquid into a small bowl: hot water (not boiling) is fine for diamonds, otherwise use lukewarm water.

2   Soak for 15 minutes to loosen the dirt.

3   Rinse.

4   With a small soft brush — for instance, a baby's toothbrush or a paintbrush — work detergent into the crevices.

5   Rinse and dry on a lint-free cloth such as a tea towel.

DO NOT WASH

The following substances are relatively soft and may absorb not only water but also chemicals, including soap or other cleaners.

- Amber
- Bone
- Coral
- Ivory
- Lapis lazuli

- Malachite
- Mother-of-pearl
- Opal
- Shells
- Turquoise

CLEANING JEWELS THE OLD-FASHIONED WAY

Store very precious jewels in cotton wool in their cases. To remove tarnish, prepare clean soap suds from fine toilet soap. Dip jewels — gold, silver, gilt and precious stones — into the suds. Dry with a brush of soft badger's hair or a fine sponge. Polish with a piece of fine cloth and finally with a piece of soft leather.

Caring for pearls

Wearing pearls often is said to be the best way to care for them, as the oils in your skin give them a gentle lustre.

- Do not wrap pearls in cotton or wool as the extra heat this generates can dry them out and cause cracking.
- Dampen pearls from time to time in lightly salted water.
- After wearing pearls, wipe them with a soft cloth or chamois leather, dry or damp, to remove traces of perspiration, which, being acidic, can damage the pearl surface.
- If your pearls are really dirty, wash them in water and a very mild soap, then clean them with a soft cloth. Lay them on a moist kitchen towel to dry. The pearls will be dry at the same time as the towel.

Caring for wooden beads, bangles and brooches

Wipe with a damp chamois cloth and rub well with a little olive oil. Finally, buff with a soft cloth.

Caring for glass beads

Shake glass beads in a plastic bag with 2 tablespoons bicarbonate of soda. Dust with a soft brush and buff with a damp chamois cloth.

Leather bags and luggage

Before cleaning an item of luggage, check the manufacturer's care label as both leather and suede are available in two different types — one can be washed but the other should be dry-cleaned.

Use different methods of cleaning for different types of leather.

- **Brush suede with a suede brush or an off-cut of suede.**
- **Finish leather with wax polish to keep it supple.**
- **Smear petroleum jelly on patent leather then buff it dry.**

LUGGAGE DEODORIZER To rid a trunk or suitcase of a musty smell, place an open tin containing clay-type cat litter inside. Close the trunk or case lid and leave it overnight.

Leather bags

- **Rub leather bags over with neat's-foot oil from time to time, or polish with boot polish.**
- **To renovate an old leather bag, use a warm, not hot, solution of washing soda to remove grease and dirt. Apply it with a soft rag or a brush if it is very dirty. Oxalic acid, used after the soda, may remove stains. After cleaning, wash with lukewarm water, place in a warm spot to dry and once dry, treat with a wax polish.**

the outdoors

Clever housekeeping outside as well as indoors makes sense on health, environmental and aesthetic grounds. Surfaces and materials get an extra battering from the elements; wet pavers and paths can be alarmingly slippery after the rain if they're covered in mildew; cleaning routines with garbage bins and correct composting keep pests down, while alternative methods of controlling weeds reduce the amounts of potentially toxic chemicals around your living areas.

In fine weather *the old gentleman is almost constantly in the garden…He has always something to do there, and you will see him digging, and sweeping, and cutting, and planting, with manifest delight…*

Charles Dickens, *Sketches by Boz* (1839)

the outdoors

The clever garden

A carefully planned garden is an enticing haven for its inhabitants as well as environmentally friendly.

- **Shrubs** **around the house will have a cooling effect on your home as plants don't absorb and retain heat as much as concrete.**

- **Trees** **provide shade, and act as a windbreak and noise and air filter.**

- **Deciduous trees** **near north-facing windows in the southern hemisphere, and south-facing in the northern hemisphere, allow the maximum amount of sun in the winter when the branches are bare. In the summer they provide shade.**

- **Pergolas and trellises** **covered in trailing deciduous vines add shade in the summer while allowing light through in the winter.**

- **Native bushes** **between the house and road absorb noise and fumes as well as attract native birds to the garden.**

- **A compost heap and worm farm** **are used to recycle biodegradable household waste and garden clippings into a natural fertilizer and mulch that can be put back into the garden.**

- **Mulch** **is used on garden beds to maximize water retention and to suppress weeds.**

- **A rainwater tank** **augments the town water supply.**

- **Grey water** **is channelled onto the lawn rather than wasted.**

- **A fixed watering system** **delivers water directly to where it is needed without wasteful run-off.**

- **A small kitchen garden** **provides an abundant supply of fresh herbs and salad vegetables.**

- **Companion planting** **helps to deter pests without the use of chemicals.**

A safe, organic garden

Efforts to reduce your home's impact on the environment are particularly rewarding in the garden: there are many ways to reduce the amount of water you use; kitchen scraps and other biodegradable household waste can be composted and returned to your garden. With a little extra care and observation you can grow a more abundant, healthy garden without relying on pesticides and herbicides.

Health and safety measures are especially important in the garden. Great care should be taken with correct storage of the many dangerous chemicals that lurk in the shed or garage. In many places fences around pools are required by law. There's little point worrying about indoor pollution if you regularly pour toxic chemicals on your garden paths and flower beds and take no precautions when you use them. Regular cleaning and tidying outside also uncovers maintenance jobs that you can attend to, preferably before they become major undertakings.

BASIC GARDEN CLEANING EQUIPMENT

- Wire brush
- Scrubbing brush
- Outdoor broom
- Bucket
- Hose
- Rags
- Newspaper
- Sponges

GARDEN FURNITURE *The important points about garden furniture are that it should be light to carry, should stow away into a small space when not required, and that any fabric used for it should be durable, damp resistant and bright in colour.*

The Concise Household Encyclopedia (c. 1940s)

Clean and pleasant gardens

Gardens are usually more relaxed places when it comes to cleaning and tidying. But keeping things looking their best often prolongs their life too, saving us the expense of replacements.

Barbecue

The heat of a barbecue burns off old grease and dirt, but you can prevent the build-up of burnt remains in the first place by doing a little cleaning up after a cooking session. Brush off what you can with a wire brush, then wipe with scrunched up old newspaper. Give metal cooking plates an extra rub with a little salt or sand while they're still warm and oil them before storing.

Bricks and stone pavers

Usually brushing with an outdoor broom is enough to keep bricks and stone pavers looking good, especially as a little weathering improves their appearance. If mould and mildew become a problem, however, scrub the bricks and pavers with a mild solution of household bleach, leave for 48 hours, then rinse with a hose.

Removing weeds between pavers mechanically — digging, snipping or pulling out — is kindest on the environment. You can also try killing them with hot water. Borax is a low-risk weed killer, but don't use it where it could leach onto beds or lawn as it is poisonous to all plants and does not discriminate. Soap herbicides, with the active ingredient of fatty acid, are also safe for the environment. See page 327 for advice on using these.

Canvas awnings and umbrellas

Brush off any dirt and debris then scrub with a hard-bristled brush dipped in warm water and detergent. Rinse. For stubborn stains, sprinkle with bicarbonate of soda, leave for five minutes, then rinse with the hose or a bucket of clean water. This will also help remove musty odours.

Remove mildew stains with a weak solution of bleach, but test for colourfastness first. Leave the bleach solution for 48 hours, then rinse. If you prefer to avoid bleach, try rubbing the mildew with half a cut lemon dipped in salt. Always allow canvas to dry completely before putting it away.

Concrete paths and paving stones

Sweep concrete paths and pavers regularly with a stiff brush and occasionally wash them with hot water and detergent. To spruce up concrete, sprinkle cement powder over wet concrete and leave for about ten minutes before sweeping up the excess.

Driveway

If you always park your car in the same spot and you're concerned about drips of grease and oil, place a shallow metal tray filled with sawdust or fine sand under the engine area. To remove oil stains, first blot any excess with something absorbent such as old newspaper or cat litter (work it in with a stiff broom), then blot again with a rag soaked in a grease solvent. Suitable solvents include methylated spirits and turpentine. You can also try a strong household bleach cleaner. Make up a high-strength solution according to the manufacturer's instructions, apply liberally on the stain, leave for ten minutes, then wash away.

Flyscreens

First, remove dust and cobwebs from flyscreens with a soft brush, then wipe over with a sponge dipped in warm water. Rinse with clean water to which a few drops of citronella or tea-tree oil have been added.

Garbage bins

Regularly washing your garbage bins with detergent helps to keep the smells at bay. Scrub off hardened dirt with a stiff brush and rinse with the garden hose. To deter flies, wipe around the top of each bin with citronella or tea-tree oil. Alternatively, soak strips of old sheet in a repellent solution made from 10 drops citronella oil and 3 drops peppermint oil mixed in 1 L (13/4 pt) water. Hang the strips inside the bin.

Garden furniture

- Furniture made from sealed wood should be wiped with a damp sponge dipped in a detergent solution. Keep an eye on cracks in the sealer and renew it regularly to maintain effective protection.

- Give unsealed wood a protective coat once a year by rubbing in a mixture of 4 parts raw linseed oil and 1 part turpentine.

- Wash cane furniture with warm salty water and leave it to dry in the sun. Protect cane pieces by painting them with an outdoor lacquer.

- Wash canvas furniture as you would canvas awnings (see opposite).

- Lubricate metal hinges with oil or petroleum jelly.

- Use a chamois cloth to wipe over metal frames. Liquid wax polish helps prevent rusting.

Guttering

The only gutters worth having are clean ones: leaf- and dirt-filled ones don't work properly when it rains and are a fire hazard in dry hot weather. To prevent a serious build-up of leaves and other debris, fit mesh along the gutter. This will protect the downpipes from blockage.

Clean gutters regularly. Use a trowel, plastic scraper or stiff brush to remove debris and built-up dirt, then give the gutters a good hose. Check the downpipe on a regular basis for blockages; use hot water to loosen any encrusted dirt before flushing the pipe with the hose.

Ponds

A healthy pond looks after itself: its ecosystem of plants and animals acts like a living filter. But if this system gets out of balance and the pond becomes choked with vegetation, or fish become diseased, you need to take action. Seek the advice of an aquarium expert before emptying the pond and possibly fitting a filter.

Spas

Regularly empty and clean your outdoor spa by following the manufacturer's instructions. If you plan to keep the spa constantly full, you'll need a filter system.

Swimming pools

You'll need plenty of equipment to keep your pool hygienic and clear of leaves and other debris. Chlorine or other chemicals keep bacteria and algae counts down. You can test for the right chlorine and pH levels with special kits. Scrub algae off the steps and pool sides with a nylon brush. Specialized vacuum cleaners and filter systems clean the water but you'll also need to regularly skim a leaf net over the surface.

Keeping the area around the pool tidy and free of leaves will help keep the pool clean too. Sweep regularly and keep plants trimmed, and make sure pavers are free of mould by cleaning them regularly with a mild solution of bleach. Leave for 48 hours, then rinse and brush with a stiff outdoor brush.

Ventilators

Vents in your house walls need checking and cleaning so air can breeze through. Make sure you prune nearby trees and shrubs. Clean small holes with a bottle brush.

Cleaning windows

There is something very satisfying about seeing sun stream through a gleamingly clear pane of glass. Like any job, you need the best tools to do it properly.

You'll need the following equipment.

- **Steady ladder to reach higher windows. Call a window cleaner if you're unsteady on your feet or suffer vertigo.**
- **Bucket of cleaning solution – a commercial one, or see the home-made alternatives on page 308**
- **Sponge**
- **Squeegee – handle with a thin stripe of sponge on one side and a rubber strip on the other**
- **Clean cloth**
- **Newspaper**

WINDOW TIPS

- To prevent windows from fogging, rub over a little glycerine after cleaning them.
- For a quick clean, when the glass is not too dirty: try wiping windows first with wet newspaper, then with dry. The ink on the newspaper gives them a polish.
- Never try to clean a window with a dry cloth as the dirt could scratch the glass.
- Never use soap on windows as it leaves smears that are very difficult to remove.

Cleaning solutions

Commercial window cleaners contain a combination of water, alcohol and ammonia. They do not contain any abrasives that might scratch the glass, nor soaps and detergents that could leave a film on it. The ammonia helps lift off greasy dirt while the alcohol removes other types of particles and aids in evaporation of the solution from the window.

Getting started

If you plan to clean or wash the window frames too, do these before you wash the glass. Wipe or dust the frames first and if that's not enough, follow with a wash and wipe dry. The best sort of day to wash windows is a cloudy one as sun on the windows causes the glass to dry too quickly and unevenly, resulting in streaks.

First, starting at the top of the window, wash the window with a cloth or sponge. Some people swear by rinsing with clean water then a wipe of chamois, others not. It probably depends on how dirty the windows were to begin with and whether this is a grand annual ritual or a fortnightly routine. Following the wash or the rinse, squeegee the surface or dry it with a clean dry, lint-free cloth.

For really dry, sparkly windows, polish with a few sheets of newspaper.

REMOVING MARKS FROM GLASS

TYPE OF MARK	METHOD
Wet paint	Wipe with a cloth dipped in the appropriate solvent — turpentine for oil-based paints, water for water-based paint
Old paint	Gently scrape the paint with a razor blade, taking care not to scratch the glass
Putty marks	Wipe with ammonia or cold tea

HOME-MADE WINDOW CLEANERS

Recipe 1

1 cup white vinegar
4 L (8½ pt) water

Recipe 2

½ cup white vinegar
½ cup household ammonia
4 L (8½ pt) water

Recipe 3

1 cup methylated spirits
1 cup water
¼ cup household ammonia

From kitchen to garden

By far the largest proportion of household rubbish consists of kitchen scraps, which are highly biodegradable and can be composted or processed by a worm farm. Worm farms take up very little space, so even someone living in a flat or apartment can use one. Composting takes a little more room, but as well as diverting rubbish away from landfill or garbage tips, composting provides you with valuable fertilizer for your garden. Alternatively, your local authority may know of community gardens that would welcome composting materials.

Constructing a compost heap

The secret to good composting is layering. Whether you create your own heap in a corner of your garden or use a special compost container from a gardening store, start with some basic layers, as follows.

1   **Start off with a layer of woody prunings to raise the heap and allow air to circulate.**

2   **Next, add garden trimmings such as prunings and old plants, plus fruit and vegetable peel.**

3   **Add a third layer of grass cuttings and leaves.**

Repeat these three layers to speed up the rotting process.

Finally, cover the heap with a piece of old carpet or straw to prevent moisture escaping and to keep heat within the compost heap.

As you add to the compost, intersperse moist and dry layers. Keep the heap damp but not wet to encourage the breakdown of material. Turn the heap regularly to improve aeration, which in turn speeds up the rotting process.

TEMPERATURE TIP If your compost is attracting cockroaches, maggots, rats or mice, add grass clippings to raise the internal temperature of the heap and keep pests at bay.

COMPOSTING CHECKLIST

Almost any biodegradable household waste can be composted.

- **Fruit and vegetable peelings** Some are particularly valuable. For instance, banana peel is high in potassium.
- **Tea and coffee** Tea leaves are rich in nitrogen. Coffee grounds contain protein and oils.
- **Waste paper** Cardboard and paper are useful because of their carbon content. Place cardboard at the bottom of the heap or packed around the sides. Paper works best if shredded.
- **Meat and fish** As these are organic they are suitable for composting but they tend to attract flies and sometimes vermin. Place them directly in the inside of an already composting heap and the heat will be sufficient to break down the flesh and kill maggots, while a covering of soil and grass clippings or sawdust will deter flies.

The lowly worm

Gardeners already know the value of the earthworm, toiling away aerating and refining the soil. In worm farms, they are also fastidious recyclers of kitchen waste and will turn your scraps into rich soil you can use in the garden or indoors for houseplants. Local councils often have information on worm farms or factories and may even provide subsidized ones.

A typical worm factory consists of a series of stacked plastic trays inhabited by a starter population of, for instance, 1000 worms on a compost-like bedding. These are compost worms, which naturally exist in the top 30 cm (1 ft) or so of soil, as opposed to earthworker worms, which burrow much deeper. Compost worms eat almost anything of plant or animal origin, converting it to castings and liquid fertilizer, which is drained off through a tap at the bottom of the trays. Once they have adapted to a new food source, worms eat up to their own body weight every day. As they eat the food in one tray, they move up to the next, leaving their castings or poo behind.

Here are a few tips for successful worm farming.

▦ **Mashed please** Worms eat more scraps if they are mashed or blended! While this may not be practical, it's worth bearing in mind that they prefer soft foods. Food for them can include: vegetable and fruit scraps and peelings, tea leaves, bags and coffee grounds, vacuum cleaner dust and hair or fur clippings, soaked and torn newspapers and cartons, and crushed egg shells.

▦ **Acids later** While they will eat them, worms will leave acidic foods such as orange peel or onion skins until other, preferred food is eaten.

▦ **A little lime** Garden lime helps counteract the effect of acidic food – a handful or so every few weeks is sufficient.

▦ **Mature manure only** Worms can process manure from horses, cattle and dogs, but it's best to let them mature for 1–2 months as chemicals in fresh manure could kill a whole worm farm in a day.

▦ **Breeding like worms** A worm farm takes 2–5 years to mature, at which point it may support up to 20 000 worms.

▦ **Holiday haven** Worm farms can be left for 3–4 weeks without you having to add food as long as they already have a good supply, and are left in a cool spot under cover with the tap open.

GARDEN SAFETY CHECKLIST

▦ Make sure pool fences are maintained and gates closed when young children are about.
▦ Lock garages and sheds.
▦ Keep play areas well away from driveways.
▦ Keep play equipment in good condition.
▦ Trim branches at children's eye level.
▦ Keep pathways clear.

Water wise in the garden

Around a third of household water is used in the garden, so any steps you take outside to reduce your usage will have a big impact on your overall household water consumption. By choosing fewer thirsty plants you can reduce the amount of watering your garden requires. You can ensure plants get the maximum drink by watering at optimum times of the day. Collecting rainwater for watering the garden, and with more care, for drinking, takes the pressure off the public water services, while using grey water — the term coined for water that's already been used in the home, for instance, for washing clothes — is an especially useful type of recycling.

Gardening with less water

Here are some ways to avoid excessive use of the hose in your garden.

- **Natives Native plants, whether they are shrubs or trees, tend to need less water than exotics.**

- **Windbreaks Plant windbreaks to reduce the drying effect of the wind, and cover bare soil either by planting or by placing pavers and boulders. Bare soil heats up in the sun, drawing moisture from underneath to the top, where it evaporates.**

- **Mulch Mulching garden beds with clippings and leaves will help stop the soil from drying out and reduce your watering needs.**

- **Maximize Efficient watering makes the most of the water you use.**
  - Avoid using a hose in the middle of the day, when water will evaporate quickly.
  - Fit timers to sprinklers.
  - Choose sprinklers with big drops, not fine mists, which are blown away.
  - Consider installing a fixed watering system with drip-feeders that deliver water directly to plant roots and eliminate wasteful run-off.
  - Group plants together according to their watering needs.
  - Water slowly to allow water to soak into the soil rather than run away.

- **Train Give your garden a good soak once a week rather than a daily drip. This effectively 'trains' your plants, encouraging bigger and deeper root systems and thus hardier plants. Frequent watering results in shallow roots, which aren't so good at seeking out water.**

■ Sweep **Use a broom, not a hose, to clear paths and courtyards.**

■ Green grass **Lawns tend to be thirsty and mowing them often uses polluting fuel. Consider grasses that need less water and different kinds of ground cover altogether. If you stick with a lawn, keep the grass on the long side, say about 2 cm (3/4 in), to shade the ground. Water no more than twice a week even when it's hot. Where possible, wash the car on the lawn and give the grass a watering at the same time.**

Raindrops keep falling: Collecting rainwater

At its simplest, rainwater can be collected straight from the sky into bins and barrels for watering the garden or washing the car. But much more can be obtained by channelling it from the roof into a tank. If you are thinking of installing a rainwater tank, check with your local authority about restrictions on size, height and location of the tank. Depending on what you intend to use the water for, you'll also need to consider the capacity of the tank. The average household uses hundreds of litres or gallons of water a day; rainfall varies considerably from place to place. Some local authorities may advise on choosing a tank.

WATER FROM HEAVEN

A sophisticated rainwater collecting system could work like this.

■ Rain falls on the roof and enters covered guttering. Covered gutters keep out any leaves and other solid matter that is on the roof.

■ Water flows from the downpipe through another type of mesh that acts as a backstop to keep out any leaves which somehow entered the gutter.

■ The first 10 or so litres (2 1/2 gal) of collected rain wash straight to the garden, and only after the roof has had a good clean is water diverted to another filtering device, called a sump, and then to the rainwater tank.

■ A pump attached to the rainwater tank allows you to use water from the tank for household appliances such as washing machines and dishwashers that require a minimum water pressure to operate.

■ Regular testing of the collected water indicates how suitable it is for drinking. Filters can also be fitted to taps to eliminate any lead in the water that may be present in the rainwater or leached from piping in the house.

Other considerations include what the tank is made from — usually concrete or galvanized iron (although other materials include fibreglass and recycled plastic); where the tank will be positioned (either buried or raised); and what it is lined with (linings may increase the life of the tank and enhance water quality). Whatever you choose, you need a non-porous tank interior to discourage algal growth.

With storage tanks and pumps, rainwater can be used in the house, for washing clothes or flushing the toilet, for instance. If tests show it is clean and uncontaminated, it can even provide drinking water.

Toxic tip

Rooftops make fantastic catchment areas for water, but you need to be careful about roofing materials that can contaminate the water.

Don't use:

- **Lead-based paints**
- **Tar-based roof paints**
- **Asbestos**

Do use:

- **Ceramic tiles**
- **Slate tiles**
- **Galvanized iron**

Use cement and metal tiles as long as the first few rainfalls are diverted to the garden, as new cement leaches lime and new metal may leach heavy metals.

MOSQUITO PREVENTION Rainwater tanks are potential mosquito breeding grounds. To keep mosquitoes out, ensure that any tops, lids, covers and inlet pipes are close fitting; fit a removable screen to the water inlet and overflow pipes; and make sure the tank is properly sealed.

A bright future for grey water

Water used in the house — in the kitchen, the bath and shower, the toilet and the washing machine — can, in theory, be used again in a useful manner, reducing the amount of water the household uses overall. The garden is an obvious recipient. How readily recyclable your used water is depends on what it contains — that is, what you've put into it.

- Laundry water may contain soaps, detergents, water softeners, bleaches, lint, dirt, skin and faecal matter.

- Bathroom water can hold soaps, shampoos, hair, skin, oil, faecal matter and urine. Water from the basin may contain toothpaste, mouthwash, shaving cream and other toiletries.

- Kitchen water usually contains detergents, soaps, food scraps, grease and oil.

- Toilet water contains bacteria from faeces and nitrogen from urine as well as toilet paper, disinfectants, toilet cleaners and fresheners.

It doesn't take a degree in environmental health to realize that reusing water safely takes some planning and forethought. Quite apart from the risk of catching nasty diseases, the problems include the following.

- Salts in detergents — particularly powders, cleaners and softeners — may alter the pH of the soil, making it more acid or more alkaline. This can affect how the soil drains, especially if used water is adding to already present salts in the soil. Indications that problems are afoot include water sitting on the soil rather than soaking in, 'burnt' leaves and stunted plants.

- Boron in some laundry products may poison plants.

- Bleaches and disinfectants can poison plants and destroy useful micro-organisms in the soil.

- Nutrients such as phosphorus and nitrogen in the used water may be beneficial for some plants but harmful to others, so you need to be selective about where water is used.

- Oil and grease in kitchen water may form a waterproof barrier over the soil, preventing water seeping into the soil in a normal fashion.

Laundry and kitchen water are more suitable for recycling if you use low-phosphate detergents or soaps (see 'The laundry', page 124). Liquid detergent, especially concentrate, is preferable to ones with fillers and softeners. Adding organic matter and gypsum to the soil will reduce problems, as will mulching the soil. Grease-laden kitchen water can always be used on a compost heap without problems.

WANT TO KNOW MORE?

Many issues regarding collecting rainwater and reusing household water are quite technical. It's important to obtain the right information and advice that is relevant to your area. Some of the following may be able to assist with technical publications, practical knowledge or may point you in the right direction of experts who can help.

- Environment groups such as Friends of the Earth
- Local water suppliers
- Environmental protection agencies
- Local government

Getting your grey water to the garden

You know what you want to do with your grey water, but how do you get it from the bathroom or laundry to where it's needed in the garden? The answer can be as simple as carrying it in a bucket…or something a little more sophisticated.

- Bucket **Scoop used water from the bath or laundry tub and carry it outside. If you can disconnect the drain, place a bucket below the sink under the plug hole.**

- Siphon **Siphoning aids, available from hardware stores, will let you take water straight outside from the laundry tub to the garden via a hose.**

- Washing machine to large hose **Fit a flexible drain hose to the outlet of your washing machine.**

- Inspection hole funnel **There is usually an inspection hole at the point where drainpipes leave the house. A specially designed funnel can be fitted to this hole, then attached to a hose that will take water to the garden.**

■ Valves Valves such as a Suldi valve or a combination called a T piece and gate valve let you choose when to divert water to your garden and when to let it run down the drain. They can be installed below the laundry tub or where the plumbing leaves the house.

■ Surge tank This lets you slow down the flow, or hold used water in, for instance, a large drum, before releasing it to the garden. Filters can be fitted to remove lint or other solid matter.

■ Sand filter Filters made by filling a drum with layers of sand and gravel can remove bacteria and some nutrients.

■ Grease trap Available from plumbing suppliers, a grease trap separates grease and oil from kitchen water. The grease rises to the top, solids sink. The outflowing pipe is located in between.

■ Pumps Various pumps are available where gravity alone will not move water to where you want it. These include sump pumps which can be installed under the laundry tub or in a holding tank.

ENCOURAGE WILDLIFE INTO YOUR GARDEN

■ To encourage birds, let a few plants go to seed, or install a birdbath, bird table or feeder in your garden.

■ Ponds, and the plants around them, provide food and shelter for frogs, bees, dragonflies, birds and lizards.

■ Rocky outcrops attract lizards.

■ A small sunny spot is ideal for a patch of unmown grass that will attract butterflies and other insects.

■ Moss-covered walls and old tree stumps provide shelter for numerous mini-beasts.

Allergies in the garden

Allergies strike outside as well as in. Pollen from garden plants and trees may be a problem for those suffering from hay fever. Some people are allergic to stings from insects that are attracted to gardens. Gardens may also be home to numerous moulds. Contact dermatitis – an allergic reaction caused by touching a trigger substance – can be activated by plants or chemicals.

There are many ways you can reduce your exposure to allergens in the garden.

■ **Clothing** Wear sunglasses to protect your eyes. A mask made from a headscarf will protect your nose and mouth, while a headscarf or hat keeps pollen out of your hair. Long-sleeved clothing and trousers protect limbs from coming into contact with irritants and allergens as well as insects. Change your clothing after a spot of gardening or a spell outside, and wash it regularly to minimize pollen levels on the clothes.

■ **Lawn lore** Mowing the lawn frequently keeps pollen down. Ideally, choose a low-pollen grass that does not need frequent mowing. Replacing lawn with a rock garden or patio reduces the pollen level even more, while also cutting down the need for pesticides. Avoid using a strimmer or whipper-snipper as sap can fly up onto your skin. Remove grass cuttings from the surface of the lawn.

PROTECT YOUR EARS If you have a large lawn that takes a while to mow, protect your ears with ear muffs to avoid long-term damage.

■ **Pollinated pets** Pets bring pollen into the house on their fur. If you suffer badly from allergies and have pets, you might consider either keeping them out of the house or – more appropriately perhaps for dogs than cats! – rinsing them before letting them inside.

■ **Hair** Washing or rinsing your hair after being outside for a while removes pollen and reduces longer-term exposure.

■ **Floors** In any room with access to the garden, use easy to clean, hard flooring, such as vinyl, linoleum, wooden floorboards or ceramic tiles. By doing so, you can remove dirt, pollen, mould spores and animal hairs that blow in or are walked in from the garden.

■ **Shoes off** A 'shoes off in the house' policy helps allergy sufferers as well as housekeepers by reducing the amount of dirt and other materials that leave your shoe soles and enter your living spaces. Make it easy for everyone by placing shoe racks by the front and back doors to hold shoes, boots and slippers.

■ **Commonsense compost** If someone in the house is allergic to moulds, you need to take extra care with a compost heap. Using a closed system – for instance, some of the special boxes or bins that garden centres sell – will help prevent spores flying off into the surrounding air. Turning the compost regularly prevents fungus growing by bringing new material into contact with the air. Anyone who is prone to allergies should be let off compost-turning duties (or should wear a mask recommended by their doctor) and avoid areas of the garden where compost has recently been spread.

■ **Playtime** For children with grass allergies, play areas can be covered with rubber tiles instead of grass, or artificial turf, both of which can be cleaned with a garden hose to remove dirt, pollen and spores. A sand pit is another alternative, but install a cover to keep out cats when it's not in use.

■ **Stinging strategies** Insect bites and stings are always irritating and sometimes painful. But for those who are allergic to them, stings can be extremely painful and occasionally fatal. To help prevent stings, bear these factors in mind.

- Many scents attract wasps – for example, perfumes, hairsprays, strongly perfumed sunscreens and shampoos, and even sweat.
- Neutral, green or brown clothes are less likely to attract insects than brightly coloured ones.

FIRST AID FOR BEE STINGS AND WASP STINGS

■ **Bees** Remove the sting by scraping it sideways. This reduces the chance of more venom being released. Wipe the affected area clean. Apply a paste of bicarbonate of soda and water to the sting site. Wrap a bag of ice in a towel and hold it over the sting.

■ **Wasps** Daub the sting area with cider vinegar. Wrap a bag of ice in a towel and hold it over the sting.

Pests and diseases

If you are making the effort to minimize your exposure to chemicals inside your home, it makes sense to extend the same care to your outdoor areas too. Reducing the use of harsh chemicals to control insects, weeds and other pests is better for you and better for your home. You will also be doing the wider environment a favour. You may need to experiment with alternative methods and some of them may need more frequent application than strong chemical pesticides, but the rewards are a safer place for you and your family and a more welcoming environment for all the local wildlife.

PERSONAL INSECT REPELLENTS

Available as lotions and sprays, personal insect repellents are designed to keep flies, mosquitoes and other insects away from the body. Ingredients can include Deet (N, N-diethyl-m-toluamide – banned in the United States), di-n-propyl isocinchomeronate, ethyl hexanediol and dimethylphthalate. Some formulas contain pyrethrum and other synthetic pyrethroids.

Natural repellents include the essential oils – tea-tree, eucalyptus, sassafras and pennyroyal – all of which can be toxic in large amounts.

It is always better to try other means of repelling insects – covering up with clothing, for instance. If you do use a product, choose a lotion rather than an aerosol as you will be able to apply it more precisely, thus using it sparingly.

Choose your plants wisely

With some forethought you can create a garden that automatically needs less chemical help. For instance, some plants are bred for resistance to attack by particular insects or to a disease. Ask the staff at your local nursery when buying plants and seeds.

■ Lawns are big users of water as well as chemicals such as herbicides and fertilizers. These chemicals tend to leach off the lawn during rain, potentially polluting water systems. You could decide to reduce your lawn area or forget it entirely.

- Some plants help keep bugs away. These include chrysanthemums and pyrethrum daisies, and herbs such as garlic, chives and nasturtiums. Many gardening experts recommend companion planting to reduce pests — for instance, planting nasturtiums among tomatoes and Brassicas (the cabbage family) is said to protect against whitefly. It's certainly worth trying.

SHOO FLY! Place fly-deterrent plants at doorways, on verandahs and so on. These plants include lavender, sweet woodruff, lemon verbena, mint, thyme, rosemary, bay, chamomile and basil.

- Planting ground covers rather than leaving soil bare not only reduces moisture loss, it also leaves less room for weeds to grow, reducing the temptation to use herbicides in the garden.
- Choose plants that are best suited to your soil and local conditions rather than struggle on with unsuitable plants, which are more likely to surrender to fungal or bacterial disease or pest infestation.

Biological battles

Your next line of defence against pests in the garden is to call in a natural army of parasites and predators. Many pests have natural enemies that, if encouraged, can keep them in check. Useful garden insects include ladybirds, wasps, assassin bugs and lacewings.

Other wildlife to encourage are spiders, birds, lizards and frogs. One of the disadvantages of using insecticides, particularly broad spectrum ones, in your garden is that you may kill off these helpers too.

Conversely, controlling ants will assist in aphid and mealy bug control, as ants protect both of these pests in return for the honeydew they excrete.

Local organic gardening clubs or even your local nursery may be able to advise on methods that work for your area.

EARWIG TRAP Place a hollow sunflower stem, piece of straw or piece of sponge among the earwigs' flower of choice (dahlias or chrysanthemums, for example). Examine the traps each morning and blow any 'prisoners' into boiling water.

Mechanical prevention

Next in the plan of attack should come non-poisonous pest control practices.

- **Barriers** Fences and electrical fences keep off larger animals. Well placed nets stop possums getting at fruit trees. On a smaller scale, protect seedlings from caterpillars by cutting the bottom out of a yoghurt container and placing the container over the seedling.

- **Water** A strong jet of water dislodges aphids.

- **Removal** Prune and either burn or compost diseased plant clippings. Remove and destroy fruit fly-infested fruit to reduce fruit fly in the garden. Remove weeds that support pests and diseases – this is particularly effective in reducing caterpillar pests, which use weed species for breeding. Pick off bugs where you can, or spot spray. Remove caterpillars or rub off butterfly eggs before they hatch. Cut citrus gall wasp swellings off trees as soon as they appear and burn them.

- **Rotation** By changing your planting seasonally, like farmers who practise crop rotation, you can disrupt the breeding cycles of many pests.

- **Sumptuous soil** Soils rich in organic matter deter many soil diseases and pests such as nematodes. Heavily mulching your beds prevents

MINIMIZING MOSQUITOES

Eliminating the breeding sites is the key to reducing mosquito populations.

- Check the garden, daily if necessary, for small pools of water. Mosquitoes breed in the tiniest amounts of water, such as in plant saucers, paint tins, empty pots or plastic sheeting.
- Stock your pond with frogs and fish, which feed on mosquito larvae and help keep them under control.
- If you're in the garden after dusk, protect your skin by wearing long sleeves and long trousers.
- Flyscreens are the best way of keeping mosquitoes out of the house.
- Coils that burn allethrin repel mosquitoes to some degree.
- Citronella and lavender oils may be used as repellents with some success.

other pests – for instance, the potato moth – from laying eggs near plants. Good soil with the right balance of nutrients also means healthier plants that are better equipped to keep diseases away.

■ Traps Try this trap for fruit flies. Make a funnel entrance by cutting a plastic 2 L (2 qt) bottle in half, then place the top half inside the bottom, with the neck pointing downwards into the rest of the bottle. Try various baits: yeast, yeast extracts, beer or citrus skin. These traps can be hung in a tree or among plants at an angle. Traps are also effective for snails and slugs.

Low-risk pesticides

With a few basic ingredients you can make a range of non-toxic, economic, effective pest control solutions to use in the garden (see page 326). Less toxic methods may need more frequent application – for instance, controlling aphids with soap or garlic sprays may necessitate spraying every three days. You may also need to exercise a little more care during the application process – for example, when spraying the underside of azalea leaves if they are being attacked by azalea lace bug.

SLUGS AND SNAILS: SEND THEM PACKING

■ If your garden is small enough, picking off slugs and snails every night will considerably reduce the damage done by them. Just squash them under your shoe or boot.

■ Dig traps made from plastic bottles into the soil (see above). Open up the neck so that snails can crawl in but can't crawl out.

■ Beer in a saucer is another effective trap; empty it every morning.

■ Soft mollusc bodies don't like crawling over scratchy stuff such as crushed egg shells, slaked lime, salt or sawdust.

■ Snails and slugs will not cross copper because it gives out a weak electrical charge. Trees can be protected with a band of copper, but make sure you allow room for a little growth.

Recipes for natural pest sprays

Green pest sprays have many advantages. They rely on a limited range of easily obtainable ingredients, and they are cheap and relatively non-toxic. For this reason, many of them are traditional.

Spray for ants

INGREDIENTS

500 mL (2 cups) water

1/4 cup kerosene

1/4 cup detergent

4 dessertspoons vegetable oil

METHOD

1 Mix ingredients together.

2 Spray this mixture within a 0.5 m (20 in) circle of an ant's nest. Pour 1/2 cup water into the nest and spray ants that leave it. Can be used in conjunction with bait.

Bait for ants

INGREDIENTS

3 cups water

1 cup sugar

4 level teaspoons boric acid or borax

METHOD

1 Stir all ingredients together until they are dissolved.

2 To make a bait, half fill a screw top jar with cotton wool then pour in about 1 cup of the solution to saturate the cotton wool. Tape the lid on tightly and pierce it with 2 or 3 holes in the centre.

3 Place 3–6 baits like this near trails and nests for up to three days.

Soap spray for sucking pests like scale and aphids

INGREDIENTS

50 g (1 3/4 oz) soap

7 L (15 pt) water

130 g (4 1/2 oz) washing soda

METHOD

1 Grate soap into a bowl.

2 Bring 1 L (2 pt) of the water to the boil in a saucepan then remove it from the heat.

3 Add washing soda to the hot water and stir until it is dissolved.

4 Add the soap to the solution and stir over heat until the soap has dissolved.

5 Add this mixture to the remaining water. Use undiluted.

Soft soap insecticide

This is an all-purpose general garden insecticide for aphids, mites, azalea lace bug, white fly and leafhoppers.

INGREDIENTS

56 g (2 oz) soft soap (from chemists)

4.5 L (9 1/2 pt) hot water

METHOD

Dissolve soft soap in the hot water and allow it to cool. Use undiluted.

Garlic spray

Use this spray for aphids, mites and small caterpillars. Garlic also provides some natural fungicide protection.

INGREDIENTS

85 g (3 oz) chopped garlic bulbs

2 tablespoons mineral oil

7 g (1/4 oz) soap

600 mL (1 pt) water

METHOD

1 Soak garlic in mineral oil for 24 hours.

2 Dissolve soap in water and slowly add to garlic mixture.

3 Strain through fine gauze, and store in a china or glass container.

4 Dilute 1 part mixture to 50 parts water.

Need something a little stronger?

You may have an infestation of some pest that simply does not respond to your natural remedies. You still don't have to resort to highly toxic chemicals. Other relatively low-risk options include these.

- Pyrethrin, from the pyrethrum daisy, is a broad-spectrum insecticide that is also toxic to fish and cats.

- Derris, often supplied as a dust made from the derris root, is a broad-spectrum insecticide usually used against caterpillars, and beetles and other crawling insects. It is moderately toxic and kills ladybirds, lacewings and other beneficial insects. It is very toxic to fish and pigs.

- *Bacillus thuringiensis* (*Bt*) is a bacterial preparation toxic to caterpillars but not other organisms, although it may kill some butterfly larvae.

- Methoprene and hydropene are insect growth regulators that keep insects in the juvenile, non-breeding stage. There is no known effect on humans. They are considered an ideal alternative to most other pesticides as they act only on target organisms.

- White oils and other petroleum and vegetable oils work by suffocating the target pest. These are worth trying on aphids, scales, spider mites, sawflies, azalea lace bugs, caterpillars, mealy bugs and whiteflies. They are relatively safe for other organisms and humans, although they may kill beneficial insects if they are sprayed directly on them.

- Sulphur is toxic to mites, powdery mildews and rust, and it has low toxicity to humans and animals. It may be toxic to some beneficial insects when it is sprayed directly on them and may damage sulphur-sensitive plants.

- Chilli and pepper can be sprinkled as a deterrent to cats and dogs who find it distressing to smell.

Zero tolerance

You may decide to shrug your shoulders and live with some garden pests but poisonous ones, such as funnel-web spiders or redback spiders, need action. Funnel-webs like moist conditions, on or in the ground, while redbacks are often found near rubbish heaps and in concealed places like old tins. Regularly cleaning up such spots in your garden will help keep populations at bay. Pour boiling water down funnel-web burrows and cover with earth.

If you wish to use an insecticide, permethrin, bendiocarb or chlopyrifos are the most suitable (see pages 348 and 350). Treat likely redback harbouring areas with permethrin. A household surface spray insecticide containing pyrethrins or pyrethroids will kill a redback if you spray it directly on the spider. (Sprays are only effective if you manage a direct hit as the bristles on spiders' feet that enable them to walk over webs also allow them to walk over sprayed poison.) Remember that large-scale spraying – for instance, under houses – only encourages spiders to seek safer homes, increasing the likelihood of an encounter with you. In addition, such blanket spraying is detrimental to a host of other organisms.

The more powerful bendiocarb or chlorpyrifos, which are moderately toxic to humans, will kill a funnel-web spider.

When the going gets tough

If you decide to use stronger chemicals to control garden pests, you need to take extra care when handling them. For information on the types of pesticides available and their toxicity see 'What's in a name?', page 347. To ensure safe handling, follow these precautions.

- Read the label carefully so you understand exactly what it is you are dealing with, and follow the manufacturer's directions correctly for both usage and disposal.
- Use only as much as is required.
- Never eat, drink or smoke when using pesticides or immediately afterwards as you increase the risk of ingesting the chemical.
- Wash your hands immediately after application and, depending on the job, wash your clothes and take a shower too. Wash immediately if a chemical gets on your skin.
- Wear protective clothing appropriate to the job in hand.
- If possible, spray on windless days. If you have no choice, spray so that the chemical is blown away from you.
- Clean all spillages.

TERMITES

The chemicals used to prevent termites (also called white ants) are highly toxic and should only be used when a professional pest control operator has identified an infestation. The following measures cut down the chances of termites moving in.

- Make sure ant caps have been installed. These sheet metal shields prevent termites moving from the soil under a building into the timber frame. They should be built into walls below the building's timber construction, or should cover piers and the stumps supporting timber floors. The termites are then forced to build tunnels around the stumps, making it easier for you to spot an invasion. As well as barricading a building against attack by termites, ant caps prevent moisture from seeping up piers into the structural timbers, discouraging fungal decay, which attracts termites.
- Inspect the areas near your building and destroy any termite nests.
- Make the most of underfloor cross-ventilation if you have a timber-floored building, as this prevents the damp conditions in which termites thrive.
- Remove builders' debris and any timber that is in contact with the soil under the house.
- Keep points of inspection access clear.
- Periodically rake the soil under the house to deter termites.
- Check the guttering, downpipes and water pipes to make sure they are well maintained and don't leak. Fit agricultural drains around the house where groundwater seepage results in constantly damp soil.
- If you find termites, you could try less hazardous treatments such as specially formulated synthetic pyrethroids. Research into low-toxicity termite treatments continues and it is certainly worthwhile looking into what is currently available. (In Hawaii, for example, barriers of crushed basalt and granite are built under and around foundations.)

ON MOWING THE LAWN *It is not possible for any machine to cut wet grass satisfactorily...Moderately dry grass is the best for mowing and, if there is any choice in the matter of time, the cool of the evening will cause less discomfort to the operator of the machine.*

The Practical Home Handyman (1946)

The garden shed

All too often the garden shed or garage becomes a dumping ground where all the nasty stuff you don't want to keep in the house gets stored: solvents, paints, weed killers, insecticides and sharp, heavy tools. The chemicals are potentially hazardous when inhaled or ingested, or when they come into contact with the skin; they are also a major cause of accidental poisoning, particularly among young children. A tidy shed is not only more efficient — it is obviously much safer as well.

Commonsense storage

If you have children, the best protection is a good lock on the shed door.

- **Never store flammable substances near heating devices or open flames.**

- **Take care that pressurized containers are not punctured or subjected to undue pressure (don't put a heavy tool box on top of them).**

- **Never store petrol in plastic containers.**

- **Never store dangerous chemicals in empty soft drink bottles or food containers. Keep poisonous substances in their original containers.**

- **Contact your local poisons information service about the safe disposal of chemicals you no longer require. Under no circumstances should you put them down the drain.**

Terrific tools

Keeping your tools clean and sharp makes them safer to use and extends their life.

- **Clean tools by wiping them with a damp cloth or, if necessary, washing them in a detergent solution. Dry them with a clean dry rag and hang them up if possible.**

- **Disinfect pruning saws and secateurs after use to prevent the spread of fungal diseases.**

- **Keep a tin of rough grease or oil with a rag in it and rub it over the metal parts of tools to prevent rusting.**

- **Wipe over the wooden handles of tools with linseed oil every few months.**

- **Sharpen the backs of cutting edges by rubbing them on a sandstone or an oilstone every year.**

what's in a name?

You might well be suspicious of something called carboxymethyl-cellulose, if only because you can't pronounce it, much less know what it is or does, but would you be equally suspicious of something as innocent-sounding as air freshener? Probably not — it sounds as though it can only be benign — and yet most of us have absolutely no idea what our most frequently used household products contain and whether they're actually harmful, either personally or environmentally.

This chapter will help you to make sense of those unfamiliar names and substances, their functions and effects. Use it as a reference to learn what's in a range of products that you might be using already or considering using — from household cleaners to pesticides — then make an informed decision about whether you really want to use them, or consider an alternative.

We've also provided a glossary of terms that you might be unfamiliar with but which would be helpful to know.

EVERYONE *can keep house better than her mother till she trieth.*

French proverb

what's in a name?

Is it harmful?

Authorities find it difficult to be precise about the danger of many chemicals found in household cleaners, pest control products and chemical aids. This is partly because the products usually contain a mixture of chemicals at low concentration rather than one major ingredient, and toxicological data is often missing for mixtures. How toxic a substance is depends not only on its chemical make-up, but also on how often it is used, in what quantities and under what circumstances.

Toxicity is described in terms of carcinogens, which are cancer causing; neurotoxins, which damage the nervous system; and ones that affect the reproductive system, causing infertility and birth defects.

There is also the concept of acceptable risk. We accept the notion of toxicity in some contexts more readily than in others. The alcohol ethanol, for instance, which is found in disinfectants and other products, is a carcinogen and central nervous system depressant, with long-term effects of weight loss, liver cirrhosis and mental deterioration. It is also the active – and attractive – ingredient of the alcoholic drinks that many of us are happy to imbibe on a weekly, if not daily basis!

The chemicals of household cleaning

Cleaning is big business. Supermarkets stock a huge range of chemicals designed to help us keep the type of home we want. But what's in these products and do we need them all? The following list outlines many common household products and some of their ingredients, some of which are completely non-toxic, others that need to be handled with great care – or not at all.

Abrasives The hidden muscle power in cleaners that physically grinds off dirt, abrasives are usually small particles of hard minerals such as calcite, feldspar, sand or silicates. At the tough end of the spectrum are large-scale abrasives used in the home, such as abrasive paper, steel wool and metal mesh cleaners. At the gentler end are abrasives found in non-scratching cream cleansers and powders and, the gentlest abrasive of all, bicarbonate of soda.

Acids Chemicals with a pH (measure of acidity and alkalinity) of less than 7 are acidic and good at cleaning scum and hardened water deposits, hence their usefulness in bathroom cleansers. White vinegar is a mild acid, while sulphuric acid, found in some toilet cleaners, is a very strong acid.

Aerosols When you use an aerosol product, a cloud of tiny droplets forms not only on the target, but also around the user. This increases the chance of inhaling the microscopic particles that can harm lung tissue and be absorbed into the bloodstream. Some aerosols may ignite and explode when exposed to intense heat.

Air fresheners Available in aerosol and block form, air fresheners contain solvents, perfumes and sometimes hydrocarbons (see below) as propellants. Some contain paradichlorobenzene, which is an organochlorine chemical that accumulates in the body. Paradichlorobenzene has been linked to liver and nerve damage.

Alcohols Alcohols — such as ethanol and isopropanol, found in disinfectants (*qv*) — are a central nervous system depressant and carcinogen. They can be absorbed by the body through the skin and by ingesting and inhaling.

Aldehydes Ingestion of aldehydes causes central nervous depressive symptoms. Formaldehyde and glutaraldehyde, two aldehydes found in disinfectants and some cleaners, are strong irritants which affect the eyes, mucous membranes and skin.

Ammonia A strong alkaline cleaner (the opposite of acidic), ammonia (NH_3) is also a mild bleach and grease solvent. It cuts through much of the grease, dirt and body debris which is acidic and finds its way onto laundry, but as it produces irritating fumes, make sure there is adequate ventilation when you use it.

Amphoteric detergent This is a mild detergent used in shampoos and personal care products as well as some household detergents.

Anionic detergents Ordinary, high-sudsing detergents used in laundry and all-purpose detergent products, anionic detergents can be slightly deactivated by hard water. (See also Non-ionic and Cationic detergents.)

Antibacterial products Antibacterial products claim to kill household bacteria and keep your house cleaner. These products contain antibacterial agents such as triclosan, which can inhibit growth temporarily but don't necessarily kill bacteria. In addition, they may encourage the growth of resistant bacteria, including antibiotic resistant strains. Using such products is no substitute for thorough cleaning coupled with good hygiene practices, such as: washing your hands frequently with soap and water (the soap washes bacteria down the drain); avoiding cross-contamination in the kitchen by using separate boards for, for instance, salads and raw meat; and rinsing cloths, then allowing them to dry. In the home, these practices are usually sufficient to keep bacteria growth to safe levels.

Anti-moulds Usually anti-moulds consist of a thick bleach, such as chlorine bleach and a thickener. White vinegar, diluted eucalyptus oil and bicarbonate of soda also inhibit mould.

Anti-redeposition agents These keep the dirt in the water and prevent it from re-depositing onto the clothes.

Bathroom cleaners This is usually a thick liquid, paste or powder containing bleach, abrasives and detergents with an overall acidic composition.

Bicarbonate of soda Also known as sodium bicarbonate and baking soda, this is a gentle, moderately alkaline, non-toxic abrasive that cuts through grease and oil because it reacts with the fatty acids to form mild detergents. It also absorbs odours by reacting with the odour-making molecules (which are often strong acids or alkalis) and chemically neutralising them.

Bleach Used to remove colour, stains and mould, bleach is also used to disinfect, clean and kill dirt. Bleach contains chemicals such as chlorine and chlorine-containing compounds, perborates, peroxides, oxalic acid and oxalates. If used in small quantities, bleaches are not harmful to the environment. But if too much is used, free chlorine reacts with organic matter in the sewage, forming organochlorines, which are very dangerous, highly persistent chemicals. The two main types of bleach are oxygen and chlorine, usually a 5.25 per cent solution of sodium hypochlorite, which is a relatively strong household laundry bleach that can clean and kill micro-organisms. Other bleaches include lemon juice and hydrogen peroxide, a so-called oxygen bleach recommended for delicate fabrics as it is milder. It can also be used for stain removal and bleaching. Strong bleach might contain a blend of surfactants (see page 124) and sodium hypochlorite. Bleaches can cause irritation to the skin, mucous membranes and the respiratory tract. If ingested they can be both irritating and corrosive to the digestive tract. Whether they are ingested, inhaled or absorbed through the skin, oxalic acids and oxalates found in some bleaches are highly toxic. Some forms of manufacture of bleach produce mercury as a waste product.

Blue This gives a blue tinge to white clothes and, by a trick of light, makes them appear whiter. Blue may be found in laundry detergents.

Borax A strong alkali that softens water, borax is a disinfectant, stain remover, deodorizer and water softener; it may be used as a laundry booster when added to detergents. It can be used for soaking nappies, but is not suitable for delicate fabrics such as silk or wool. It also has uses in pest control as it is poisonous to plant life and to ants. Borax is sold in powder form or as a colourless crystalline salt.

Builders These are substances added to a detergent to improve the way it works — water softening, deactivating acids, buffering the washing solution so it remains effectively alkaline and preventing the re-depositing of soil.

Carpet cleaners Sold as a liquid, powder or foam mousse, carpet cleaners contain detergents and solvents. Powder formulas eliminate wetting which can leave water marks. Take care not to use alkaline solutions on wool carpets.

Cationic detergents Quaternary ammonium compounds (qv) are cationic detergents, which are used in disinfectants (qv) because of their strong anti-bacterial qualities. (See also Anionic and Non-ionic detergents.)

Caustic soda Also called sodium hydroxide, caustic soda is a strong and corrosive alkali often used in drain cleaners and oven cleaners. Concentrated solutions of caustic soda are harmful to aquatic life. Australian-made caustic soda contains traces of mercury, which is toxic and accumulates in the food chain. The presence of heavy metals such as mercury prevents sewage from being treated for use as a fertilizer. Other countries produce caustic soda using methods of production that exclude mercury contaminants.

Chlorhexidines Found in disinfectants, chlorhexidines cause damage to the oesophagus and liver if strong solutions are ingested. They are also irritating and corrosive to the eyes, skin and mucous membranes, and may induce contact dermatitis and photosensitivity.

Chlorinated solvents Animal studies suggest that exposure to chlorinated solvents such as dichloromethane and 1,1,1-trichloroethane used in spot fabric cleaners may cause birth defects, but research into people who have been exposed to high levels through their jobs has not been conclusive. These two chemicals are progressively being replaced with glycol ethers and organic acids.

Cleaning liquids These can vary considerably; some contain a concentrated mixture of surfactants (see page 124) and solvents (qv) with an overall acidity. All-purpose bathroom and kitchen cleaners tend to contain detergents, ammonia or solvents and sometimes a mild abrasive.

Cleaning sprays Such sprays contain surfactants (see page 124) in a viscosity that allows them to be sprayed.

Cloudy ammonia This is a mixture of ammonia (qv), at a concentration of around 10 per cent, and soap.

Cream cleansers Cream cleansers contain a mixture of detergents — for instance, a cream cleanser may contain anionic (qv) and non-ionic (qv) detergents, finely ground calcite for abrasion, plus perfume.

Degreasers A degreaser may be a product itself, designed to strip surfaces of oil and grease. Found in toilet bowl cleaners and drain cleaners, a degreaser may consist of various acids and alkalis, and may include phosphoric acid, sulphamic acid, sodium and potassium hydroxide. These acids and alkalis are highly corrosive to tissue, such as the skin, mucous membranes and the respiratory tract.

Detergents Detergent is a surfactant (see page 124) made from petrochemicals. Chemicals in detergents can kill good bacteria, which are necessary for decomposing sewage.

Dishwashing liquids These are blends of detergents and other chemicals such as stability aids, fragrances, preservatives and additives for mildness.

Dishwashing machine powders These powders contain oxygen-based bleaching agents, low-foaming alkaline detergent, phosphates (qv) and silicates. They can corrode glassware, aluminium and glazes, and can harm some plastics.

Disinfectants There is a variety of disinfectants available. They kill germs on household fabrics, dishes and other surfaces. The ingredients in commercial disinfectants include chlorine bleach, hydrogen peroxide, phenol, chloroxylenol, quaternary ammonium compounds (qv) and triethylene glycol. Natural disinfectants include white vinegar, lemon juice, tea-tree oil and eucalyptus oil.

Drain cleaners Usually, drain cleaners contain a concentrated solution of lye (NaOH) and aluminium. The lye produces heat when it dissolves and the aluminium produces bubbling. The heat dissolves the grease blocking the drain while the bubbling agitates it. Drain cleaners can also dissolve hair. Less toxic drain-cleaning methods include a sink full of hot water and washing soda, or a combination of bicarbonate of soda and white vinegar.

Dry-cleaning fluids Toxic solvents (qv) are used in the home to spot clean clothes and upholstery.

Enzymes The three enzymes protease, lipase and amylase are found in some washing detergents and help break the stain into smaller pieces, aiding stain removal. Cellulase enzymes remove tiny cotton fibres from the fabric surface to improve its look and feel.

Eucalyptus oil This should be used very sparingly as it can kill many beneficial animals, plants and micro-organisms. Use it in doses of drops as even 2/3 teaspoon (3 mL) can be fatal.

Fabric softeners These contain waxy lubricants that coat the clothing fibres to make them feel soft and smell perfumed.

Flammable solvents These should be treated with caution.

Floor cleaners A typical supermarket floor cleaner contains a mixture of nonionic and anionic surfactants, quality control agents, colour, perfume and water.

Floor polishes Floor polishes contain solvents, waxes or oils, and perfumes.

Fluorescers These make white fabrics appear whiter in the presence of ultraviolet light, found in daylight and fluorescent light. They are also called optical brighteners, brighteners and fluorescent whitening agents.

Hydrocarbons Hydrocarbons are a vast group of chemicals made of hydrogen and carbon only. They include petroleum distillates such as kerosene, naptha, paraffin wax and tar; and chlorinated hydrocarbons such as the pesticides chlordane and lindane. Hydrocarbons feature in many household products — for example, solvents, furniture polishes and adhesives. Toxicity depends on the hydrocarbon in question, its viscosity (the thinner it is, the more toxic, as it spreads easily), but many can damage the lungs, nervous system, heart, gastrointestinal system, kidneys and skin. Most hydrocarbons irritate mucous membranes and are absorbed across tissue layers; many can cause chemical burns. Some of the volatile hydrocarbons are central nervous system depressants.

Hydrogen peroxide This is commonly found in 10 per cent solutions for bleaching hair, and in higher concentrations as a mild disinfectant. It can irritate the skin, eyes and mucous membranes. As it breaks down into oxygen and water, it is considered a benign alternative to chlorine bleach, both in industry and in the house.

Ironing aids These can be used to keep the iron sliding easily, or to give shirts extra stiffness. Spray starches contain, for example, corn starch to provide the fabric with body; silicone to stop the iron sticking; fabric softener; borax to stabilize the starch; preservatives; and fragrance. On the other hand, sizing may contain cellulose gum instead of starch for a lighter fabric body.

Lather controller As it prevents too much foam being produced, a lather controller may be used in detergents for front-loading washing machines and in dishwashers.

Laundry detergents Available in tablet, powder or liquid form, laundry detergents often contain enzymes (qv) to attack stains and a range of other additives, including bulking agents, water softeners, bleach activators, perfumes, optical brightening agents and foam suppressants. The liquids are often concentrated; these contain fewer additives.

Lime scale remover Used to remove mineral deposits and other stains from bathroom fittings and kettles, lime scale remover contains corrosives and abrasives (qv). Some brands may also contain acids and detergents.

Liquid detergents Found in laundry detergents, floor cleaners and general cleaners, these can cause skin irritation or sensitization in some people. If swallowed they can cause diarrhoea and vomiting. They include alkyl benzene sulphonates, sodium lauryl sulphates, alcohol sulphates and alcohol ethoxysulphates.

Metal polishes Brass and copper polishes contain abrasives (qv) such as pumice, plus solvents (qv), ammonia (qv), kerosene and white spirits (qv). Silver polish is more acidic.

Methylated spirits 'Metho' (also known as rubbing alcohol) is pure alcohol with additives to make it unpalatable. As a household cleaner it can remove stains, wash windows and glass, and polish chrome, jewellery and ivory. It is highly flammable and can cause skin and respiratory problems. It should not be poured down the sink as it pollutes waterways.

Nappy soaks Nappy soaks sterilize and whiten laundry items such as soiled nappies, stained clothing and tea towels. They often contain sodium perborate (a mild bleach), water softeners and detergents.

Non-ionic detergents These are low-sudsing laundry detergents and dishwasher detergents. They work well in hard water and are effective on most types of dirt, especially oily dirt. (See also Anionic and Cationic detergents.)

Oven cleaners Sold in aerosol, paste or vapour format, oven cleaners contain strong chemicals such as sodium hydroxide, anionic surfactants (qv), polycarboxylates and solvents (qv). Non-caustic ones contain strong alkalis such as ammonia (qv).

Paradichlorobenzene PDB is an organochlorine used as a deodorizer in air fresheners and as a disinfectant in toilet cleaners. (It is also used as an insecticide.)

It works by preventing the formation of bad-smelling compounds by bacteria in stagnant urine — mainly ammonia and other amines — and by masking odours with its own strong smell. PDB has been linked to liver and nerve damage, its fumes are toxic and it will cause cancer if inhaled in high concentration over long periods.

Phenol Also called carbolic acid and often used as an ingredient in household disinfectant, phenol is a strong disinfectant (*qv*).

Phenolic compounds Highly toxic when swallowed, phenolic compounds include phenol and cresol, which are used in disinfectants. They damage the central nervous system, heart, blood vessels, lung and kidneys. They are also corrosive to the skin and respiratory tract.

Phosphates Found in detergents, laundry powders, liquids and shampoos, phosphates are used as 'builders' (*qv*) to boost the cleaning power of the surfactant (see page 124) by softening water (they react with the ions in hard water that interfere with cleaning), increase alkalinity and help suspend the dirt in water. Problems occur when there is too much phosphate in water systems: it encourages excessive growth of algae and weeds, robbing less aggressive plant life and animal life of oxygen.

Polymers These large molecule compounds are used in washing liquids to thin them, or as a deflocculating (dispersing) agent in concentrated liquids.

Pre-wash stain removers Available as sprays or bars, pre-wash stain removers may contain ingredients such as solvents (*qv*), sodium percarbonate, hydrogen peroxide (*qv*), surfactants (see page 124), perfumes and water softeners (*qv*).

Quaternary ammonium compounds Corrosive at high concentrations, these compounds are eye and skin irritants. If swallowed, they can cause vomiting and diarrhoea, and depending on the dose, coma, convulsions and shock. They are found in strong cleaners and disinfectants.

Rinsing aids Rinsing aids contain detergent to break water tension and stop water clinging to crockery, promoting more even drying.

Scouring powder Containing bleaches and abrasives such as silver sand, pumice and whitening as well as perfumes, scouring powder may scratch many surfaces, including enamel, bathroom and kitchen fittings and sinks.

Soap As soap is 100 per cent biodegradable, and does not pollute the environment, environmental groups recommend it in preference to washing detergents for washing clothes. Available in supermarkets, soap flakes are ideal for the gentle washing of clothes that may be damaged by strong detergents – for instance, silks and wools. Laundry soap is also available in blocks and may contain additives such as borax (*qv*), bleach (*qv*), sodium phosphates and perfumes. Unlike synthetic detergent, soap does not dissolve well in cold water.

Sodium perborate A mild bleach.

Sodium percarbonate Considered environmentally friendly, sodium percarbonate is used in laundry and other cleaning products for its cleaning, bleaching and stain removal abilities.

Solid detergents Found in laundry powders and dishwashing detergents, solid detergents are highly corrosive and irritating when they are ingested or inhaled or come into contact with skin. When combined with phosphates (*qv*) they are highly toxic. They can cause dermatitis and chronic skin irritation.

Solvents Water is the most common solvent, a liquid capable of dissolving another substance. There are several types of solvents, each capable of dissolving different substances. Hydrocarbon solvents include paraffins, naphthenes and aromatic hydrocarbons. Chlorinated solvents are synthetic solvents mainly used in dry-cleaning and degreasing. Alcohol is the main constituent of methylated spirits. Ketones are excellent solvents for fats, resins and lacquers, and include acetone, found in nail polish remover. Others are plant-derived solvents. These include turpentine from pine trees and terpenes, non-toxic and readily biodegradable, which originally were derived from plants. The solvents present in dry-cleaning fluids, pre-wash treatments, spot and paint removers, and furniture polish are usually volatile and harmful if you breathe them in for any length of time.

Stabilizers These prevent chemical instability in a washing powder by stopping metal ions (electrically charged particles) reducing the effectiveness of bleach.

Stain removers Used in dry-cleaning and spot stain removal, these may be neurotoxic (poisonous in a way that affects the nervous system) and hepatoxic (damage the liver), depending on how long and how severely someone is exposed. The body can absorb these solvents through the skin and by ingesting and inhaling. They include chlorinated and non-chlorinated aliphatic and aromatic hydrocarbons.

Sugar soap This is not a soap at all but a strong synthetic detergent which is corrosive and good at cleaning grease and built-in dirt, especially as a preparation for painting. It is alkaline, contains surfactants (page 124) and also removes moulds.

Toilet gels These products may contain strong acids that dissolve scale. They may also contain non-ionic (*qv*) surfactants (see page 124) and bleach (*qv*) in the form of an oxygen-based bleaching agent.

Washing soda Otherwise known as sodium carbonate, washing soda is a mild alkali available in a crystal or powder form. It is a good stain remover and is used as an additive in commercial laundry products. Use it with soap for laundry, as a tarnish remover on silver and to help unblock drains. Washing soda is not dangerous to the environment but it is harmful if swallowed.

Water softeners These remove or deactivate calcium and magnesium ions present in hard water, and so make detergents work better. Some contain phosphate.

White spirits These solvents are petroleum distillates. Also known as mineral turpentine spirits or petroleum spirits.

Window cleaners A window cleaner may contain ammonia (*qv*), solvents (*qv*) and detergents (*qv*).

Wool washes A gentle surfactant (see page 124) mixture for washing wool, wool wash avoids alkalis, which can affect the dyes in wool, damaging the wool and causing running and fading.

The chemicals of pest control

Flies, mosquitoes, cockroaches…the list of unwanted visitors is long. The trouble is, many, although not all, of the chemicals we aim at them are unwanted too. Some of these chemicals are listed below.

Aldrin (and dieldrin) These are organochlorine (*qv*) insecticides once widely used but now banned in some countries. They are still sometimes used by licensed operators for termite control. Aldrin is converted into dieldrin in the body. Dieldrin is a carcinogen. Both chemicals can cause liver and kidney damage. Dieldrin persists in the soil for up to 20 years and is highly toxic to most living organisms.

Allethrin A first generation pyrethroid (*qv*), allethrin is of low toxicity to people because it is broken down quickly in the body. Allethrin also decomposes quickly in sunlight.

Bacillus thuringiensis This is a bacterial insecticide used mainly against moth and butterfly caterpillars. One strain can be used on mosquito larvae. It is regarded as almost non-toxic to other organisms.

Bioallethrin See Tetramethrin.

Bioresmethrin See Tetramethrin.

Carbamates This group of chemicals is based on carbamic acid and is used in insecticides, herbicides and fungicides. It includes carbaryl, used in garden insecticides, flea collars and animal shampoos. Toxic to bees, earthworms, some fish and other marine life, carbaryl breaks down in 16 days in the soil. Carbamates also include bendiocarb, which is found in surface sprays used to control household pests such as fleas, silverfish, ants and cockroaches. It is moderately toxic and skin contact should be avoided. It has a residual life of several months and is dangerous to fish, birds and some mammals.

Chlordane (and heptachlor) Both these chemicals are organochlorines (qv). Once used against borers, common ants, cockroaches and spiders, they are still used against termites. They are extremely hazardous due to their long residual life: they bind to particles in the soil and may persist for decades. They are eaten by animals and can build up in the food chain. They are moderately toxic to aquatic animals, livestock and birds, and may affect reproduction in animals and humans.

Chlorpyrifos This is a chlorine-containing organophosphate (qv), which is found in a wide range of insecticides for use against ants, spiders, ticks, lice and locusts, in cockroach baits and against termites. It is highly toxic to fish and other aquatic organisms and should not be used near water bodies. It is also toxic to bees.

Cypermethrin (and deltamethrin/decamethrin, fenprobathrin, flucythrinate and fluvalinate) These are fourth generation pyrethroids (qv), used in the pest control industry when long-lasting residual insecticide is required to control ants, cockroaches and other household pests. These highly effective insecticides act as nerve poisons in insects and are also more toxic to humans than other pyrethroids. They may be carried by water or air to places where they may harm birds, reptiles, fish and plankton but because they are so effective, only small amounts need be used in very specific areas.

Deltamethrin/decamethrin See Cypermethrin.

Derris An extract from the root of certain legumes, derris's active ingredient is rotenone. A contact and stomach poison, it is moderately toxic to mammals, including humans. When it is exposed to sunlight derris breaks down in three days. It kills bees, fish, lacewings, ladybirds and parasitic wasps.

Diazinon This chemical is used by pest control companies against cockroaches, fleas, ants and spiders. It is a contact poison that is readily absorbed through the skin. It can remain active in the soil for several months and is extremely toxic to bees, birds and fish.

Dichlorvos An organophosphate used in insecticides, pest strips and flea collars, this chemical can also be used as a fumigant. It may be listed on packaging as 2,2-dichlorovinyl dimethl phosphate, DDVP or Vapona. Strips and flea collars impregnated with dichlorvos continuously emit it, exposing not only fleas but also the pets wearing the collars and their owners. It carries with it a number of health risks, and although it breaks down rapidly, dichlorvos is highly toxic to bees, birds and fish.

Dieldrin See Aldrin.

Fenprobathrin See Cypermethrin.

Fenvalerate See Permethrin 25/75.

Flucythrinate See Cypermethrin.

Fluvalinate See Cypermethrin.

Heptachlor See Chlordane.

Hydropene (and methoprene) These are insect growth regulators that keep insects in the juvenile, non-breeding stage. There is no known effect on humans. They are considered an ideal alternative to most other pesticides because they act only on target organisms.

Malathion Considered to be one of the less toxic organophosphates (*qv*), malathion is used in insecticides for the house and garden, in flea shampoos and powders for pets, and in head or body lice treatments for humans. Although it is regarded as having low acute toxicity to humans, if you are pregnant it is best to avoid it since there is little data about its effect on a foetus. It is highly toxic to bees and harms almost all insects. It decomposes quickly and completely breaks down in the soil within about two weeks.

Methoprene See Hydropene.

Organochlorines Sometimes abbreviated to OCs, organochlorines are organic chemicals that contain chlorine. They include polyvinylchloride (PVC), chlorofluorocarbons (CFCs), many solvents, dioxins, polychlorinated biphenyls

(PCBs) as well as pesticides such as DDT and the cyclodienes, aldrin (*qv*), chlordane (*qv*) and heptachlor. They are toxic and hazardous, highly stable and chemically inert so they have long-lasting effects on the environment. They are also persistent in the food chain as they build up in animals' fatty deposits (they are often found in human milk).

Organophosphates Also known as OPs, these are organic compounds that contain a phosphate or thiophosphate group. They were specifically developed as insecticides but are also related to some nerve gases. Readily absorbed through the skin, they are safer than organochlorines (*qv*) because they are much less toxic to humans than to insects. In addition, they are less persistent in the environment and do not accumulate in the body or the environment. They kill beneficial insects such as bees, ladybirds and lacewings as well as pests.

Permethrin 25/75 (and fenvalerate) Third generation pyrethroids (*qv*), these are nerve poisons that cause hyperactivity and convulsions in affected insects. They are not highly toxic to humans because they are broken down rapidly in the body. However, they are toxic to non-target insects such as bees, and also to fish. Permethrin is used as a surface spray and remains active for several weeks after application. It is also used as a wettable powder in the pest control industry.

Phenothrin See Tetramethrin.

Piperonyl butoxide This is often added as a 'synergist' to insect sprays containing pyrethrin (*qv*), pyrethroids (*qv*), rotenone or carbamates (*qv*). It makes these substances more toxic to the insect by inhibiting the enzyme that breaks down the poison. The long-term effects of its use are unclear, so avoid the use of sprays containing piperonyl butoxide near people, particularly children.

Pyrethrin See Pyrethrum.

Pyrethroids These are a group of synthetic insecticides based on the structure of the naturally occurring pyrethrins. They are classified in four 'generations' according to when they were developed: (1) allethrin (*qv*); (2) tetramethrin (*qv*), resmethrin, bioresmethrin, bioallethrin and phenothrin; (3) permethrin 25/75 (*qv*) and fenvalerate; (4) cypermethrin (*qv*), deltamethrin/decamethrin, fenprobathrin, flucythrinate and fluvalinate.

Pyrethrum (and pyrethrin) A natural insecticide extracted from the flowers of a daisy-like member of the chrysanthemum group, pyrethrum and pyrethrin are used in many household insecticide sprays and aerosols and in some mosquito coils and mats. They are not highly toxic to people or other mammals; however, pyrethrin formulas nearly always contain piperonyl butoxide (*qv*) to enhance its effectiveness.

Resmethrin See Tetramethrin.

Tetramethrin (and resmethrin, bioresmethrin, bioallethrin and phenothrin) Second generation pyrethroids (*qv*), they are used in household aerosols such as fly sprays and for mothproofing. While they are not acutely toxic to humans, avoid exposure as their chronic effects have not been exhaustively tested. They pose little threat to the environment as they break down quickly in sunlight.

What's in the products?

Reading labels on sprays and other pest control products does not always give you the full story. Here's a brief outline of some popular pest control methods.

Surface sprays

Some surface sprays contain bendiocarb, a moderately toxic insecticide. Others may contain dichlorovos or the persistent pyrethroid permethrin, which can remain active for several weeks as a contact poison.

Termite treatments

- Organochlorine insecticides are sprayed on the soil below and near buildings. These aren't necessarily very effective as the spots most difficult to reach are the very ones most prone to infestation.
- Creosote can be painted onto both vulnerable and infested timber, but it must be done every 12 months. Creosote can burn the skin and is possibly carcinogenic.
- Arsenic trioxide dust can be injected into active termite workings. It is carried back into the nest where it may kill the entire colony. This is one of the least hazardous treatments as the household is not exposed to the chemical.
- Liquid treatments include the very hazardous cyclodienes (aldrin, dieldrin, chlordane and heptachlor) and the less hazardous chlorpyrifos, which can be injected into building construction material.

Zappers and coils

Plug-in mosquito repellents and coils may contain a variety of pesticides but often include allethrin. Critics warn against prolonged, long-term use of zappers and coils near children — for instance, in bedrooms every night — because children are more vulnerable than adults.

Glossary

Acaricide A chemical that kills members of the *Acari* family, including dust mites and ticks.

Allergen Any substance that might trigger an allergic reaction.

Biodegradable Biodegradability refers to the degree to which a substance can be decomposed by the action of bacteria and other living organisms, such as fungi.

Corrosive Many strong cleaning agents are also corrosive or caustic — that is, they can burn the skin, eyes and even internal organs if ingested or inhaled by accident.

Flammable Easily set on fire.

Irritant Many substances are irritating to the skin, mucous membranes (these are the moist surfaces lining, for instance, your nose and your gut), the respiratory tract and, especially, the eyes.

Surfactant Soaps and detergents contain surfactants, which clean in three ways: they help water wet a surface by reducing its surface tension; they help remove the dirt; and they keep the dirt in the washing water and stop it from being re-deposited on the laundry. Some soaps and detergents are surfactants themselves — the terminology is not precise. Without surfactants the strong surface tension of water — the property which causes it to form droplets — tends to bead up on greasy objects rather than wet them and carry off the dirt.

Volatile A substance that turns to gas at room temperature.

Volatile organic compounds (VOCs) These compounds contain carbon (hence the term 'organic'), and evaporate easily at room temperature (hence the term 'volatile'). They include formaldehyde, many pesticides, solvents such as benzene and perchloroethylene, and a number of cleaning agents.

Index